'With descriptions as rich as the biogeography of Prespa and with a powerful sense of place, *Lifelines* is much more than a delight, it is a book that will draw you in, again and again. Julian Hoffman's prose is poetic, joyful and filled with love for the natural world and his chosen home. I too, yearned to be there and meet true wilderness in the form of a bear!'
Annie Worsley, author of *Windswept*

'*Lifelines* describes a homecoming to a place that, as the story opens, has yet to become home. It is both an inner journey and a journey of discovery, rich in event and beautifully crafted. Crucially linked to this is Hoffman's deep connection with the "more-than-human world": the creatures that live alongside him and the landscape they share. At a time when the planet is at risk, Hoffman's passionate sense of place is both a celebration and an alarm call.'
David Harsent, author of *Skin*

'A tender, powerful story of love for a place and a way of being, and a bracing call to the barricades – for enemies are closing in. An urgent, important and compelling read.'
Charles Foster, author of *Cry of the Wild*

'*Lifelines* elegantly and sensitively describes the pathways that all living creatures travel to get to where they belong – the "lifelines" taking them "home". In rich and moving prose Julian describes these odysseys, infilling with past and present events and circumstances, from the Greek Civil War to the spectre of climate change, and how they impact the journeys. He shows where the pathways cross and entwine, posing challenges and opportunities for humans to co-exist with the wild world. Pulling the whole story together is the best explanation of biodiversity I have ever come across. I thoroughly recommend it to anyone interested in our place in the wider community of life on earth.'
Lee Durrell, MBE

Lifelines

Searching for Home in
the Mountains of Greece

JULIAN HOFFMAN

a story of shelter shared

Elliott&Thompson

First published 2025 by
Elliott and Thompson Limited
2 John Street
London WC1N 2ES
www.eandtbooks.com

Represented by:
Authorised Rep Compliance Ltd.
Ground Floor, 71 Lower Baggot Street
Dublin, D02 P593
Ireland
www.arccompliance.com

ISBN: 978-1-78396-864-0

9 8 7 6 5 4 3 2 1

A catalogue record for this book is available from
the British Library.

Map and illustrations by Matina Galati
Typesetting: Marie Doherty
Printed by CPI Group (UK) Ltd, Croydon, CR0 4YY

For Nina Mesner,
whose beautiful light lives on

Will there be a world
to lament?
Celebrate?

Su Hwang, 'Witness Marks', from *Bodega*

There is another world, but it is in this one.

Paul Éluard

Contents

WRENS I

It's one of those sharp winter days that make the nights tremble with light. When no clouds conceal the vastness to come, so that the gathering dark is shot through with a cold so deep and clarifying that our galaxy seems sleeved in silver ice. When stars shine with the intensity of fireworks.

I open the front door to haul in enough firewood from the porch to last until morning. Outside, in the lowering of late afternoon, a pair of ravens row through the deepening blue to their roost. As I bend to the wood, something moves to my right and disappears. A swift brown blur and whirling of wings. I carry the split beech inside and drop it into the wood basket beside the fire. Although I'm unsure about the species, garden birds do occasionally descend to the front steps, foraging for spilled seed whenever deep snow makes it easier for me to remove the feeders from their place in a tree and reload them on the swept stone. I can only assume another seam has been exposed.

Opening the door for more wood, I expect the birds to have scattered. Instead, three wrens swirl like moths about my head, as though circling a sudden flame. I retreat indoors and let the wood fall with a thud, listening in silence to see if the world outside resettles.

This time I open the back door and follow the stone wall until I'm flush with the front of the house. The day is dying away. Sunlight crowns the mountains, turning the snowfields around their summits to a dazzle of shining light. The highest spires glitter

and glow as if they've been dipped in gold. Around the house,
though, the shadows are lengthening.

In the dimming light, I watch the front door and adjacent
woodpile. Everything is silent and still. Compressed. Just as I'm
about to give up and return to the warmth of the fire, a sharp
clacking bursts from the stack of dry beech. In the dark slots
between logs, I can just make out the brown cloak of a wren, its
stubby tail tilted upwards.

Wrens are among the most solitary and territorial of European
songbirds. They're a creature devoted to dark corners; and the
Greek name for them, *tripofraxtis*, or the hedge-hole dweller,
speaks to such seclusion. But as I watch the shadowed bird,
another wren sweeps over my head and twirls around the corner.
Then a third sinks through a sky of shifting shades, deep blue
feathering to violet and orange at its edges. From the tangled
streambanks of ground elder and nettles beside the house vaults
another wren, flashing low over the garden grasses. All of them
calling in the same insistent register, their voices like ice cubes
clattering in a glass.

Even the highest mountains are sliding out of the light when
from the woodpile the first wren blurs towards the house. There
it fastens itself to the wall, swivelling its head to assess the degree
of danger it faces from being this openly exposed. A second wren
hits the house, nearly inseparable from stone in the waning light.
From the neighbouring meadow, another hurtles past me. They're
convening like tributaries at the sea, funnelling in from the over-
grown hazel coppices and bramble thickets where they've foraged
throughout the day. One slants over my shoulder towards the
woodpile. Another arcs like an arrow above the roof, dissolving
into darkness as it descends.

I shift my feet to keep warm and feel the grasses already stiff-
ening with frost. It'll be a night of river ice and glazed fields ahead
of us. From its spot on the stone wall, the first of the wrens flares

sideways to the wooden trim of the front door. It then quickly finds the frame of the inset window. Seen from inside the house, it would appear as though pinned beneath glass in a collector's case. And then the bird is gone, fanning upwards like a wind-lifted leaf to vanish inside a cup no larger than my hand. A small bowl of hardened mud that has hung empty above our front door for years.

A rush of late motion marks the end of day. A black twist of jackdaws cackles overhead and our neighbour whistles home his goats, their passage a river of bells through the meadow. Then the next wren makes its move, tracing the same flight as the first, crossing from stone to door to window. And there it pauses, as though settling between waves before riding upwards on a crest. Disappearing like the other. I can barely see now as darkness closes up the sky. But I can still hear the wrens, their flurry of wings sketching a map of movement made readable by ear, as one after another they whisk up into the safe shelter of a long-abandoned swallow's nest.

Beginnings:
An Introduction

On a small hill beside the lake, the March sun was warm on my skin. It was the vernal equinox and almost a week into the closure of the country. Shops, restaurants and cafés shuttered and still. Schoolchildren sent home and the streets eerily empty. Borders sealed amid the unfolding pandemic. A world of scrolling light on our screens, the lit figures unreal and rising.

It was the first day of spring. A beginning, but also an end.

I'd climbed through lengthening grasses to reach the top of the hill. Underfoot, the small white blades of star of Bethlehem split the damp earth. The changes felt sudden and unexpected, as though each circling of the year were still a surprise. Wild plum trees exploded into snow on the flanks of the hill and a drowsy billow of bees honoured the blossom. From the blue water below lifted the liquid laughter of little grebes. Somewhere to the west, an early cuckoo called its name.

From the top of the hill, I could see the evocative ruins of the basilica built over a thousand years earlier by Tsar Samuel of Bulgaria when he made the island of Agios Achilleios the capital of his once expansive kingdom. Beyond the basilica, large birds were gliding over the water towards an archipelago of small white islands beside the tawny sweep of an immense reedbed. Even within a vast basin of water, where encircling mountains reached high into the blue sky, these white islets dominated the scene. Most of the movement around the lake that day originated there. Pale brown and largely unnoticed for several months of the year, their bleaching meant that pelicans were with us again.

No matter how long I end up living beside the Prespa lakes in northern Greece, the presence of pelicans will never fail to move me. Not only does their grace in the air encourage a mysteriously durable form of awe, impervious to the kind of dulling that the repetition of experiences can often occasion, but they lend the landscape a palpable antiquity. Their flights convey something of another age, as though towing an invisible line behind them that reaches all the way back to the dinosaurs. There's that slow oaring of the air on wings that have barely changed in structural essence since the bird's earliest ancestors. Or the wondrous doubling of forms when skimming so low over the lake that you could barely slide a knife between the bird and its reflection. Taking advantage of an aerodynamic phenomenon known as ground effect, in which air flowing between the surface of the water and the surface of a bird's wings creates an invisible cushion that keeps the pelican suspended mere inches above the lake, the great evolutionary aim to conserve energy whenever possible produces a simultaneously potent visual poetry. And in summer, when heat haze rises off the water in rippling waves of light, it's hard not to imagine those pelicans being held in place solely by a spell.

Every spring I climb the hill to see these returning birds. But on that equinox day in 2020, the visit felt undeniably different. By then, Covid-19 was raging throughout southern Europe. Acutely attuned to the crippling financial crisis and stark economic contraction that Greece had endured since 2009, there was an early consensus – both politically and among citizens – that the state's fragile public-health system would swiftly collapse if case numbers rose rapidly. All week we'd heard that the closure of shops and schools wasn't sufficient to quell the increase in transmission rates and that the implementation of a strict lockdown was imminent, placing severe restrictions on personal movement. In light of that prospect, I came to see the pelicans on their nests that day knowing it might be my only chance to observe the colonies for a considerable period of time.

I heard a pelican hidden by the overhang of the hill. Uncloaking into view, it glided through the sharp, silvery light. Up close in my binoculars, the image of an earlier era only intensified. Dalmatian pelicans have eyes of such tremulous glacial depths – the bluish-grey sclera like an ice sheet being cored by the black iris – that they appear to hold entire worlds inside them. And, in a way, they do. Like the great white pelican, the Dalmatian pelican's brethren species that nests alongside it on this lake but arrives later in spring, these birds traverse broad valleys of oak and mountains thickened with beech trees and pines to reach here. They sail over remote upland villages and lonely, winding roads. They spiral high above the milky wash of deltas running quick with meltwater into the sea. They trace a geography of longing with those audible wings, because within each of these journeys is concealed a code. Something untranslatable by us. A string of genetic memory and meaning that brings them home each and every year to these islets on a Balkan lake, guiding them back across that expansive aerial map to the same place of shelter we share. And that spring, in a world so radically altered and uncertain, those journeys home and the constancy of connection they detailed resonated more deeply than ever.

The pandemic – as catastrophic events have a tendency to do, tearing us away from our regular, concealing rhythms – showed us just how much illusion we live with, revealing countless cracks across the surface of the world. Cracks that have long existed, of course, fissuring through any truly cohesive and equitable vision of society, but which were exposed in a sharper and more penetrating light by the unrelenting focus and fallout of the crisis.

That while 40 million Americans filed for unemployment during the first five months of the pandemic alone, billionaires in the United States saw their total wealth grow by a further $637 billion. Or that thousands of empty aircraft were kept airborne in order to retain lucrative landing slots in the future, burning fuel on 'ghost flights' in the midst of a climate emergency, shedding carbon emissions while carrying few, if any, passengers. And these stark disparities and dissonances were no different when it came to shelter, one of the wider themes of this book.

Early on in the pandemic, citizens of San Francisco and the Bay area in California were asked to shelter in place – to seek safety by staying put in their places of residence. Over the following months, people right across the globe were told, at varying times and to differing degrees of intensity and enforcement, to remain at home in order to aid others. Here in Greece, the slogan and message were clear: *Menoume spiti*, or *We're staying home*. This, then, was shelter as refuge and sanctuary. Shelter as safe haven. But while sheltering in place was possible for those with safe homes to be in, for others, like the 36 per cent of 750 Greek women who replied to an online survey to say they'd suffered domestic abuse at some point during the forty-two days of the country's first lockdown, home meant anything but shelter. Or for the tens of thousands of day-wage migrant workers in India forced to walk long roads home when Prime Minister Narendra Modi shut down the public transport system in March 2020 in response to the pandemic. Shorn of desperately needed earnings and safe spaces to stay, these labourers – some with children at their side – embarked on gruelling journeys to reach places of refuge that were frequently in other states, walking the edge of motorways or the curving bed of rail lines, hitching lifts if they were lucky, or crossing fields, marshes, forests and plains on foot if not, to reach a shelter of their own. Some of them never made it.

Critically, shelter isn't solely a human concern. As the origins of the pandemic continue to be investigated, there's a very real possibility that it stemmed, like Zika, Sars, Nipah, AIDS and Ebola before it, from the destruction of wild places that enabled a zoonotic disease to spill over from ever-shrinking wild domains into humans. Such devastating viral flows cast a harrowing light on the ceaseless ravaging of natural habitats and homes around the world and the disruptive encroachment on the vital shelters of others. Acts that not only undermine the ability of these places to exist as dwelling grounds for forms of life other than our own but unquestionably corrode our common shelter in a planetary sense as well. If shelter is meant to be something safe and secure – a refuge or sanctuary – then we are destabilising the very thing that enables human societies and the more-than-human world to live well.

This book, however, isn't about the pandemic. The stories it relates of homes lost, found and reimagined – alongside the conflicts and possibilities bound up in the greater issue of human existence with the wild world – were already in place and unfolding long before the appearance of Covid-19. But neither does the book avoid the pandemic, because this crisis dramatically altered our understanding of what shelter means, making possible, I hope, a larger conversation about how we might live in a shared world at this particular point in time. Nor, in all honesty, *can* this book ignore the pandemic, because the world we once knew is no longer here. Acknowledging that fundamental shift is a necessary step towards a potential realignment of relationships. Until that happens, we'll watch whole other worlds we once knew become memory too, because this isn't the first, nor will it be the last, to go. Worlds we once thought stable, permanent or, to borrow that understandable but misplaced pandemic word, *normal*, are being eclipsed and made relic by the twin emergencies of climate change and the Sixth Extinction of wild species. Instead, this book is a reflection on our place in a shared but shifting world at a time when our path into the future could take us any number of ways. When the choice, for the moment, is still ours to make.

It was the wrens that brought the idea of exploring lifelines at the personal, cultural and ecological level into focus for me. Their second winter with us ended just as the pandemic was beginning. That ability of theirs to divine the arrival of potentially killing cold, and react in a way that was completely out of sync with their isolationist tendencies, made me realise how reimagining shelter on this shared planet is key to forging a common path into the future. On each of the nights they flickered upwards into the old swallow's nest, we were separated by only the stone walls of the house. In one corner of our bedroom, where the floorboards pleat with the wooden beam beneath which they roosted, we were little more than an arm's reach away. The distinction between our needs on those nights, when the valley was crystallising with frost or snow fell so deeply that it dampened even rivers to a rustle, seemed just as thin. And when as many as fourteen wrens crowded into that old earthen bowl, I realised how close I felt to those birds. Not just physically, or even through the extraordinary wonder their presence generated when we watched their arrival at dusk, but through a sense of kinship and connection. It felt as though our lifelines had been intimately aligned.

A fortnight after the warmth of the spring equinox the lake basin filled with late snow. All day the world through our windows had whitened, blurring the promise of blossom to almost nothing. By then, our strict lockdown was in place. The hill on which I'd stood above the thriving clamour of the pelican colonies wasn't far from me at all, but – as anticipated – it existed beyond the limits of allowable movement. Throughout the day, as garden branches sagged

and snapped with the gathering weight, I found myself thinking about the pelicans on their nests. Many of them tended eggs;
others already huddled close to young. As snow deepened across the
mountains and lakes, there was nothing for them to do but endure.
To make shelter in a storm, protecting what they'd only just made
or were beginning to raise. And that evening, after an absence of
several weeks, wrens returned to the nest above our door.

The greater watershed of the Prespa lakes has been my home
for well over two decades now. Shared by three countries – Greece,
Albania and North Macedonia – this place exerts a powerful hold
over me. In part because of its remarkable biodiversity and wild
beauty, sheltering not only those pelicans and wrens but also
brown bears in the beech woods, otters along the rivers and shores
and golden eagles in the mountain sky; and in part because the
region's complex human histories, cultures, ecologies, animosities
and compromises, shared by nations with at times acrimonious
ties and divergent political visions, are written vividly into the
place itself. And, like all places, it holds stories of what we get right
and stories of where we went wrong. But this crossroads region
has also been my way into thinking about home on an intimately
personal level as well. When I moved to Prespa with my wife,
Julia, we had little idea of whether it was even possible to find
shelter here. Or, as strangers, whether there was any way for us to
put down roots in a place that we knew only from reading a book
about the area. But the extraordinary and unexpected welcome we
were shown on arrival, and the generous ways in which we were
made to feel part of a small rural community, illuminated for me
how deeper relationships to the wider world around us might be
built and sustained. This, in essence, is a book of homecoming.
And by telling our story of coming to live in Prespa, I hope to tell
a larger story about living in a shared world.

That story is told in three distinct sections in *Lifelines*. The first
– 'Grounding' – braids our journey from London to a mountain

village high above the Prespa lakes in Greece with the broader stories of people and place that converge in this transboundary region. At the heart of the book's middle section – 'Shifting' – are stories of imbalance between human cultures and the natural world. While still anchored by the Prespa lakes, we move outwards to other wild shelters – the relic woodlands of southeast Australia, a tributary of the Brahmaputra river in northeast India and an active volcano on the island of Bali – to explore some of the most pressing issues and threats of our age. Finally, the closing section of the book – 'The Shared World' – shifts the focus of *Lifelines* towards renewal, resilience and radical hope. Chronicling close encounters around the Prespa lakes with species as varied as fireflies, brown bears and Dalmatian pelicans, together with the human communities of these borderlands, it argues that the lifelines of the world hold together the greater home of us all.

On the morning after the storm, we woke to a changed place. The snow glared like summer off a lake and the sky shone a brilliant, bewildering blue. From the porch steps I glanced up at the old swallow's nest, once more amazed that such a small thing could be refuge for so many. Reaching for my shovel, I started clearing a path through the garden, imagining the pelicans on their nests being indistinguishable from the snow of their islands. And it was then, as sunlight began dismantling the storm, peeling back winter to a resurgent spring, that I started this story of shelter shared.

An end, but also a beginning.

I

GROUNDING

1

Sheltering

The sky was a harbour all of a sudden. Wherever you looked, wings furrowed wakes in the air. Having sailed north over the Sahara and the Mediterranean to reach here, swallows and house martins swirled through pools of clouded blue. They'd arrived in days of dancing light, when the oak leaves were so thin that they glowed like stained glass. When you could see spring laddering higher into the mountains by the hour, the rising line that had kept two seasons separate finally erased when the winter peaks were swept by greenery.

It was a time of shelter. Nests, burrows, dens – the clearing out and the building anew. Throughout the valley, those late snows of April had seeped away and signalled a shift towards dwelling. Alongside the returning swallows and house martins, who spent their first days back in the basin inspecting last year's nests under the eaves of village houses, field crickets spaded thumb-sized chambers in the soil with their back legs, smoothing flat the outer lip as a stage to sing from to prospective mates. Golden orioles wove bowls of wool, feathers and grass in the willows, while hoopoes examined trees for a perfectly shaped cavity. Even those with little time left spent what remained in search of refuge. From the woodpiles and shed tiles that had housed them all winter, peacock butterflies emerged to track down nettles in their last flights, gluing a new generation of eggs to the undersides of leaves. A quest for a future shelter that

seemed all the more moving because it was steeped in such clear
and limitless light.

We had an idea of what it was like to arrive here in need of shelter.
In the summer of 2000, when we found ourselves at a crossroads
in our lives, Julia and I left London to traverse the same mountains
that those swallows and house martins had just flown over on their
journeys north, unsure of what we would discover on the other
side. All that we knew about this place on the borders of three
countries had been gleaned from a book that had been glowingly
reviewed in the RSPB's magazine in 1999. Although we'd never
heard of Prespa until then, the reviewer's description of stone villages in the mountains, brown bears in the beech woods and two
expansive lakes in the basin, on which nested pelicans, great white
egrets, squacco herons and little bitterns, made it sound like an
ideal destination for a holiday. Imagining a week of long upland
walks, birdwatching around the shared waters and evenings of local
food in village tavernas, we'd ordered the book as soon as we'd
both finished reading the review.

At the time, having finally acknowledged just how unhappy
we'd become in London, we were looking for ways to change our
lives. Our days in the city, as they are for so many, increasingly felt
as if they consisted of little more than being worn down by work
and long commutes; me as a painter and decorator and Julia as an
organiser of corporate events after a long spell in the theatre industry. Come evening, we lacked the energy and desire to engage
with any of the things we'd once felt so passionately drawn to in
the city, going out to its cinemas, restaurants, museums and music
venues less and less frequently. We were changing in ways that left
us out of sync with that urban world and increasingly knew, at
some deep but still evolving level, that it was time to move on.

We'd even begun talking more openly about leaving England altogether to experience living in an entirely different country and culture. To see if we could find some inner space again in a landscape less familiar to us. But we kept circling around the same, seemingly unresolvable, question: where would we go?

A fortnight after ordering the book we returned from work to find a parcel at our flat. As soon as we'd started dinner and opened a bottle of wine, we slipped *Prespa: A Story of Man and Nature* from its packaging and sat down with it in the living room. Although we hadn't given any real thought to the timing of a holiday, we wanted to see what this place was all about after the excitement of reading the review. Holding the book between us so that we could each see its images, we began reading passages aloud about mountains, pelicans and lakes. Slowing down to savour vivid descriptions of people and place. The author of the book, the Greek biologist and conservationist Giorgos Catsadorakis, wrote openly and honestly about the human and ecological complexities of Prespa, its rich and sometimes troubled history, its natural wealth and fragile future. He captivated us right from the start, pulling us inside this small part of the world so completely that by the time we'd finished a second bottle of wine and reached the end of the book we'd decided to ditch the plan for a holiday in Prespa and to leave London to try to make a home for ourselves there instead. We were heavily hungover the next morning, but nothing could mar the distinctive lightness we felt at the road of possibilities suddenly opening into view ahead of us. We now had an intention, if not quite a plan, to change our lives.

In the summer of our leaving London, we laboured with over-loaded rucksacks – one on the back, another on the front – their side pockets bulging and the straps loosened like belts after a Christmas meal. Inside was all we thought we'd need in the new lives we were about to begin: a selection of summer and winter clothes; books, journals and conservation textbooks; a pocket-sized CD player, portable speakers and a few CDs; walking boots; a first-aid kit; two pairs of binoculars and a basic set of utensils. There was also a heavy laptop that I'd insisted would be a waste of space given everything that we had to carry – a line of reasoning that Julia, sensing how rapidly the still-emerging online world was changing, thankfully just ignored.

Those packs were with us the whole way, from the June day when, experiencing a tearily intense blend of exhaustion and exhilaration, we finished closing up our flat on a North London council estate in the early hours of the morning. With no sleep at all, we had repainted the final rooms and scoured clean every last surface for the incoming tenants while snacking on takeaway pizza and draining a bottle of cheap fizz. The packs were with us as we journeyed down the Adriatic coast by boat, the rocky, pine-studded islands of Croatia appearing as if mirages against the deep well of blue, and on a hot, oily ferry crossing from Bari in Italy to the port of Igoumenitsa in Greece, the crew kicking us awake on the floor of the ship's bar still sticky with spilled drinks, where we and a few others had slept as best we could above the incessant grumbling of the engines. They were with us when we boarded a bus rolling north into the steepling green mountains of the Pindus range in western Greece, the sun fevered and fierce through the windows, the conductor approaching us with a smile down the aisle, slinging a few sentences our way that made all the Greek we thought we'd learned at night school in the weeks before leaving suddenly feel as though we'd been enrolled in the wrong class. The packs were with us on the afternoon a taxi corkscrewed us ever higher into the mountains towards the northwest corner of Greece, winding down the other side in a series of spellbinding switchbacks, oak forests greening the slopes as two stunning blue lakes opened like eyes in the vaulted light of the Balkans. And they were with us when the driver dropped us in the quiet square of Agios Germanos, the village we'd decided on because of a particularly stunning photo of it set against the mountains and lakes of the basin that we'd seen when reading the book about Prespa back in London.

It was mid-afternoon, a sky of hot light and silence. We'd arrived, but didn't really know where. We soon found the guest house I'd discovered in the *Rough Guide to Greece*, one of the few lodgings around at the time. The owner, Vassilis, showed us to our room and suggested we rest after our journey. In an hour, he said, opening the door to a simple, white-tiled and white-walled space, he'd bring us tea and we could complete the paperwork for our stay.

Sure enough, an hour later we heard a rapping at the door. The three of us settled on wicker chairs on the veranda. The guest house looked down over the valley, where a winding line of trees marked the course of a river that spilled into the lake. The water shimmered with summer silver, the sun riding the high blue sky as the imposing peaks of Albania dimpled into the distance.

Vassilis poured mountain tea, the herby scent of an alpine meadow rising from the liquid. As he handed us our cups, I noticed how tall, graceful poplars studded the valley and rustled in the hot air, so that their leaves flashed silver and green, as though spun from a dream. 'So,' Vassilis began, placing a glass bowl of sweet, stewed plums between us with a set of spoons, 'how long are you thinking of staying?'

Much that seems minor in the moment can become magnified over time, so that any particular experience takes on the accrued depth and contours that only hindsight and history can give it. It's like walking yourself backwards through all the choices you've ever made, carrying on further and further into the past and finally realising that personal decisions only ever played a partial role in configuring a course through life. The rest was determined by circumstance and serendipity; by the combined decisions of family and ancestors that brought you to that particular point in time; by remote events you had no control over but that helped sculpt the context of your options; and by an unfathomable number of people whose paths run parallel to yours. All coalescing into something we tend to call self-agency but which is in fact the sum of compound and interconnected actions, responses, desires and deliberations. Our lifelines aren't ours alone.

This was certainly true for us when we arrived; those first hours in Prespa on that summer's day well over two decades ago set the tone for our future here. We could simply have told Vassilis we weren't sure how long we planned to stay and remained non-committal about our intentions until we had a better feel for the place, or chosen a random number of days for the sake of convenience. But having gone to all the trouble of closing up our lives in one part of the world to try to begin new ones in another, it didn't seem to be in the spirit of things to be secretive and aloof. And so I said the words on that veranda above the lakes.

'We've decided to move here, Vassilis.'

Even now, all these years later, I'm still not sure what I'd expected, but Vassilis's response wasn't it. There was no pause or hesitation from him; no frowning or furrowing of brows. He simply set his cup down on the table and said, 'Then you should finish your tea so that we can start finding you somewhere to live.'

That evening, in the glorious shine of an alpine summer, we rattled up rocky tracks in an old, beige Toyota pick-up, winding ever higher into the pleated granite folds, us in the back and Vassilis's small and beloved dog Boubou up front in the passenger seat, skirting the stone ruins of shepherds' huts into a world where wildflowers still stood their ground in the cooler climate of the highlands. We stopped at remote outbuildings on steep, thyme-cushioned slopes to speak to cattle-herders Vassilis thought might have a room for us to rent in the village below. Others we flagged down as they descended the pitted mountain tracks for dinner at home. They all listened with what appeared to be a mixture of friendly curiosity and courteous uncertainty, their eyes shifting between us and the man who had taken us under his wing. Not that we could decipher the true meaning of the conversations until Vassilis had translated them for us back in the truck. Though sometimes he didn't need to, as the shaking of heads was understandable enough.

We stayed at Vassilis's guest house for six weeks that summer. They were long, light-flooded days of discovery. We would climb in the encircling mountains and slowly acquaint ourselves with the paths traced across them over time. We'd sit on the veranda and watch short-toed eagles comb the rocky slopes through our binoculars, or stare at the shifting blues and greens of the sunlit lakes. We'd return from the woods with tubs of wild raspberries gleaned from the smashed canes after bears had clawed up their fill, giving whatever we hadn't eaten to Vassilis's mother. Chrysoula would then tip them into a pan heaped high with sugar to simmer down for winter, when that raking summer light was just a memory to be savoured on a spoon. And all the while Vassilis kept looking for shelter for us, knocking on our door in the evenings to share any news, or calling up to the veranda when a new idea occurred to him. When it did, we'd immediately hop into his truck and roll slowly along back lanes where cats and chickens convened in the neighbourly shade or go off to other villages in the basin, entering the homes of strangers to enquire about a place to rent. For all kinds of reasons these other ideas never quite panned out – there was no running water or we'd have to share a room with the retired owners when they returned from the city on weekends – but Vassilis was determined. He'd made it his mission to find us a home.

On an afternoon at the end of August we returned from a walk in the hills, their grasses now as pale as straw from a punishing summer and the birds we'd begun to learn already leaving for seasons to the south of us, to see a note pinned to our door. *I've found you somewhere to rent*, it said. Set to one side of the village square and with a small garden out front, the stone house he showed us that evening would become our home for the next fourteen years. The longest I've ever lived in one place in my life.

While we now rent a house at the very edge of the village, where meadows rise into mountains and those wrens roost in an old swallow's nest above the door, the house by the square was our way into another world. Not only did it give us somewhere to be, but it gave us a reason for staying. And like all good shelters, it grounded us in the specificity of a place and community. Raised from granite hauled from the local mountains and riverbeds, the knapped stone shone a mineral gleam of pale russets and varied greys when struck by sunlight. As with other traditional houses of the village – many of which in the past had sheltered farm animals on the ground floor while people lived above – each of its commanding walls was nearly two feet thick, to exclude the worst of the winter cold and keep the rooms cool at the height of a burning summer. And like layers of cream in a cake, two thin bands of wood had been inserted into the lower half to ensure the building remained elastic during earthquakes, absorbing the shaking seismic pressure and letting the house move naturally with the turbulence. Built around 1920, the period when so many of the village's remaining buildings date from, the house was a compound reflection of local climate, geology and terrain; shelter as an essential, but also intimate, interpretation of place.

On our first night there, we cracked open cans of beer and sat in the garden beneath an umbrella of astonishing stars. All summer we'd marvelled at them. With little light pollution cast upwards from the small settlements and the mountains acting as an intensifying frame of focus, they offered a particularly resonant sense of depth to the visible universe. As we sat there in the dry tangle of grasses with the evening sounds of the summer square close by, that night sky of starlight and moon glow lent clarity to our decision, even if we had no concrete idea of what we would do next, or how we would even begin to earn a living here. But shelter was a significant start. Later that night, we went inside and piled the belongings we'd carried with us in one corner of a room. It didn't look much, nor did it feel as though it equalled the weight of the rucksacks on our shoulders that summer, but it was a small beginning to the making of a home.

Although we knew little about Prespa beyond what we'd read in the book that brought us here, the village soon began yielding its particulars. As with so many southern European settlements, its square is the animating heart of the small community. Not only is it a physical focal point, which all roads and lanes ultimately gravitate towards, but it's also a place of trade and practical exchange, of fellowship and social cohesion, of celebration, politics and conversation, and, not uncommonly, of disagreement and feuds. Its varied seasonal uses reflect the working patterns of the settlement, reliant on the soils, woods and waters surrounding it. This was even more the case when we arrived, as the square has since been transformed to make it more attractive to tourists and residents alike, gaining a distinctive aesthetic appeal but losing something of its open and unadorned honesty in the process.

During our first autumn, as we dug the garden in preparation for growing as much of our own food as we could the following spring, the square clanged with the bells of donkeys and mules being led up into the mountain beech forests to carry out wood for winter fires. A week or two later, a middle-aged Roma couple set up their mobile workspace at the foot of our drive. There they kindled a fire and fanned the small glow until the flames took hold. Then they set to work, receiving copper pots, bowls and basins eased out of kitchen cupboards and lifted from nails in village sheds to be walked towards the square. While the woman continually fed the fire with dry wood, her husband spun each vessel at speed on a rotating metal clamp above the flames, scouring the interior with a stiff wire brush and a few drops of liquid cleanser. Once clean, he heated a lozenge of tin until it bubbled in a pan over the fire, tipping the molten metal into the copper vessels and relining them to a silver shine. By Christmas Eve, a tower of cut logs and evergreen branches was lit in the square. We all gathered close, passing around bowls of bean soup and topping up cups of red wine siphoned straight from barrels in winter sheds. And then the dances would begin. Reflecting the knitted histories of the village, the music was a blend of Balkan brass band and Greek clarinet, the raucous and the melancholy. As the circle of dancers opened and closed with each new arrival, enlarging around the smoking pyre as orange sparks flew upwards through the cold and snow, it sealed inside it some essential element of collective connection.

It wasn't only humans who were connected to the village square, however. Across from our house stood the village post office. We were separated from it by a narrow stream that rippled through a deep channel seeded with willows. Through the leaves we could watch the congregations of spring. From their arrival in the middle of March until the end of August, when they lined up on electricity lines like dominoes readying to fall into their southward flights, house martins and swallows – red-rumped as well as barn – wove a score of extraordinary beauty through the air above the square and the post office, where dozens of mud nests bulged from the underside of the building's eaves. And in those summering months, for the five days a week that the post office was open, the world of humans and the world of hirundines visibly melded into what this whole world really is – a planet that's shaped by a spectrum of presences and shared beyond measure. Farmers shouldered sacks of produce inside to be shipped onwards to shops as swallows swung upwards past the steps, carrying beakfuls of mud to shape their suspended dwellings. Older folks cashed their pensions and sat chatting with the postmen as young house martins begged from their nests. And during sudden rainstorms, birds in their dozens would flatten themselves against the walls of the building while customers inside peered out of the windows until the weather had passed. Seeing these birds in such close and easy relationship with human spaces was a reminder of just how woven our lives are with some wild species. Their definitive attachment to our architecture, particularly in rural areas where sourcing mud is a relatively simple task, not only makes their gracefulness accessible to a wide range of people but is also remarkably confiding and trusting, too. Much wildlife exists at the edge of human perception unless actively sought, but these birds, pouring in on the winds of spring, fill the empty centre.

We rely on these rituals of return to steady our place in a shifting world. To shore up foundations gone wobbly in winter, when the wet gales and short dark days can tumble us into a funk. With the arrival of these birds the last of the winter light broadens out into another pattern of the turning earth. They bring life from elsewhere, having only weeks earlier swept through the salted air above the Cape of Good Hope or felt the cold over the slopes of Kilimanjaro. They join up far places in the way that a constellation of named stars transforms before our eyes into one of the recognisable shapes of the sky. And it feels like a kickstart to the heart when they appear.

Sometimes, though, birds don't arrive.

On 6 April 2020, when we were deep into the most restrictive period of our first pandemic lockdown in Greece, lives other than human experienced an awful limiting and suspension of movement, too. Unseasonable cold weather mantled the southern Balkans, ushered in by persistent northerlies that raked the Mediterranean just as migrating birds peaked in their crossings. There they met an immovable force. The extraordinary ability of birds to fly and move vast distances in sync with the seasons and supplies of food, the thing that makes them so compelling to the human imagination, also leaves these wild lives particularly exposed and vulnerable to weather. I'll always remember taking a bus from the city of Malmö in Sweden on a day of leaden skies and punishing rain to watch the spectacle of autumn migration from the headland of Falsterbo, the last spur of Swedish land before the beginnings of the Baltic Sea, and passing a field containing hundreds of crouched buzzards on the dark, runnelled mud, their drenched feathers pasted flat and forlornly to their bones. Without waiting out the torrential rain, their crossing of the cold sea – where no thermals are generated to help them ride the skies – could be perilous; wait too long, however, and they might be too weak to span the distance. For years I've wondered how long those buzzards stayed hunched in that sour field.

On that April day in the first year of the pandemic, though, the hirundines streaking northwards were already in the air and en route to their summer grounds when the winds set in. It must have felt as if they'd hit a wall. Unable to continue, countless birds were brought down out of the sky that day and night. Beaten, exhausted and hungry, they had few options but to go to ground. When they fell, the lucky ones hit a hard surface; the rest were lost at sea. On the following morning, people across southern Greece woke to a bewildering scene. Thousands and thousands of swallows carpeted the sodden roads and verges, some of them already crushed beneath the wheels of cars. House martins clung in their hundreds to the edges of roofs, desperately hanging there like colonies of bats. Swifts sheltered beneath all manner of outdoor objects – doormats, patio rugs, furniture cushions – having crawled there on what passes for their legs and crept under to keep warm together. Some birds regained the air only to discover that the flying insects they depend on for food were grounded too. All they'd consumed across the southern deltas and savannahs of Africa to prepare for their gruelling flights had run out just when they needed it most. Nothing could have foretold them of their fortunes ahead.

We take them for granted up there: their songs, their splendour, their grace. That admirable ability to stay afloat and angle upwards, or to sheer clear through the air without resistance, as though made of wind or light or water. They belong to that vast sheltering sky we can only dream of without the aid of technology, but it's a sky that can also break them like sticks. And in an age when Earth's atmosphere is being cooked by fossil-fuel emissions, triggering winds and storms not only more common but also increasingly violent and unpredictable, our feathered kin are rendered that much more vulnerable. Their plight reminds me of how many other lives wink out in the same desperate way. A world traced with the footfalls of fellow humans fleeing war zones, poverty, persecution and violence. Largely unrecorded for posterity, their crossings are no less fraught than those of migratory birds; and, like those swallows, swifts and house martins streaming north on the promise of an unfolding green spring, they sometimes meet with terrible and haunting endings.

On the first of March, in those strange days in the earliest stage of the pandemic, when we watched a virus spread along the aerial arteries we've created by mimicking the flight of birds, Julia twined

two lengths of wool – one red, the other white – around my left
wrist. This is the custom of *Martis*, named after the month of
March in which the first swallows typically arrive in Greece after
their migration from Africa. While the tradition is thought to have
an obscure ancient lineage connected to the Eleusinian Mysteries,
and is celebrated in various parts of the Balkans in a wide spectrum
of ways, symbolising anything from the safeguarding of houses to
the protection of children's faces from the warming sun, the most
significant aspect of the ritual for me, in these parts at least, is that
the bracelet is worn until the first swallow of the season is sighted,
at which point it's cut free and placed in shrubbery or a tree to
provide nesting material for the newly arrived birds. Although
I rarely witness a swallow taking up the offer of the bracelet to
line its nest, the fundamental heart of this iteration of the custom
is that it involves people in the lives of fellow species, making a
compact that marks each yearly return. Similarly, in other parts of
Greece, children still sing an ancient song called 'Swallowing' on
the first of the month, going carolling from house to house with
a wreath or basket of early wildflowers while carrying a dummy
swallow fashioned from wood on a stick. Traditionally, they would
receive fresh eggs, coins or, in an apt blending of traditions, the
white and red bracelets of *Martis* at each household. While it
has long been understood that swallows suppress disease-carrying
mosquitoes and garden pests from the surroundings of a house,
meaning their desire to live alongside us has largely been encouraged across multiple cultures, these customs, like all rituals that
effectively celebrate the vernal return, appear founded on deep
respect for the birds themselves, the paths of our lives converging
in a season of communal renewal.

But even this ritualised embrace can be fragile. While far from
common, I sometimes see the remains of a destroyed nest. A tracery of dried mud where the entire shelter should be: an echo of
what was. Although nests naturally fall as they age, to see entire

rows of these imprints on a building typically means the solid cups
have been bashed down with a stick or scrubbed off with the stiff
bristles of a broom, scouring away all the ingenious labours of a
house martin or swallow that has painstakingly beaked from puddle or pool hundreds if not thousands of mud pellets to be shaped
and pressed into as much certainty as a small bird can ever hope
for. It's usually at the beginning of the breeding season that they're
dismantled, just as birds are completing their arduous journeys.
Such removals are meant to discourage further nesting attempts
in a particular place, but occasionally it's later in the season that
they're felled, so that eggs or fledglings tumble with the crumbling
mud. I've witnessed ghost-nests on hotels, tavernas and municipal
buildings; I've seen them on apartments, houses and bus stations.
It's almost impossible to erase entirely the evidence of past tenancy.

Such eradications aren't specific to any region or country.
A simple online search for ways to prevent swallows from nesting reveals the widespread presence of the practice. But there's a
single line, from a page called 'How to get rid of swallows' on an
animal-control website in the United States, that has stayed with
me since I first carried out that simple search:

Another reason to prevent swallows is their love for home.

A barn swallow of the Americas, a sub-species of the European
swallow that in flight flashes redder underparts and a paler blue finish above, could have journeyed from as far as southern Argentina
to arrive at a clapboard house in Wisconsin or an adobe mud
home in New Mexico to raise a brood in the same nest it cared
for its young in the year before. Its attachment to place is extraordinarily precise, staying faithful to a dwelling that can be used by
a pair and their descendants for ten to fifteen years, though the
longest recorded use of a European swallow's nest is an astonishing forty-eight consecutive summers. What is frequently elevated

in human cultures as a virtue – a sign of deep roots and respected generational legacy – is frowned on in this instance. Instead, the animal-control company warns of an 'infestation' if you allow the birds to nest, one that could 'reduce the value of a home or property by 5–10 per cent':

> Swallows can be discouraged from returning to an area by knocking down nests either before they're occupied or after the swallow has migrated. Continually losing your home would be enough to keep most animals away from an area.

It's the casual ease of the phrasing that troubles me most; the way in which a light-hearted tone makes the destruction of dwellings so much gentler on the ear. The removal of nests is a small matter in comparison to the greater, systemic pressures these birds face, but there's an analogy at the heart of such acts that goes some way towards understanding the role of humans in the biodiversity crisis, while also reminding me that if we hadn't left the unused swallow's nest above our door that those wrens would have had to search elsewhere for a place to roost against the winter cold. Erasing our common connections to the natural world by favouring the sterile separation of species is one of the underlying triggers for making large parts of the world unliveable for other forms of life. That inability to consider the needs of others, or to focus entirely on a value only financial in measure, failing to take into account any of the other attributes the presence of swallows might occasion in a home, such as beauty, wonder and joy, risks the further leakage of species and meaning from the world.

It's hard to imagine a world without swallows, but it could come to pass. For nearly thirty years now, Alejandro Onrubia has monitored the passage of migratory birds across the Strait of Gibraltar in both spring and autumn from the low hills of

Andalucía in southern Spain. As one of only two primary crossing points between Europe and Africa for journeying birds (the other being the Bosphorus Strait at Istanbul), the Strait of Gibraltar acts as a vast funnel for birds breeding across western, northern and central Europe in their continental exchange. The regular monitoring of the strait enables a complex picture of migratory trends and population figures to be built up for a significant portion of Europe. In the three decades that Alejandro has glassed the skies for weeks on end in his work for the environmental organisation Fundación Migres, he's witnessed a cumulative rise in the numbers of particular species. Storks have made noticeable gains, as have those raptors whose lives are closely tethered to woods, which appear to be trending positively in response to an overall uptick in European forest cover in recent years. But Alejandro has also chronicled the sharp and unequivocal dwindling of passerines in that time, too.

'Numbers of songbirds here are declining dramatically,' he said when I passed a scorching autumn morning with him at his vantage point in 2018, the blue waters of the strait glistening beneath us and the sky above clouding with eagles, vultures and storks. 'Compared with the data from the 1970s, we are counting an eighth of the swifts and only a third of the barn swallows now.'

While there's still much to be learned about the precise causes of these declines, it appears that a heating climate is at least partially responsible for the losses. Increasingly hot and dry summers are leading to plummeting insect numbers across large parts of Europe, thereby reducing food availability for hirundines; more sporadic rains in spring make it difficult for swallows and house martins to locate the muddy pools and scrapes that are the source material for their nests; while agricultural fields drenched in toxic pesticides further winnow the birds' food supplies. Both in Europe during the breeding season and on their wintering grounds in Africa, these species face a litany of interconnected threats.

As hard as it is to imagine a world without swallows, it's just as difficult to conceive of one without elephants or fireflies or sharks. A world without dolphins or giraffes. Each of these wild species is an emblematic and recognisable part of the patterned world. And yet, not so very long ago, it must have been equally hard to imagine a world without passenger pigeons, without great auks, without buffaloes. Of these, only the last is still with us, having hung on by the slenderest of threads during the savage slaughter of its kind, when tens of millions of these animals were massacred across the plains of North America by white settlers in the nineteenth century. The other two, along with numerous other species differentiated only by their relative anonymity, departed this world after a dedicated period of attrition. If abundance in nature has taught us anything in relation to human pressures, it's that there's never enough of a thing. No numbers were sufficient to ensure the collective existence of those lost species, and given the astounding plenitude of some of them — enough to darken a prairie sky of an afternoon in the case of the passenger pigeon — it's clear that abundance alone is neither safety net nor shield. Extinction shows us that nothing is infinite; that no shelter can be absolutely secure. Without a desire to reconfigure relationships between the human and more-than-human worlds so that they lean towards kinship and reciprocity, so too could swallows go the way of the passenger pigeon. Without acknowledgement of a shared planet and its intrinsic limits, those red and white threads on a wrist might never get cut. Because what breaks isn't the world but the lives it holds.

I still think about Vassilis's reply when we told him of our intention to move here. Not only did he not waver or hesitate before suggesting we begin looking for a house, but he didn't ask any of the questions I might have asked if our roles had been reversed.

What for? What will you do here? Are you sure about this? Instead, on that veranda above the lakes and encircled by summer mountains at the meeting point of three countries, he responded with an extraordinary degree of openness and an enlarging gesture of welcome. He offered fellowship before even knowing who we were.

I'm sure there were easier ways to find a home than rocking wildly in a pick-up truck whose suspension had long since been run into the ground, the wild uplands and tumbling rivers unfolding around each bend as the sun fell slowly over the basin, its light angling outwards and reflecting over everything – the rustling beech trees and rugged rowans, the small pale stones in the glowing streams, the grasses in their evening sway – but I now realise that Vassilis wanted to open the door for us personally. And it was this immediate and unwavering embrace that showed us how home, at its heart, should really be thought of as a verb – something that requires action for it to become real. And that the act of making one can be shared.

In a similar spirit of kinship, I've witnessed creative and caring ways for living alongside swallows and house martins. I've seen wicker baskets hung beneath nests to catch droppings, or signs explaining why a dining table is set at an odd angle on a restaurant veranda; I've seen netting slung like a hammock to catch any prematurely fallen young; and I've seen nests left in peace in the reconstructed Minoan palace of Knossos on Crete, where rooms open to the air might well have been shelter to the birds' ancestors over three and a half thousand years ago. We will always live in some kind of contradiction with the natural world; the question is *how do we live with it well?* Because when we lean into the presence of other lives, we ensure that the shared world is infinitely richer. I remember sitting outside our village taverna in late March some springs ago when my friend, Nikos, whom I'd never known to show any particular interest in nature, shouted over from another table to ask why I was still wearing my red and white bracelet.

'I haven't seen a swallow yet,' I said.

'Haven't you been looking?' he asked, laughing and holding up a wrist free of threads. 'They've been with us for days.'

That afternoon, just as Nikos had already known, swallows were flickering over the village when I looked up, their journey to an ancestral shelter complete for another season.

Within weeks of us moving into the house by the square, Vassilis's mother had brought round cuttings of evening primrose and lilac from her garden, jabbing the stems into the early-autumn earth with little ceremony beyond a sturdy knowledge of what worked and when. Although we no longer live in that house, and Chrysoula died many years ago, her cuttings still flower to this day, a connection between her home and what had been ours. And whenever I walk past it, especially when swallows are with us again and the nests fringing the post-office eaves clamour with the voiced needs of their young, these gifts of hers – some of them re-rooted in our current garden at the edge of the village – remind me of the grace and solidarity of acceptance. If it hadn't been for people like these at the very beginning of our journey, our story here would have been radically different. And there's no way of knowing whether we'd still be in Prespa at all. In their generous embrace of our desire to home here, we were shown shelter when we least expected it.

2

Above the Lakes

Mountains give shape to these lakes. Rising from a plateau in the southern Balkans, they wrap the basin like the sides of a bowl. And inside that bowl sits a vast well of water some 3 to 5 million years old. While most of the world's lakes are relatively recent endeavours, particularly in the northern hemisphere, where the grinding actions of glaciation forged depressions that brimmed with meltwater when the last ice age began receding from the land around twelve thousand years ago, there are some twenty lakes of geological antiquity scattered across the planet that have each carried water for more than a million years. Predominantly tectonic in origin and known collectively as 'ancient lakes', this rare vintage includes – together with the Prespa lakes – Lake Baikal in Siberia, Lake Titicaca in Peru, Lake Tanganyika in eastern Africa and nearby Lake Ohrid in North Macedonia and Albania. Age has lent each of these bodies of water a characteristic richness, like the creases of experience written across an elder's skin. Not only do they chronicle the deep-time changes of the planet at a geological level and through the archiving of past ecosystems in the lake bed's sediment, but in modern times they typically nourish a distinctive flora and fauna. Their historic isolation and longevity have frequently created the conditions for endemism to take root, meaning that certain species have evolved in that specific location and are found nowhere else in the world. And in the case of the Prespa lakes, mountains aren't merely the dramatic backdrop for the complexity of biological expression found within the water-shed, but one of the fundamental reasons for its presence.

To understand these mountains, you need first to see inside them. Imagine slicing a line down the middle of the basin as you would with a cake. Then tease the two halves apart, so that its interior is fully revealed. Instead of the same substance to either side – lemon sponge, let's say – you'll discover two completely unrelated flavours. On the eastern flank of the basin, dark brood-ing granite is the primary ingredient of its geological recipe, while pale and porous limestone makes up the western half. Each side holds light and water differently; each responds to heat, wind and ice in its own unique way. But in the collision of these dis-tinct foundations entirely unalike habitats are nurtured in a single place, so that plant and invertebrate communities that prefer one geological shelter and soil type over another can co-exist in the same watershed. It's this physical diversity, rising from lake level at around 850 metres right through to the mountain peaks, that enables 1,815 wild plant species to make a home in the Greek part of the basin alone, or 31 per cent of the country's flora across just 0.3 per cent of its land surface.

These mountains have also contoured the cultures of the shared lakes, from the spiritual seclusion of Christian hermits in Ottoman times to pastoralism in the more recent past, when Sarakatsani and Vlach transhumant shepherds guided their flocks on foot from the southern coasts and lowlands of Greece to seek out forage in these uplands. Around the peaks – Kitsevo and Belavoda in Greece; Mali i Thatë in Albania; and Mount Pelister on the Baba massif in North Macedonia, which, at 2,600 metres, is the highest in the whole basin – snow holds fast until June. Then the slopes flare into a short, hot summer, their grasslands a storm of wild-flowers and butterflies. In winter, the upper reaches are owned by others: ravens, wolves, horned larks and lichens. The occasional wakened bear. Up there, on the rim of the lifted earth, winds cut the snowfields like blades. And when they finally fade, the angled land becomes a kingdom of piercing white silence and ice.

Mountains give shape to these lakes. They always have and always will. Together they work the sky into a smaller thing, collapsing views like a camera shutter stuck half open, so that the intensity and aspect of light flooding through is rearranged. They generate their own weather, atmosphere and climate; they encircle our lives. And in their legacy of differing stones, they hold close entire stories of shelter.

I pulled over by a small church on a limestone ridge above the lakes. Beside it a rough mountain track bedded with pale pebbles. Spring was spiralling into sound as songbirds spun lines into the cool, morning air. I walked up into a deep-green world where immense junipers towered over the church like living cliffs. Many of the trees had forged expressively idiosyncratic paths as they'd risen, their branches spoking at unusual angles, or the trunks twisting like rags being wrung free of water, so that fissures in their bark corkscrewed around the limbs. Others had bellied outwards, or were leaning back as if some invisible weight was pressing on them. In one thing they were united, though: they all gave off the heavy complexion of persistence, something resinous and compressed. Something enduring. Inside the grove, things felt different from outside it. Distinctive. Even the sounds of insects and birds were amplified by the living shape of the space, as though they were being listened to in a small room. A room you could enter and leave without need of a door.

Prespa is a crossroads place. As we've already seen, it's where limestone collides with granite, generating a cosmopolitan citizenry of plants and associated invertebrates. It's where three countries come together around two lakes, the invisible borders slicing through lake water, uniting through its natural watershed a range of languages, histories, religions, traditions and ethnicities. And it's where heat-adapted Mediterranean ecosystems meet their cooler, Balkan relatives. The junipers on this mountain are the western exemplars of juniper woods more commonly found in southeast Turkey and the Near East. Composed primarily of Greek juniper, along with some stinking juniper, this particular grove is an assembly of remarkable rarity because of its species composition and the size of its trees – not only in Greece but throughout all of Europe. These ancient trees rise up to 25 metres tall, revealing the profound potential for juniper growth when these organisms are allowed the opportunity to express themselves unhindered.

These elders are with us today solely because that small church at their centre gives them shelter. As with other sacred spaces in remote valleys or on the islands of the Aegean, the trees benefit from the protection historically accorded spiritual sites in Greece and elsewhere, like the remarkable church forests of Ethiopia, small oases of biodiversity scattered across vast seas of agricultural plains. Considered seamless aspects of the landscape of faith, they consequently come under its care. The church on this site today is a relatively modern structure, which means the junipers predate it by hundreds and hundreds of years. *They* are the lingering physical tie to the earth at the time of the original church's founding. Sanctity in the shape of living trees. And they exist because the relationship between natural world and sacred space, in this place at least, has been sustained.

We often talk of the resilience and endurance of long-lived wildlife, from towering redwoods that were alive before the time of Christ to the Greenland sharks believed to have roamed the cold seas for up to half a millennium each, but what can be equally resilient and enduring is our respect for the wild world. Sacred sites show that our systems of thinking are capable of dissolving the distinctions so frequently employed to demarcate boundaries between humans and the natural world, seeing them instead as linked, interwoven, inseparable. Understanding them, as many Indigenous cosmologies have long done, as connected elements of an indivisible world.

I stepped out of the shadow of the ancient junipers and zig-zagged through spring along the ridge. While the beautiful bells of the snake's head fritillary had already fallen, the shaded places beneath trees were still lit by the purple glow of pyramidal orchids. Owlflies, appearing like a strange and wondrous cross between a butterfly and a dragonfly, their antennae tipped with small black pompoms and their transparent wings glinting in the gathered light, jetted over the wild grasses. The sharp scent of junipers clotted the air. All around me grew younger relatives of the sacred grove. In leaving the old trees behind, I'd crossed a cultural border – and the distinction was easy to see. In both texture and mood, the brocade of the landscape was more open and available to light. And the junipers were scaled to a size that didn't edge out the sky, because this is where livelihood rather than sacred association was entwined with the wild.

Beyond the church, the ridge's juniper woods have been worked and grazed in the way of forests the world over. Juniper's resistance to rotting made it the ideal material for the construction of Prespa's traditional boats and houses, while the branches were harvested for fodder and used in the construction of fishing traps called *pelaizia*. You can still see the old cuts, hardened and healed over. But despite being worked trees rather than spiritually protected, the younger junipers – probably no more than 150 years old at most – have helped nurture and sustain an extraordinarily vibrant and unique ecosystem, sheltering 800 different plant species on this mountain alone, including exceptional European rarities, and an enormous variety of butterflies, beetles, dragonflies and moths. I say *helped* because human communities have played a vital role in defining the nature of these sun-filled slopes, creating and maintaining glades through regular cutting and traditional grazing, enabling a spectacular gallery of wildflowers to open each spring within what is listed as an EU priority habitat.

Rising through the trees, I began encountering flushes of sapling oaks. While both oak and juniper were once leaned on heavily by local communities as essential resources, the junipers responded far better to the exploitation. As oak shoots are a favourite food of goats, making their grace period for regrowth typically brief, over time the junipers came to dominate this landscape. And in response to the presence of these evergreen trees and the abundance of light at the heart of them, a remarkably rich ecosystem of plants and invertebrates evolved on the mountain. But the gradual decline in woodcutting and grazing as a result of depopulation, combined with an economic shift from pastoral subsistence to the production of agricultural beans as a cash crop on the plain below, has created a curious ecological conundrum. As the oaks naturally recover, springing up in thick, ground-blanketing masses, the junipers are being squeezed out, and a unique spectrum of species reliant on the light and space they provide is at risk if this ridge gives way to the greater shade of an oak wood. We are repeatedly told about the many burdens that humans place on the planet, but this is only one strand of our conjoined story, because human withdrawal and the absence of traditional practices can be a pressure too, potentially reducing the biological complexity of a place significantly.

Above the ridge, alpine swifts scythed through the brimming blue. Between the trees I caught glimpses of the lakes and the green glow of the rising spring reeds. Snow still capped the mountains of our village on the granite side of the water. Ahead of me, through a screen of junipers, a set of stone trenches came into view, where the soil had been dug to a depth of a metre and the hollows lined with roughly stacked limestone, creating a warren of simple capillaries threaded through the earth. This, too, was shelter – but shelter of a very different kind.

When the fragile truce that had existed between Greece's left-wing and right-wing resistance movements during the Second World War irreversibly fractured, the Greek Civil War exploded across the country. Having notionally coalesced in opposition to German occupation, each saw the possibility of remaking the nation in its own image, capitalising on the political vacuum created by the Axis withdrawal to establish their respective ideologies. A desire that eventually led to a horrific fratricidal conflict that cost an estimated 158,000 people their lives. Greece assumed a toxic, haunted atmosphere – socially, politically, psychologically. Whole villages were abandoned, especially here in the north, their residents uprooted and made refugees. Suspicion and fear ran rife. Death squads on both sides of the ideological divide carried out reprisal attacks against opposing communities. And in 1949, as the war between the Hellenic Army of Greece's right-wing, royalist government and the Democratic Army of the anti-monarchist Communist Party of Greece neared its terrible end, Prespa was key to its coda. From here – where the General Secretary of the Greek Communist Party, Nikos Zachariadis, directed the Democratic Army from his headquarters in a hilltop cave just a few kilometres from the trenches on this limestone ridge – refugees and fleeing left-wing soldiers desperately tried to escape the country when the Communist forces finally collapsed. As they did, the Greek Air Force, reliant on planes, equipment and training supplied by the British and American governments, rained bombs across the Greek portion of the basin in an attempt to disrupt the flow of escapees. And napalm was unleashed on select landscapes of the north. Just a short way up the ridge from the trenches, the large panel of a rusted canister that once held this savage form of fire leans against a twisted juniper tree.

If a single mountain ridge could ever symbolise this place, it is this one. Its underlying limestone is prone to dissolution, being worked by water over fathomless spans of time so that any natural cracks, hollows and fissures are gradually opened and enlarged through the slow process of erosion. It feels as though the stories of these varied shelters – of sacred trees, livelihoods, traditions, war and exodus – have been poured whole into the stone. The entire mountain a vessel of memory. But the stories of these shelters aren't yet complete: they're still in motion, continuing to reshape our lives just as clearly as water reshapes these stones.

When I was a boy, I was fascinated by outer space. It was an interest initiated by a coffee-table book about the universe that I pored over obsessively in our living room in a small town in southern Ontario, staring at the remarkable illustrations of the planets, trying to fathom the staggering size differential between Jupiter and Earth. I peered at the eerie reflective radiance of nebulae in the dark unimaginable reaches and wondered what it would be like to pass through the gasses of the planetary rings, naively thinking the experience was comparable to being enclosed by scrolling mists on autumn fields. By Grade 7, when I would have been twelve, I even dedicated an essay to the mysteries of our galaxy. Reading it today, the blue ink of my handwritten words a little faded but still clear, an awestruck tone shines through the youthful academic reserve.

A few years later, when I was in my mid-teens, something shifted for me. I altered my allegiance from the book about the universe to an atlas of Earth. It was our home world rather than everything outside it that increasingly fascinated me as a teenager; but even so, it was still the Earth as seen from out there, as perceived from space. It was the Earth of the Blue Marble image that I dearly loved, in which our globe is pictured afloat in the darkness, captured from a distance of 29,000 kilometres by the crew of Apollo 17 on 17 December 1972. Or, later on, the Earth as a Pale Blue Dot, the extraordinary image coordinated by the astronomer and author Carl Sagan in conjunction with NASA. Captured by the Voyager 1 space probe on 14 February 1990, just before the spacecraft exited the solar system, it shows our planet as a barely visible mote in a dark and incomprehensible vastness. Earth is suspended in a wan beam of lightfall caused by lens distortion in the camera, which makes it seem as though our smallness is being spotlit on a spectacular celestial stage. Taken from a distance of 6 billion kilometres, the Pale Blue Dot image reduced our world to the nothingness that it is in universal terms. These images of Earth appealed to me for reasons not dissimilar to my earlier fascination with outer space, but they also fundamentally re-centred my perspective. They held the mystery of what we as humans are a part of but which is simultaneously beyond us too, immersing us – physically, psychologically, intellectually and spiritually – within a far greater realm. And they were extraordinary in their enlarging register of awe. But I don't know that these images ever encouraged me at the time to consider what happens *on* this planet at an ecological or even societal level. Or to explore the closely related range of mystery, wonder and awe found here because of life itself and the presence of a wild world. That all came much later, when wild things – by happenstance rather than planning – gradually became a source of joy in my life. But back then, on the verge of adulthood, those remarkable images made distance more appealing than intimacy.

There has been much written about the momentousness of the Earthrise moment, that inner transformation occasioned in some astronauts when apprehending our planet in all its unlikely and luminous beauty from space; how it can induce a sudden and humbling reverence for our home world for the few people fortunate enough to have seen our planet framed against the darkness in person. But in an essay written in response to the optics of belonging as portrayed by environmental organisations and at climate conferences when the globe is used to telegraph a sense of moral relationship, Anna Pigott, a lecturer in Human Geography at Swansea University in Wales, asked whether such popularised images of the planet as the Blue Marble 'help to inspire humans to take better care of their one, fragile home'. She argues that such projections ensure that 'humans appear on the outside looking in . . . a perspective that expels humanity from the lifeworld'. She then goes on to say this about such externalising depictions of the globe: 'Rather than the environment surrounding us, it appears that it is us that have surrounded it. From such a perspective, humility is difficult.'

For a few years I ran a camera trap in Prespa with my friend Chris Mounsey. Together we would scout out potential sites to place the infrared device according to season, topography and the visible signs of animals and their paths, and then leave the camera strapped to a tree or a post to record the passage of wildlife. There was only one hard and fast rule to our joint endeavour: we would always watch the footage in the field, no matter the time or weather conditions that day. We did this because one of the joys of trying to capture wild animals on remote cameras is experiencing their presence in relation to the home they inhabit, seeing the way they interact with it and respond to changes over time. Going through the footage *in situ* broadened our involvement with the place, enabling us to appreciate small details of animal behaviour or the physicality of the landscape better – scents, winds, sounds, movements, temperatures – that might otherwise have gone unnoticed if we'd brought the SD cards back with us and reviewed the video clips in the comfort of one of our homes. But within that living system, we might find ourselves sat on the same patch of new ice in the reedbeds where a recorded wildcat the night before had jerked its paw back in momentary surprise at the sudden coldness of the surface, or we'd rub our fingers over the smears of drying mud left by a family of wild boar brushing past the lowest oak leaves after rootling in a forest waterhole. We would match the movements on screen to the scene in front of us, a set of interactions that ultimately enabled us to read the signs of passage in other parts of the basin better and to understand what animals were present. It felt like it narrowed the space between species, even if only a little.

One June afternoon, Chris and I pulled over below the small church and its sacred grove. On the other side of the road and downslope of the stone trenches, we pushed through junipers and young oaks for about 50 metres to the spot where we'd set our camera a couple of weeks earlier. The path had looked promising when we'd first found it – worn in, we believed, by animals descending to drink from the lakes as summer evaporated any lingering forest pools.

'Brilliant,' said Chris, bunched up on a rock, his laptop balanced on his knees, 'we have a hundred videos.' I sat down beside him to see what had passed by in our absence, thrilled, as always, by the mystery that brought us out each time. The first minute-long video was of waving wildflowers and grasses, the camera sensors triggered by their near motion. The second clip the same. Third and fourth, no different.

'Shit,' both of us muttered. What we'd failed to consider was the explosive growth of vegetation at that time of year, which had swiftly risen within range of the camera. We skimmed through more of the footage, increasingly frustrated. No. 40, 60, 80 – all empty except for the sway of stems. I'd walked away by then, pissed off that we hadn't thought more carefully about our camera positioning. As was sometimes the case, there was to be no magic to follow the mystery that time.

'Shit,' said Chris again from behind me.

'More grasses?'

'You'll want to get back here.'

No. 99. A massive female brown bear passes directly in front of the rock we're sitting on, her shaggy coat glowing with summer light. She turns her head so that we can see her black eyes; they're so clear that it feels like she's looking into us. Her dark, doglike nose gathers the air and all that it tells her of what's been this way and when. She's so close to the camera that she fills nearly half its frame. All energy and attentiveness. Sentience. Her muscles ripple through her legs and flanks as she shakes her body, pausing and panting in the heat. And then she moves out of view to our left. But, as she does, the footage is suddenly shaky and unfocused. Shuddering. Something, it seems, is pressing against the camera, flicking it upwards so that we get swift, oscillating visions of sky and trees, a whirling blur until everything goes black. Strange scrapings are heard through the darkness, then loud slappings and cracks as the camera gets knocked against the tree. Finally, the light returns, opening wide onto something else: a snout, an eye, an ear. The camera lens clouds with breath as a bear cub peers back at us on the laptop screen.

Chris let out a deep breath, as though he'd been holding it the whole time. 'I've just seen the time stamp of the video,' he said. 'This was just half an hour ago.'

With tingling skin, I rose from the stone, thinking of all that passes so close sometimes. I tried to work out where the mother bear had gone after she'd drifted out of view while her cub played with the camera. I estimated her paces, her angle of leaving. And then I saw it: the limestone boulder torn from its socket of earth and pushed to one side. In the hollow where it had been, a nest smashed open. Hundreds of ants still massed around the breached shelter, carrying away eggs to safety, excavating collapsed chambers and shoring up slumped tunnels. They must have been as oblivious as us when an earthquake rocks our homes.

I still remember the extraordinary degree of humility I felt as we stood in the presence of bears that weren't there. It was breathtaking, unnerving, astonishing. The swaying grasses, the glowing light – everything seemed so vivid and charged. It was the middle of a summer's afternoon, merely 50 metres from a well-used road connecting Prespa villages. Standing there, with the shared world so viscerally revealed, I was reminded of how I'd once felt looking at those images of Earth from a distance. Or at those illustrations of the planets and nebulae in the book I pored over as a child, when I first began to realise how much more there was out there and beyond us. But on that limestone ridge above the lakes, it was brought home to me just how much more there is in here – within the world we're held by.

Just days after our arrival in Prespa, Vassilis took Julia and me to meet the man he called Grandad. Though the two of them weren't biologically related, the relationship they'd forged while running the village distillery from a mudbrick shed at the back of Germanos's garden was noticeably close. You could infer the deep bond from the way they moved around one another as they worked the still, as though each had foreknowledge of the other's next step. It was like a casual dance to a song only the two of them knew.

Germanos was inspecting his vegetable patch when we arrived, lifting back the leaves of courgette plants with the wooden cane he was so rarely without. He wore a summer outfit that I later discovered differed little from his winter attire: an old brown jumper and faded blue trousers, a fraying green work apron and a paling blue cap that looked as if he'd lifted it from the head of a train engineer. He shook our hands with formal authority as Vassilis introduced us and told him our story. We'd practised a few more words of Greek just for the occasion, letting him know what a pleasure it was to meet him and how wonderful his garden looked. I was quietly pleased with our efforts, but Germanos clearly felt otherwise.

'You goddam dirty bastards!' he roared at us, smacking his cane against the earth.

We were stunned into silence. It felt as if the sun was burning right through us, until laughter broke free of Germanos's chest, his cane now pattering at the soil. It was a laughter we would come to know well, when our visits to his house were a slapstick sketch of sign language and fumbled vocabularies as we helped out around the distillery and garden, but that day, having never met before, it made no sense to us. Turning to Vassilis in the vague hope we could amend the misunderstanding, we saw that he couldn't speak for laughing either. And so we joined in, nervously at first, not really sure what we were laughing at but feeling it was all we could do to help hide our confusion. Eventually, when the two of them had quietened down, Vassilis explained that those were the only words of English that Germanos knew. He'd heard them in a John Wayne film, he said, too long ago even to remember the name of it; but the words – and the reaction to them on screen – had so deeply impressed him that he'd held onto them, waiting for decades to deploy them in conversation.

Waiting was an essential aspect of Germanos's character. He pursued patience at the distillery as though it was the aim of his labours, waiting out the slow transference of fire from the stoked blaze of wood as it passed through a mash of grapes to the alcoholic heat of *tsipouro*. You'd step inside the outbuilding when snow lay thick on the ground and the wall of warmth would knock you back on your heels. As your eyes adjusted to the glare of the single bulb suspended from a beam, you'd invariably find Germanos through the swirl of cigarette smoke in the corner by the fire.

That was his place, where he sat on an old wooden bench with his cane by his side. He'd always spot you and smile, then raise a hand, beckoning you close through the knot of people piling in with snow on their coats and a few drinks already inside them, patting down a place beside him on the bench. We were his congregation inside there – devoting our hours to a different kind of church.

In his early eighties, Germanos was no longer strong enough to do the heavy lifting around the fire, but his knowledge of distillation was essential. He understood the timings, degrees of heat and percentages of alcohol. He recognised the raw liquor's subtle gradations of clarity as it dripped from the spout into a copper basin. And he still tended to the dozens of wooden barrels packed with grapes in the barn next door, capping and sealing each with sheets of newspaper and a splodge of cow dung mixed with water. You were part of an older world inside these mudbrick buildings, but you never heard Germanos talk about his own past in any detail. Never. No matter how many winter nights you spent warmed by the distillery fire.

Germanos was one of the thousands who fled Prespa at the end of the Greek Civil War, when trenches such as those on the limestone ridge above the lakes were abandoned as the Hellenic Army surged northwards, pushing Communist fighters and civilians out of this corner of the country. From a pre-war population of around 11,000 residents, only 3,000 remained in Greek Prespa at its end. The rest, if they were lucky, fled – escaping into the mountains of Albania or Yugoslavia, carrying children, provisions and anything else of significance that they could. Once on the other side, out of reach of the aircraft whose pilots tried to obliterate the isthmus – the flat and sandy stretch of land that separates the two lakes – they fanned out across the Eastern Bloc, beginning journeys that for some would last the rest of their lives. Odysseys of exile that took them to Skopje, to Warsaw, to Budapest, to Sofia. Journeys that took some of them as far as Tashkent.

I don't know exactly how Germanos ended up in Tashkent, 5,000 kilometres due east of the village distillery and on the far side of both the Black and Caspian Seas, but a common route at the end of the war was to pass over the high mountains of neighbouring Albania and join a Russian timber ship in the port city of Durrës. From there the ship would pass through the eastern Mediterranean and enter the Black Sea via the Bosphorus Strait, going on to unload its passengers on the shores of Georgia in the Caucasus, which would still have left a few thousand kilometres to be navigated safely, either overland around the northern or southern shores of the Caspian Sea or somehow across its waters. Today, Tashkent is the sovereign capital of Uzbekistan, but back in the late 1940s the city was firmly in the orbit of the Soviet Union, a part of the connective Communist corridor radiating out from the wreckage of the lost conflict in Greece for fighters and civilians alike. Once there, Germanos joined 11,000 other Greeks sheltering in the city after exiting villages such as ours.

Vassilis always said that Germanos wasn't allied with the Communist cause, which might or might not have been true. Given the suspicions hanging over exiles returning to a deeply divided nation firmly refashioned in a right-wing mould, it's hard to imagine openly admitting to past left-wing allegiance, especially when examples were being made of the losers. Either way, Germanos eventually ended up as an internal political prisoner after he came back to Greece, incarcerated on one of the barren rocky islets of the Aegean that the government used to house its ideological enemies. The topographical distance between Tashkent and that Aegean island is as unimaginable for me as what happened to Germanos and others in those inescapable places. Because this was shelter as hell.

We pass over hidden damage and hurt all the time. Outside of the most remote corners of the polar regions, few places on the planet have gone without some kind of violence being carried out on them. For trauma to be part of their soils, even when invisible or unspoken. Germanos never mentioned to us the torture he'd endured on the island after returning from exile in Tashkent. What took place in the stark shelter of that prison he kept to himself. Even Vassilis knew only some of the story – enough to let us know that it was unbearably grim. It's why Germanos always walked with a cane. Not because it was a handy tool to lift the leaves of courgette plants in the garden but because his legs needed help to keep moving. Whatever was done to him had left him permanently in pain.

In 2021, when climate negotiations were underway at COP26 in Scotland, Julian Aguon, a writer from the island of Guam, published an essay in *The Atlantic* entitled 'To Hell with Drowning'. In it, he charted what a shifting world meant for the people of the Pacific, where sea-level rises were wrecking livelihoods and condemning homes at the same time that politicians in Glasgow were performing a largely perfunctory exercise by promising climate action without resolving how to achieve the necessary degree of change needed. One of Aguon's many compelling lines of thought in the essay is that it isn't more information that we need to hear about the damage done by climate change but rather more stories about the places on the frontline that are lived in and loved.

We require stories about our home places, in part, because stories are so frequently silenced. Silenced for reasons of racial exclusion, cultural and class discrimination, and institutional invisibility. Silenced for reasons of fear, anxiety and self-doubt. Silenced for the sole purpose of retaining privilege and enforcing authority. Silenced because the tellers of a story are gone. Silenced because they come from places that others see as peripheral when for those living there they're the centre of the world. And silenced because sometimes silence is the story.

What is lost in this silencing is beyond measure. We lose ways of understanding some of the countless diverse experiences and interactions that make up our common world. We lose ways of recognising how power keeps systems of inequality and disenfran-chisement locked in place. We lose ways of cultivating empathy and understanding. And we lose, too, potent tools of agency and change. Up on that ridge above the lakes, where an ancient juniper grove has witnessed centuries of Prespa's turbulent history, those stone trenches symbolise a set of stories about this place that are key to its current cultural and ecological construction. And yet those stories were silenced, in a formal sense, for far too long. I remember once running a writing workshop here in Prespa for young people from several southern European countries. While exploring one of the region's villages that was abandoned at the conclusion of the war, I briefly sketched out the conflict's impact on Greece as a whole and this local area more specifically, asking the young writers to imagine the abandoned houses at a time before they had been emptied out. Afterwards, a few of the Greek participants approached me. They wanted to say thank you, they said, because they'd heard so little about the Civil War while growing up. These stories, they added, were all new to them. And the reason they were new to them is because the state had for decades adhered to a policy of avoidance, believing that by silencing discussion of the conflict you could make it feel as if it never happened. It wasn't even added to Greece's educational cur-riculum until nearly seven full decades had passed since its bitter completion. And this silencing is another kind of shelter: a place in which we hide away from things, pretending they aren't there.

In much the same way, many governments simply carried on with business as usual within days of their representatives standing up at COP26 to argue how vital it is to tackle climate change. But sheltering away from the stories of a shifting world doesn't erase the damage and changes we face, nor lessen the impact on those who'll live with its harshest realities, just as silencing the difficult stories that make up the places we love doesn't help heal their wounds. Instead, in their honesty, their sensitivity and their respect for those who've suffered or are hurting, the stories we tell of our home places can be significant acts of solidarity. By being open as well to the indelible joy and laughter that are also essential aspects of damaged landscapes and lives – as Germanos so irrepressibly expressed when he shouted *You goddam dirty bastards!* – these stories articulate claims on a greater commons, affirming the validity of varied experiences. And in telling them as carefully and inclusively as possible, so that connections and affinities are established where they might never have been previously considered, space is created for the reimagining of a shared and more equal world.

I learned this one afternoon with Germanos's wife, Theodora. Even on the hottest of summer days, when she would just loosen the hood of her shawl a little in acknowledgement of the season, Theodora never dressed in anything but black. Unlike her husband, she was quiet and withdrawn. Circumspect. She walked with considerable difficulty, bent nearly double by chronic back pain. Because of this, she spent most of her time either sitting or lying down. But none of these physical challenges stood in the way of her fierce beliefs, as we saw when friends of Vassilis had visited from Athens for a weekend. That morning, we'd gone with them on a day trip over the border to Albania at a time when the Greek media was full of stark reports about violent criminality owing to the arrival of Albanian migrant workers, even though official statistics didn't support the increasingly hysterical claims made in newspaper columns and on TV talk shows. In the garden beside the distillery after returning from our journey, one of Vassilis's friends turned to Theodora, who'd slowly and painfully risen from her seat at a table to greet us, and said, 'But isn't it true that Albanians crossing the border steal from your gardens here in Prespa?' Theodora, who had endured the Civil War and then exile in neighbouring Yugoslavia, was sharp in her reply. 'We're all from the same place here. So what if a hungry Albanian takes a cabbage from my garden? Remember that *we* were that desperate once.' I'd never heard Theodora speak like this before. She was shaking with passion. 'Remember that *we* might be that desperate again some day.'

We all have vital stories to tell of our home places and how they've come to be what they are, especially of those places and communities that have been frequently silenced. And stories not just of the past, but of the present as well. Stories of the future, too. Because in a radically shifting world, when the climate and biodiversity crises are undermining the stability of the planet itself, leading to lost livelihoods, displacement, conflicts, anxieties and the extinction of wild lives in our surroundings, stories are lifelines. Both in the agency created through their articulation and in revealing, as Theodora did that afternoon, a path of affirmation and fellowship that's open to us if we choose it. But what stories require, too, what stories have in fact always needed for them to be meaningful as forms of communication, is for them to be heard. For them to be listened to closely, carefully. Because it's in the intimate exchange between teller and hearer that stories grow into a force. An ear can be as transformative as a voice.

For as long as we'd operated a wildlife camera, Chris and I had wondered how bears moved around the lakes' basin, how they connected the granite and limestone halves in their journeys. The isthmus that divided the lakes was their common crossing point, that much we knew. Yet, given the presence of a taverna, a road and a small military post on its southern side, we speculated that they used the northern edge to join the limestone mountains from the plain, where a narrow ramp of rock and wild grasses cut through a wall of cliffs.

It was a warm summer's evening when we arrived there with our camera. Sunlight was already shrinking across the flatlands as the mountains clipped the sun. Near the foot of the rockface, a narrow stream rippled past us, carrying water from Lesser Prespa Lake to Great Prespa Lake. On the other side of it, a dense tangle of vegetation rose from the base of the cliffs, where young willows had thickened into palisades and arching brambles guarded the edges. That summer I'd had an acute recurrence of a chronic back problem, and I could already see that twisting and turning through the burgeoning scrub would only make it worse, so Chris offered to go ahead on his own, disappearing into the enclosing greenery after crossing the stream.

While he was gone, I watched the waters through my binoculars. Ancient though these lakes are, their current configuration is a relatively recent phenomenon. Prior to the last ice age, only one lake pooled in the basin – a lake in all likelihood much shallower and marshier where the smaller of the two lakes is today. But over the thousands of years that followed, day by day and grain by grain, soil and sediment were sluiced down the mountain slopes above our house and washed into the lake by way of a river, gradually accumulating and spreading out into the water a little further each day, until it eventually reached the other side, transforming one lake into two. On that isthmus between them, where refugees fled the Civil War at its terrible end as planes roared overhead, the sandy substrate reaches a depth of 17 metres in places, creating a unique habitat of desert-like conditions for an uncommon assembly of plants. To stand there, on the flattest stretch of land in the whole basin, is to stand on the tops of mountains, too.

A fishing boat cut a silver line through the water as I watched pelicans and pygmy cormorants cross between the lakes, catching the low glow of the light on their flanks. Turning slowly to scan the rest of the lake, where the slopes on the North Macedonian side rose from its shores, one of my feet touched something less yielding than sand. I looked down to see the tapered nose cone of a bomb. Although partially covered by pale grains and muddy silt, it was unmistakable in its shape and solidity. I froze completely. Dropped by a pilot all those decades earlier with the aim of severing one of the escape routes of fleeing soldiers and refugees such as Germanos and Theodora, the bomb had been sheltered by the sediment of the lakeshore until this day of resurfacing. My heart thrummed in the summer quiet as I gently shifted my weight, easing my foot off the rusting device. I held my breath for as long as I could, as if I was suddenly trapped underwater. The world slowed around me until I'd forgotten it was even there. I think it's the silence of these unexploded bombs that I find most disconcerting – as if all the grief of the war was sealed up inside them still waiting to be released. The past is never not with us.

Chris jumped back over the stream just as I was putting some distance between me and the bomb. We stared at it in the half-light, its unexpected appearance as surprising as the mother bear and her cub on the slope above us. Stories stirring on the surface of the world. The next day, a bomb disposal unit from the Greek Army cordoned off the shore made of mountains and carried out a controlled explosion, the blast rippling upwards through the sacred grove and echoing across the limestone ridge above the lakes.

3

Lines on a Map

Our breaths clouded in the cold air as we crunched across hardened snow to reach the end of the peninsula. Patches of fog scrolled past as we followed a narrow trail edged by European box and wild pistachio, where wild boars had found openings during the night to rootle down to the soil in search of edible roots. Julia and a friend had once walked this same path on a summer's afternoon and met a dog that became a bear cub as it slowly turned around, eliciting soft sighs from the pair of them until the reality of a nearby mother crystallised in their minds. That evening, when she was back at home, Julia said she'd never run as fast in her life, largely to keep pace with her younger companion, reminding us of what a friend who guides in northern Greece tells his wildlife groups with an impressively straight face at the start of each tour: 'Remember, you don't have to be the fastest in the group if you encounter a bear; you just have to be faster than the slowest person.'

At the end of the path, we emerged into a world of sky and water as the rising sun pulled mist off the lake. The basin shimmered in bright winter light. Few places on our side of Great Prespa Lake command a view as expansive and compelling as this peninsula. Cape Roti rides into the lake like the prow of a stone boat, so far out that when you're standing at its end you don't feel entirely attached to land. As if you were already partially immersed in what's below. And what's off the tip of the peninsula is the

deepest point in the entire watershed, an underwater sinkhole
descending nearly 50 metres beneath the surface.

We set up telescopes at the edge of the peninsula's cliffs and
pulled field guides and clipboards from our rucksacks. I poured
tea from a flask and then set my phone down beside it to keep
an eye on the time. While we waited, I watched the lake. A light
wind etched crests on the surface, the water changing from pewter
to dark blue with the altered angle of the sun. Cutting through
that shifting plane were the borders of three countries. The lines
– straight, angular, unbendable – are as unlike water as anything
could be, and yet there was nothing to mark the strictness of their
positions beyond their relation to significant landmarks.

As always, the island of Golem Grad drew my eye first. Rising
in the North Macedonian part of the lake, its cliffs shone like a
winter citadel on the water. Lush draperies of emerald moss thrive
on its Roman ruins and scattered stone walls. It feels like Prespa's
own Galapagos given its extraordinary vitality and striking degree
of abundance, where well over a thousand Hermann's tortoises
roam the rocky glades beneath stands of junipers holding a bustling
colony of cormorants. Golem Grad is also known as the island of
snakes, housing the greatest number of dice snakes and venomous
horn-nosed vipers per square kilometre of any place in the world. A
biologist friend of mine carrying out fieldwork on the island once
encountered a Slovenian naturist reclining on his side, his head
casually propped on his arm beside a tent, completely naked except
for a pair of socks. When my friend asked about the single item of
clothing he'd chosen to wear, the man said that he'd already seen
so many snakes that he thought he would do them less harm if he
accidentally stepped on one while wearing socks. My friend suggested it might be a good idea to dress, stressing that harming the
snakes should be the least of his worries given the extreme difficulty
of reaching medical help when stuck on a small island in the middle
of a vast lake with 1,500 horn-nosed vipers living alongside you.

Turning to the southwest, I found Golem Grad's smaller sibling. Known as Mali Grad, this island rises off the coast of Albania near the village of Pustec. Despite the presence of an exquisite fourteenth-century church inside a cave, Mali Grad stands out in memory for me mostly because of our journey there one summer morning. Midway between shore and island, water began sloshing about our feet in the low wooden boat arranged for us by a friend in Pustec. When I raised the alarm, the two boatmen shrugged their shoulders, as though sinking were just a minor inconvenience, tossing each of us a plastic pail and telling us to quickly bail. 'We're halfway there,' one of them reasoned, not unreasonably, 'so we may as well go forward rather than back.'

It was nine o'clock. I drank the last of my tea and checked to see if Julia was ready. Then we uncapped the lenses and began to scan the lake through our telescopes, knowing that others were doing the same thing from their own vantage points throughout Prespa. Looking inwards to shared water. Every year the International Waterbird Count is carried out in the middle of January to determine the population densities of wetland birds. Given the transboundary nature of the region, and the need for counts to be conducted simultaneously to avoid doubling up on birds as they move about or between the bodies of water, monitoring in the basin is integrated at the local level through the close cooperation of environmental NGOs in each of the respective countries. Though the time zone difference that catapults Greece an hour ahead of its neighbours means that those monitoring in Albania and North Macedonia had an earlier start to their day than we did.

I began by scanning the rocky shores of the peninsula, counting up great white egrets and grey herons standing sentinel on the coast and adding their numbers to a census sheet on my clipboard. Three Dalmatian pelicans broke the blue shallows near the shore as they lifted into the air. Working my way deeper into the lake,

I encountered a stunning flock of 140 shovelers unwinding in single file like a current within the water. Two goosanders streaked low, like a pair of skimming stones. I then panned towards Julia, who was already concentrating her focus on a point off the end of the peninsula, where a vast raft of great crested grebes floated on the worn glitter of the waves.

In winter, numerous birds are pulled down out of the greater cold of northern and central Europe, where they find respite on these milder waters. The harder the winters are elsewhere, the more birds we typically see in Prespa. But there's an additional lure beyond the water's relative warmth, which the great crested grebe is perfectly evolved to exploit. Even without the stunning auburn sash and electric hairdo of the breeding season, or the remarkable courtship dance between a pair, when the birds mirror each other's extravagant choreography and offer ribbons of vegetation to one another symbolic of their bond, the great crested grebe is, even in its simpler winter plumage, a beautifully elegant creature. All sleek contours and narrow curves. And with its swift, explosive motion, it's made for the deeps – like the sinkhole at the end of the peninsula. Known as an *uvala*, this karstic depression – an underwater extension of the limestone ridge on which so many of this place's stories are inscribed – shelters millions of wintering Prespa bleak and other small fish species. A treasure chest the feeding grebes unlock when they dive. We marked off their numbers as quickly as we could, watching them descend, powering down with the paddles of their webbed feet kicking deep, the whole surface in endless, shining motion. There were just over 5,000 off the tip of the peninsula that morning, though in harder winters as many as twice that number have been recorded. After packing up our gear we returned the way we'd come, following the crusted white path, the first spears of early crocuses rising in the snowless shelter of prickly junipers. The grebes were left to their place on the winter lake, gathered at the edge of three countries.

Although we didn't know it at the time, our move to Prespa had been seeded several years earlier in an entirely different part of the world. Like the rivers that spill into these shared lakes, lifelines rarely flow straight. Instead, they contain bends, meanders and loops; they hold, at times, turns of extraordinary surprise, as I discovered in late 1997 when Julia and I got together just a week before I was due to leave England for a year. My plan for the first six months of that time was to travel in India with a friend. Sid Dance and I had met in London when we were both hired to tend plants for the royal parks and gardens in a set of large greenhouses hidden by a circular screen of trees in the centre of Hyde Park. We immediately hit it off while potting up hundreds of edelweiss and watering thousands of poinsettias, quickly discovering a shared love of walking, music and mischief that continues to this day. Sid was also an excellent landscape photographer, and we were looking for ways to work together on our travels, exploring a series of ideas and landscapes that had interested us both for some time. After India, I then hoped to spend six months in Sri Lanka on my own, using whatever money I still had left over to settle down in one place and begin writing a book that I'd struggled to make time for while living and working in London. Starting a relationship just days before departure hadn't really been part of the plan.

Even though Julia and I had already known each other for several months by then, the heady thrill of a sudden and unexpected closeness spun our heads and hearts, perhaps even more so than it might otherwise have done because we both knew there was a physical and immovable limit to its growth. A border we were swiftly approaching. In the days before leaving, as I burned the candle at both ends between my day job, organising my travels, clearing out my rented room in a communal house and seeing

Julia in whatever time was left over, we talked – jokingly most of the time, but not without moments of earnest searching – about the possibilities of continuing our relationship while I was away. But the distance between us and the duration of my journey made it seem an all but impossible task. Then, one evening, as I sorted the last things in my room and readied my rucksack, placing it beside the door that I would close on that phase of my life, Julia said, 'Why don't I join you in India? I wouldn't mind getting a different job anyways, so I could just leave the one I have and look for something else. And then I'll tell them I can't start for a few weeks as I'll be away. What do you think?'

When the last ice age spread over Europe, compromising life across large parts of the continent and in particular the north, Prespa is thought to have acted as a refugium for wild species pushed out of their sheltering spaces. With localised ice sheets expanding across the high Balkan mountains and glaciers gripping the alpine valleys, numerous organisms pressed south in an attempt to outpace the killing cold. Some of them reached Prespa and other nearby areas, where the most extreme climatic expressions of the ice age hit a border, so that the region's warmest, lowest and south-facing extents escaped the worst of its reach, becoming a sanctuary for expelled species. And when that intense glacial era eventually receded, enabling species to disperse and regain northern homelands and territories once more, some of those life forms kept a toehold where they'd found refuge further south.

It's why, at times, a strange sense of bridged worlds exists here, as when you walk the forest that skirts the southern shore of Great Prespa Lake, its tangled wood of alders and willows studded with the snow-white pillars of silver birches, a tree so redolent of northern Europe that you won't find its papery bark peelings any further south than these lakes. Or when, on a winter afternoon as mists roll over the waters, the garrulous honking of Greece's only colony of greylag geese summons the shores, fields and estuaries of northwestern Europe, where these birds gather in immense numbers. The same is true of the hazel grouse, a small and reclusive ground bird deeply entangled with northern forests right across its impressive longitudinal span, being found all the way from western Europe to the island of Hokkaido off Japan's northern coast. And yet here in Prespa, at the most southern point of its species' reach, a small number of pairs dwell in dense woods of juniper and oak, a note of the north in the mountains of Greece. In this crossroads place, it can sometimes feel as though the cardinal points of the world are being spun swiftly around.

It's not only wild species that have found refuge in Prespa, because for centuries men did, too. Monastic, remote, alone. Men who'd shed some of the world in order to live with what they considered to be its essence. At the tip of Cape Roti, where those great crested grebes gather offshore, the cliffs are as pale as the winter moon. Bending south, they mottle to mineral brown. Trellised with creepers and fugitive trees, the sheer, rocky walls are fissured with caves housing colonies of chambered bats and denning otters. Sometimes an eagle owl. There too, clearly visible from the water but hidden from the surface of the peninsula, are the relics of human residency: fading frescoes of saints painted onto the rock faces and small chapels enclosed by crags. The Hermitage of the Metamorphosis was built directly into the cliffs in the thirteenth century, its solitary window framing a view of the lake and the mountains of Albania, while the Hermitages of the Panagia Eleousa and Mikri Analipsis were raised some two centuries later when this peninsula had become a centre for spiritual solitude. Encircled by high, protective mountains, and more discrete than the lowland plains when Ottoman rule swept across the Balkans in the fourteenth and fifteenth centuries, it was a place of refuge for Christian ascetics. A place where men dwelled in stone.

I've often tried imagining what it was like to live so exposed to the summer crush of light, with all the heat of the season gathered by the suntrap of the cliffs. Or how winter would swiftly harden you, snow lancing across the lake as ice took hold of the edges, the temperature plummeting as low as twenty below. Many of the monks had only the caves as shelter, just like those otters and bats and owls, while others carved beds from the cliffs that were little more than hard, ungiving lips suspended above the lake. There they would have experienced this place in all its harsh and elemental extremes. And then I think of what they would have seen as they shivered into a thicker set of robes with the coming of the cold and unmoored their dugout boats, the skin around their eyes raw from wind and fingers cracked and blistered as waterbirds poured down out of the north. They would have parted those shoaling grebes that shared the shelter of these lakes, casting nets in the same place as fishermen do today to snare the rising funnel of fish. They would have lived on these waters when no borders divided the lake. And somewhere on the peninsula, beneath mounds of piled limestone or under the junipers foresting the flats, some of these monks must still be buried. A nest of bones in a dark clot of earth, given to the place that wasn't an edge to them but the centre of their world.

'Bring binoculars with you,' said Sid over beers in a London pub a few weeks before we left for India. I remember frowning, thinking of the extensive list of things that already had nowhere to go in my pack. Because of the length of time I intended to be away, I was troubled by the glaring mismatch between what I might need and having to carry it all for so long. Items I'd thought essential only days before had already been scratched from the list.

'I don't have space for binoculars,' I said, raising my pint to clink glasses with his, 'especially as I probably won't use them.'

'You'll use them,' said Sid, who'd already spent a considerable amount of time in India. 'Trust me, you won't regret it.'

Sid and I landed in Delhi in December. After a few days in the city, we caught an early-morning train, chugging south beneath grey skies as scattered rain fell over the plains of Uttar Pradesh. On Sid's recommendation, we left the train in Agra and boarded a bus heading west to Bharatpur in eastern Rajasthan. There had been nothing to denote these lines on a map that we'd crossed, just the gradual and seamless shifts of a landscape in response to latitude, climate and geology, but I experienced the changing names of the regions with intense excitement all the same. And I remember thinking at the time that I would return to Agra to see the Taj Mahal after we'd completed this side trip to Rajasthan, but I never did. Which has never been a regret of mine, because I experienced something so life-changing over the following days that it doesn't register as a missed thing.

After an evening of spectacular storms over Bharatpur we rose early the next day and walked into Keoladeo National Park. I pulled from my pack the binoculars I'd reluctantly brought with me and hung them from my neck. Within minutes, as a marsh harrier rode in low and wavered over our heads, I had them pressed against my eyes. Suddenly the world was in sharp and wondrous motion, enlarged by small discs of glass to startling and vivid immediacy. A pied kingfisher fell fast and knifed open the lid of a pond with its bill. Flotillas of ducks whose names Sid was beginning to teach me – gadwall, teal, tufted – burst in trembling waves from a silver lake. The guide we'd hired paused by a tree and pointed to the strange and otherworldly faces of four baby owls looking down at us from their nesting hole. Everywhere

I turned, a bird seemed to fill the space; it was like shutters were being drawn open on a window I didn't even know was there, so that the place I stood in was transformed by a sudden flood of light. Even getting my rented bicycle so badly mired in a bog that I had to spend an hour hauling it out as a nervous herd of water buffalo gathered ever closer to me couldn't lessen the beauty of those days.

That was when my own world shifted – when I was twenty-seven. I can pinpoint it so precisely because until then my interest in nature rarely extended beyond an enjoyment of being out in it. Of wanting to walk hills and moors for the space they gave me rather than a desire to understand their own intrinsic value. What was startlingly different about this experience was that it entailed crossing a border into other lives – those lives we share this world with in all their extraordinary inventiveness, elegance, ferocity, fragility and fortitude. A crossing that would broaden out from that national park just 50 kilometres from the Taj Mahal that I never saw into a lifelong love of wild creatures. And from those encounters with birds, one in particular stands out as the moment when the deal was finally sealed. Sid and I had emerged from a wooded path to find a small grassland bordered by marsh and filling with mist. There in the pale grasses, nearly two metres tall, stood a pair of sarus cranes. I raised the binoculars that I'd never wanted to bring with me to my eyes again, absorbed by the graceful river bend of the birds' necks. Their heads were dipped in crimson and crowned with a silvery-gold band, and they walked on a pair of stilts for legs. I'd never seen anything quite so mesmeric in my life.

'This is amazing,' I whispered to Sid, as we knelt beside one another at the edge of the woods. He just grinned in reply. For the next minute or two we watched in silence as the cranes danced in that glade of shifting mist. Slowly circling one another, the pair of towering birds – the tallest flying bird on the planet – leapt backwards and hopped high above the grasses. They bowed in response to an ancient courtship code that has linked their kind for millions of years, and together they rolled back those riverine necks and trumpeted skywards in unison, a sound of such earthly aching beauty that those cranes found a home in my heart that day.

'I think I'll tell Julia to bring binoculars,' I said to Sid when we finally walked on, bowled over by joy.

In travel pieces and other articles about the region, Greek Prespa is often described as remote. It's hardly surprising given that it's such a tempting and evocative word to reach for, one capable of acting as a cipher for so much: somewhere untrammelled and pristine; a place that's difficult to reach; a land not entirely connected to the modern world. Historically, as when monks lived in stone shelters on the peninsula, or even after the Civil War, when a government permit was required to visit the region until as late as the early 1990s, these descriptions would have fitted the place well. But today, when Prespa is far from untouched nor particularly difficult to reach by car (though cuts to train and bus services in nearby towns have left the region more isolated and disconnected from Greece's large cities), and where our mobile and internet services are far better than in many places typically considered to be well developed, the still common use of the word tells us more about contemporary perspectives on place than it does about the place itself. The only reason Prespa could still realistically be thought of as remote is because we've internalised the topographical world according to political boundaries above nearly all else, orientating ourselves in relation to states and their centres of power and influence. Because in that sense, Prespa *is* remote – it exists as far away from Athens as it is possible to be in the northwest of the Greek mainland. It is also home to the village of Psaradhes, which is farther from the sea than any other settlement in Greece – another of those defining geographical markers of detachment, owing to the country's collective cultural connection to the Mediterranean. And as many of those travel articles like to point out, it's the very end of the country as well. Where the road runs out, taking you as far as you can go.

The political borders dividing the lakes are a relatively recent arrangement of territory, first coming into being at the end of the Balkan wars in 1913 with the final dissolution of the Ottoman Empire. The subsequent splitting of the wider lands lived on by Greeks, Albanians, Serbs, Jews, Turks, Roma, Bulgarians, Vlachs and others was then formalised with the Treaty of Versailles in 1919 at the conclusion of the First World War and later refined in 1926. Despite their historical newness, these borders still carry an especially great weight because of the sensitivity that nascent states felt towards their frontiers, seeing them, after so many centuries of Ottoman control, as sites of potential weakness. It's why the names of villages that had non-Greek names were Hellenised by the Greek state after the consolidation of national boundaries, so that in 1927 the name Nivitsa used by the local Slavic population became today's Psaradhes on Great Prespa Lake. Or why, in the aftermath of the Greek Civil War and the consequent emptying of the area, the government in Athens shored up its borders by settling 7,000 pastoralist Vlachs in Prespa – a people often seen to be among the most patriotic of the country's citizens. As borders throughout the Balkans were strengthened, frequently through policies that aggressively and sometimes violently foregrounded uniformity to the detriment of diversity, there was a hardening perception of minority languages, ethnicities and religious affiliations as potential threats to the supremacy of the state. In 1936, the Greek dictator Ioannis Metaxas even went so far as to ban the Slavo-Macedonian language common to many residents of Prespa and other parts of northern Greece at the time. As the lines on the map became darker and bolder in hue, the ways in which one could belong to a place were increasingly a question of national identity.

Given how deeply such political borders have been culturally internalised – not only here in the Balkans but throughout the world – it's hardly surprising that they sometimes manifest themselves in unusual ways. Just after Christmas during our first winter in Prespa, Sid came to stay with us. By then, Julia and I had already split ten tonnes of winter wood after it was carried out of the mountains by mules, the beech logs bandsawed in front of our yard by Nikos, the man who would, several years later, ask me why I was still wearing the red and white *Martis* threads on my wrist when swallows had been with us for days. Throughout autumn we'd overhauled the entire garden, digging it over and laying out beds separated by paths I made by laying down broken roof tiles I'd found near the house. And, with the help of Vassilis, we'd slowly started building a shed in the yard. But all this work paused when the ground began to freeze. As we didn't yet have a long-term plan for what we would do in Prespa, those winter days at the turn of the year when Sid arrived from London were still largely free for exploring.

One day, after a long walk in the valley, Sid asked if we could have a look at the cemetery attached to the stunningly beautiful tenth-century Byzantine church in our village, where frescoes fill every last wall, arch and dome in richly coloured iconography. Because of his work as a photographer, Sid was interested in seeing the personal images used to mark the tombstones, comparing them with others he'd found in his travels through southern Europe. The day was cold and snowy. We were all dressed in heavy coats, scarves and gloves, and Sid wore a tall woollen hat with long, dangling ear flaps. After wandering through the cemetery, where we'd read the names and dates on graves while stopping before some of the more poignant black-and-white images chosen by families for their loved ones' memorials, we began walking home. We didn't get far, though, because opposite the church is the village police station, where an officer was standing outside in the falling snow. Without saying a single word, he briskly waved us over.

Inside the station, the officer fired questions at us about our reason for being in the cemetery. Although our Greek was still rudimentary at that stage, Julia and I did our best to explain our interest in the images. Clearly unimpressed with our answers, the policeman demanded identification from each of us. When I explained that it was at home now that we were living in the village, he ordered us to return with it immediately.

A cigarette burned in an ashtray on the policeman's desk when we sat down again with our paperwork. This time he paid particular attention to Sid, scouring his passport and lingering over each and every visa and stamp he'd accrued on his many travels. Finding nothing out of order, he then asked Sid to go through his journey details multiple times, changing the order to check for inconsistencies: *length of stay, date of return, airline, flight number; date of return, flight number, airline, length of stay*. Failing to uncover anything out of the ordinary, he let us go.

It was such a surreal experience that we told Vassilis about it when he stopped by for his regular evening coffee with us. Not only was he just as bewildered as we'd been, but he felt personally aggrieved that this had happened to us in his village. He worked himself up into such a state that he finally picked up the phone and rang the station, asking to be put through to the officer we'd described to him.

'The English couple have lived in the village for several months now,' he said. 'Why are you questioning them like this? Is this how we treat guests to our country?'

Vassilis pulled a cigarette from a packet in his blue overalls while listening to the officer's reply. And then he laughed – a laugh as deep and uncontrollable as when Germanos had called us goddamn dirty bastards in his garden.

'So,' Vassilis began, lighting his cigarette and exhaling a wreath of smoke into the room after putting the phone back down, 'the policeman would like to apologise to you all. He wasn't so interested in you two,' he said, pointing at Julia and me. 'It was Sid that he was concerned by.' Vassilis swung his arm to one side so that his finger faced our friend. 'Because of your hat, the one with the big ear flaps.' I think he was enjoying our puzzlement, because he held back the punchline until he'd taken another drag on his cigarette, stifling a laugh to get it out. 'He said you looked like a Bolshevik. A Bolshevik from across the border, coming here to look for a place in a Greek Orthodox cemetery to bury a non-Orthodox body.'

Borders are stories we tell ourselves about what belongs and what doesn't. About who we are and who we're not. And what, sometimes, we wish to keep in rather than out. For several decades after the end of the Second World War, the Albanian dictator Enver Hoxha had his country sealed like a time capsule, protecting its frontiers from largely imaginary threats by constructing hundreds of thousands of concrete bunkers that are still scattered across the country to this day. In places, barbed-wire fences were erected along the borders. An Albanian woman on the outskirts of a Prespa village once took me to the spot where one such fence used to separate her country from ours. With the heel of her shoe, she roughly marked out where a band of soil running parallel with the fence was cleared of stones and regularly raked, creating the ideal surface for recording the movements of people. Not to track the incursions of hostile enemies, as I'd initially imagined, but to reveal the footprints of escapees. This is an extreme example of borders as sites of state violence, as the penalty for being found leaving Albania without permission during the reign of Hoxha was potentially death, but even those more benign versions lacking physical impediments can cause separation in places that were once whole.

I remember walking with friends through a mixed forest of Greek juniper and Macedonian oak on the North Macedonian side of the lake some years ago. We'd dropped out of the woods that October afternoon and entered the small fishing village of Konjsko, which held only a few permanent residents outside of summer. At the first house we saw a group of people clustered in the yard. As soon as we'd been spotted, a short, burly man in his early seventies approached us. Dressed in a striped jumper and a navy-and-grey tracksuit top over jeans and heavy boots, with a grey woolly hat tipped back on his head, he looked the spit of Lawrence Durrell if the Durrells had chosen Prespa instead of Corfu as their home. Without breaking his stride, the man spread his arms as wide as that first spring smile when you're standing in warm sunshine after a long winter, embracing each of us as though we were the lost tribe he'd been separated from for years.

'Call me Jimmy,' he said, in a deep and voluble voice bolstered by beer. By the shore of the lake that day, in the sharp autumn stillness, it sounded as dramatic as Melville's opening to *Moby-Dick*. After finally releasing us from his hold, Jimmy herded us over to a table heaped with grilled meats and saddled with an extensive collection of beer and *rakija*, the equivalent of Germanos's *tsipouro* on this side of the lakes. And like Germanos, Jimmy knew little more English than what he'd already exhausted by telling us his name, a phrase picked up while visiting New York for a month in the 1960s. But between our friends and his, who had come from towns in the region to visit him that day, there was enough commonality of language that we were able to spend the next hour chatting as food and drink was boisterously passed around and endlessly replenished.

When he asked us where we were from, I pointed across the lake to the flat-topped ridge that Julia and I call Table Mountain and which marks the border between our countries. Behind it, though unseen from that angle, was our village. That mountain landmark, which I look at every day from my desk, was enough to call up memories from each of them of friends on our side of the lake, of journeys made long ago and connections to families whose surnames we knew. Memories that momentarily collapsed the space of the watershed in a way that made even stranger and more absurd the difficulty of reaching the other countries when they sit so close. The nearest North Macedonian village to ours within the basin is just a couple of kilometres over the border, a pleasant and easy walk down the valley and along the shore of the lake if it were permitted, but given that the Prespa border has been closed since the 1960s, the only legal way to get there is a long and circuitous route that takes two and a half hours by car via cities in both countries and a recognised international crossing. We may be neighbours, but we're kept apart as though strangers by a line.

Just a few months before we moved here in the summer of 2000, the prime ministers of the three nations sharing the lakes signed a document in the village that would become our home, establishing Prespa as the first transboundary park in southeast Europe. Together they pledged 'to protect the unique ecological values' of the region through 'peaceful collaboration', though it took until 2019 for the Greek parliament to ratify a formal arrangement signed in 2010 by the countries' environment ministers that would pave the way for official cooperation through state-level mechanisms. The opening of the local border between Greece and North Macedonia, though long delayed, is still moving slowly forward since the Prespa Agreement of 2018. Signed by the country's foreign ministers in the village of Psaradhes, the agreement theoretically resolved the long-running dispute over the shared

claim to the historic name of Macedonia; though the dispute that
has soured relations between the countries ever since the disin-
tegration of Yugoslavia and the elevation of the former Yugoslav
Republic of Macedonia to a fully-fledged state in 1991 shows
little sign of abating, given the significant opposition to the nam-
ing solution in both countries. But speaking to Jimmy and his
friends on that autumn day by the lake, with their outpouring
of affectionate remembering, highlighted for me the range of
meaningful ways we can look at shared places. How they can be
re-imagined beyond that fixation with hard boundaries and identities. How they can establish the potential for connectivity rather
than disruption, not just in terms of movement, technologies and
infrastructure links, but in the deeper and more difficult acknowledgement of common ground.

Some years ago, I interviewed Myrsini Malakou, the managing director of the Society for the Protection of Prespa (SPP),
an environmental NGO on the Greek side of the lakes, about a
transboundary project the organisation was running in a village
on the Albanian side. To this day I've remembered what she said
about the nature of borders, not only within the region itself but
in terms of how, ultimately, we approach and understand them as
an idea. How we relate to them as part of a shared planet.

'You can't say that the national border is more important
than any other,' said Myrsini. 'There is a geological border here,
between limestone and granite, an ecosystem border between wetland and upland. There are borders of interest and activity – the
fisherman, the farmer, the environmentalist. Borders are a limit or
a challenge, a restriction or an opportunity. I prefer to see them
as a challenge, where opportunities can enrich.'

Since the barbed-wire fences of Albania came down, the
borders dividing these lakes are no longer physical impediments
(though it remains illegal to cross the invisible lines all the same,
a fact made clear in Greece by the large number of border police

stationed in the area). But this situation at least allows the flow of brown bears, wolves and other wildlife between the countries in what to them are naturally extensive homelands. Numerous other borders in the world, however, including in Greece along its frontier with Turkey, are increasingly being transformed into solid obstacles, visceral assertions that the national border is still regarded as more important than any other. Put in place to prevent the movement of people, these impermeable barriers also curtail the migrations of wild species. The southern-border wall championed by Donald Trump between the United States and Mexico, even in its haphazard and partial state, fragments fragile desert ecosystems and restricts the range of many vulnerable animals, including jaguars, ocelots and the endangered Mexican grey wolf, further compromising the latter's small gene pool by isolating one part of its population from the other. In Europe, the 130 kilometres of 5.5-metre-high steel barrier being raised between Poland and Belarus will split Białowieża Forest, Europe's largest remaining primeval woodland, drastically curtailing the freedom of native bison, wolf and lynx to roam their ancestral territories, while preventing the natural colonisation of the European brown bear to the Polish side of the edifice.

'Physical barriers such as fences and walls now line 32,000 kilometres of borders worldwide with significant increases over the past few decades,' wrote conservation scientist Katarzyna Nowak of the Białowieża Geobotanical Station in an article about her work in the transboundary forests in 2021. She went on to say that as many as 700 mammal species across the planet will find it difficult to move into adjoining countries because of these barriers, further undermining their ability to adapt to a shifting world as their gene pools, populations and habitats are fragmented. 'As climate change threatens to disrupt borders and migratory patterns of people and of wildlife, we will need to reform, not only policies and frameworks, but also how we perceive borders.'

As the climate and biodiversity crises make plain the separation that exists between different peoples as well as between humans and the more-than-human world, the challenge – and therefore the opportunity, as Myrsini of the SPP put it – is to find ways of moving beyond these borders. Here in Prespa, that begins by understanding the region not as a periphery, or where three countries come to an end, but rather as a place entire, a unified ecological entity in which the waters are shared solely because human history has divided them. While borders are typically regarded as sites of separation, they can also be understood as meeting points. As those monks on the peninsula would have known long ago, Prespa is only an end when you look at it from a distance; seen from within, it's a vital and irreducible whole.

It was deep into afternoon when we remembered the long walk ahead of us, having to return through the forest to our hotel higher up the lake. 'Don't worry,' said Jimmy when he heard we were leaving. 'Have another drink or look around the village if you want – I'll get you back there.'

An hour later, like those monks rowing out through the gathered grebes, we set off over the water, steered in a small red-and-white fishing boat around the shelving spur of land on which the last houses of Konjsko sat. We motored slowly into the cold wind alongside cliffs overhung with the gnarled junipers and dense oaks that we'd walked through earlier that day to reach the village. And it was then, looking up at those trees as Jimmy pointed out caves and churches along the coast while waves slapped at the hull and sent spray into our faces, that I understood for the first time how that forest was the same forest as on the other side of the lake, where the sacred grove presses high into the sky. I'd long thought of them as distinct because of the way the lines on a map encourage us to define places through ownership – *our forests, their forests* – but that day I realised that they weren't separate entities beyond our human influence on them, leading to differing cultural traditions and economies of use. Instead, there was *a* forest. And the lake wasn't an end to it either; nor was it a border as we've come to understand borders. The water was merely a pause. A held breath before the trees surfaced again on the other side.

We rounded the cliffs into a bay where late sunlight held on to the lake. Cutting the motor, Jimmy rowed us in close, carving his oars through the shallows to hold us steady alongside a thin wooden pier. We jumped off and shouted our thanks as he pulled away. When he turned a final time after firing his motor back into life, Jimmy gave us a shallow bow and then waved across the water.

After leaving Keoladeo National Park, Sid and I travelled together for another month in western India before going our separate ways when Julia arrived. It was strange being together again: after the short, intense intimacy, an extended period of absence. We had to learn each other all over again, slowly filling in the pieces as we fell in love while winding our way north through the southern heat of Kerala and Karnataka. And as we did, we realised we were falling in love with something else along the way: the birds we encountered on our journey. Whole other worlds revealed to us by grey hornbills fanning past the windows of our bus in wooded hill country and the iridescent sunbirds shimmering against flowers in the backwaters explored by boat, the spectacular dangling pendants of a racket-tailed drongo in a park in Mysore. For me, they were an entirely new country, as surprising and extraordinary as the landscapes and cultures we moved through together. For Julia, whose childhood in a small Yorkshire town held the freedom of that age, allowed to run wild and explore the nearby world on her own terms, where she was drawn to the common plants and creatures she found in the fields, it felt like coming home. She renewed a relationship with the natural world first forged long ago with the help of *The Observer's Book of Birds*, her mother's nurturing encouragement and the rooks that played in the wind on the neighbouring farm.

Months later, back in London and living together, it was the desire to pick up that thread of our journey and seek out the places of birds that led us to spending as much of our spare time as we could exploring woods and marshes and estuaries outside the city. Most of the wild species we encountered were radically different from those we'd discovered in India – far less colourful and not nearly as easy to see, especially in late winter when we first went in search of them – but they were no less captivating; because what birds ultimately taught us was that watching them was simply a way of cultivating attention, so that it was the world itself that came into sharper focus. As we tramped through muddy thickets after storms or were pulled inside the dense silence of a sunlit stand of reeds, we experienced the first stirrings of a desire to live somewhere else; of wanting to be in a place where we felt more at home and nearer to the wild than we did in London. It was seeing those other lives that encouraged us to fly.

Sid and I never did do the work we'd hoped in India. Nor did I make it to Sri Lanka, instead staying on in India by myself after Julia returned to England to start work at her new job. One morning a couple of months later I woke in the foothills of the Himalayas and knew that it was time to turn for home. It was a moment of sudden, piercing clarity, when the path ahead was unexpectedly visible in the distance. I finally understood that for the next journey to begin this one had to end.

WRENS II

It's still dark as I step outside. Silent and snowing. I find the stone wall with my hands and follow it through the garden. I'm not used to leaving the house this way, but for a week now, ever since the wrens began sheltering in the old swallow's nest, we've used the back door between dusk and dawn to avoid disturbing them, fearful they'll scatter across the freezing valley. On these long winter nights, we're intensely aware that we share this home.

The arrival of the wrens has marked our evenings with intimate wonder. We've watched them from both indoors and out, finding new angles and perspectives on their ritual of return. In some languages, the twilight time between day and dark is known as wolf-light, or the hour of the wolf. A time when all that is solid becomes mutable, when the world for humans tilts from the visibly familiar to the mysteriously wild. A time *between* times. This winter, I've come to know the gloaming as wren-light. But right now, I'm following that other phase of transformation: when darkness becomes day.

With my gloved hands I feel for the chair I put out the afternoon before at the edge of the garden. I sit down and train my binoculars on the front door, but it's still far too dark around the house to see anything. As a sudden wind slants the snow, I draw my scarf tighter and pull my woollen hat down over my ears. I have no idea how long it'll be before the wrens begin leaving the nest.

Nine months earlier, at the beginning of spring, this cup of mud was freshly fringed and lined with moss. That day, I'd been

weeding in the garden as a wren ferried the tufts of bedding up
to the nest. I'd watched with mixed feelings as it studiously flew
back and forth, preparing the softest of possible shelters. While
I was thrilled by the thought of wrens nesting so near us, I was
equally worried about the fate of their breeding attempt because,
unlike swallows, wrens haven't evolved to raise a brood so close
to humans. Given the frequency of disturbance, even if we used
the back door as often as we could, I feared the nest would fail.

The following day, the wren was nowhere to be seen. At
the time, I imagined it had abandoned the site for elsewhere,
recognising that my regular presence in the garden wasn't ideal
for a breeding site. But this past week, as wrens have slipped each
evening inside the cup of mud now lined with dry moss because
of that one bird's labours, something else occurred to me. Had
the wren even been contemplating a nest there, or was it instead
preparing for bad times in good by restoring a potential winter
shelter? And if it had been considering the swallow's nest for its
own breeding attempt, did it, all these months later, when snows
had closed in and a perishing cold front mantled the mountains,
remember its moss-lined presence? Because until that spring day
in the garden, no bird had ever expressed any interest in this long-
abandoned nest in the years we've lived here. Could coincidence
alone account for its sudden desirability?

The valley gradually brightens, a thin screen of light sliding
over a sky of snow. Against the steep walls of the mountains are
outlined the white silhouettes of trees. Everything is ice cold and
densely quiet. It's still too murky to see clearly in the shadowed
overhang of the porch, but I fasten my binoculars on the nest nonetheless. My arms soon ache from holding them steady for so long,
but just as I'm beginning to doubt that the wrens are even there, I
see movement around the rim of mud. Dim flickers and blurrings
of brown wings. A shuffling of birds, as though they're rearranging
their formation as they waken. And then all is still again.

I wait as snow falls in large, drifting flakes, swirled upwards in sudden gusts. There's just enough light now to lend some clarity to what I'm looking at when a wren pops up and settles on the lip of the nest. It glances to either side and then drops off the edge, briefly plummeting before gaining lift and streaking off into the breaking day. One after another they follow the same pattern, like parachutists jumping in sequence from the open bay of a plane. I've counted eight out of the shelter so far, each of them vanishing into snow, tracing solitary routes through the valley. But the next wren hesitates. It slips back inside the nest, as if it's decided it's not ready. Then it returns to the lip again, where it shakes and stretches its wings. Behind it, I pick out the restless commotion of birds still to come. The one on the edge is blocking their exit, until a second wren squeezes onto the rim of dried mud and pushes it overboard with a wing. The bird freefalls for a split second before curling upwards and away over the whitening meadow.

As the last wrens follow, the winter valley moves from silence to sound, the calls of other birds beginning to be heard. The falling snow curtains our world. With the nest empty again, I head back inside. I stand by the glow of the fire that I'd lit in the dark and rub my hands together to loosen some of the cold. And then I cup one of them into the shape of a swallow's nest, knowing it's roughly the same small size as the one that somehow held fourteen wrens safe that night. All of them huddled close inside a shelter of another's making.

II

SHIFTING

4

Lost Songs

On a spring afternoon when a light breeze stirred some of the internal fog of lockdown, I heard a strange song in the garden. It pooled around the heart of our hazel tree like the wheezy breathing of an asthmatic. Standing there beneath the tree, I tried separating out the bird from the suspended green world where only a week earlier I'd watched two olive metres of Aesculapian snake unfold like a river across a plain. That day, a pair of tree sparrows had bravely badgered and scolded the incomer until it made a looping descent out of the canopy to the concealing tiles of our shed. But this wasn't the sharp and ceaseless alarm call of those agitated tree sparrows. The sound more closely resembled a song, or at least an approximation of a song, because something in its slurred metallic cadence felt distinctly out of sync and unusual for a garden bird in this part of the world. Staring up into the brimming green dome was like searching through a barrel of sand for a small stone, as in the days since the snake had slid across the upper branches the tree had closed ranks, excluding anything that wasn't leaf from view. Even light was now held at a distance. While the song was clearly audible, the singer remained a mystery. Eventually I gave up and went inside.

Several days later, Julia tracked the song to its source. Unexpectedly, she announced it was a great tit. So common to our garden and widespread throughout Europe, great tits are renowned for their inventive and wide-ranging voices. They're a bird that

can frequently surprise with a sudden turn of phrase, some liquid
lilt that catches a listener off guard, especially in early spring when
the need to retune to the song register of birds is common to many
of us after so many months of quiet. But despite the variety of the
great tit's repertoire, this particular spill of sound simply wasn't part
of it. Deviating so far from its recognisable musical terrain, it soon
became clear that this bird had been born with a voice defect, or
had suffered an injury at some later stage in life.

Wheezy – as the great tit became affectionately known to
us – would frequently return to the hazel tree over the following
months. Although it took me ages to see him, his song was so
singular that it announced his arrival like fanfare. And during those
spring and early summer days, as light swelled over the mountains
and swifts and swallows sailed across the blue lid of the world, I was
able to tune in to this bird with an unusual degree of precision,
because he was no longer a species to me but an individual within
a tribe. So distinctive was Wheezy's voice that I became familiar with his specific movements – his chartable morning passage
through the willows and walnuts beyond the edge of the garden,
his predilection for a dense tangle of wild clematis at the back of
the house in the afternoons. And most evenings he was in attendance at the tree where I'd first heard him, singing that unique and
solitary song from inside a cluster of green leaves.

As the breeding season sped away towards the hot haze of
high summer, I began to feel a degree of sympathy for Wheezy.
Given the significance of song to the mating rituals of birds, it was
highly unlikely this great tit would find a suitor. His voice, in all
probability, would compare poorly with other males and make him
unsuitable as a partner. Realising this, I couldn't help but think of
Wheezy as lonely when I heard him sing deeper and deeper into
the season. Not in the sense of being sad or forlorn of course,
but literally alone. Isolated and cut off from his kind. Made distinctive for all the wrong reasons as the valley went quiet around

him. His separation began to feel like a metaphor for lockdown in light of the narrowing tunnel of opportunities it entailed. But while Wheezy was just a single, broken-voiced bird in a garden in northern Greece, nearly a year after his appearance in the hazel tree I began to understand the greater implication of the world's lost songs.

By the time I first heard about the regent honeyeater, our valley had settled into the monochrome tones of snow. The village streets were iced over and quiet. At times, only the wood smoke spiralling from chimneys told you that anyone was living here. It was against this backdrop of winter withdrawal that the story of a vanishing song emerged. Endemic to southeast Australia, the regent honeyeater is a strikingly patterned songbird. It wears a black hood that sleeks away to a pointillist design of crescent moons against the night sky of its breast. Underneath its tail shines a lemony light that leaks through to the other side and illuminates some of its primary feathers and edges. As its name suggests, the regent honeyeater has a fondness for sweet things, gravitating to eucalyptus trees for their sugary confections. With a curved black beak ideal for probing flowers, the bird uses its brush-tipped tongue to sponge up the nectar it's named after. But it was the bird's music, a curious blend of clipped robotic notes, that was the ultimate focus of Ross Crates and his fellow conservation scientists at the Difficult Bird Research Group (who have the best title for a scientific team I've yet heard) based at the Australian National University (ANU) in Canberra.

'We spent a year in the field searching out places where regent honeyeaters might be and where the habitat looked good,' said Ross over Zoom when we spoke about the group's intensive work studying endangered Australian birds. 'Which meant a lot of time just wandering around, playing regent honeyeater songs, counting other birds. You can imagine the feeling when we did actually find one – it was elation.'

Finding regent honeyeaters is so difficult for two reasons. Firstly, the bird occupies an enormous range that historically stretched from Adelaide to Brisbane; although it's no longer found in the state of South Australia at all, the area it inhabits today is still 'probably ten times the size of the UK', according to Ross. Secondly, like so many other species across the planet, the bird has suffered a calamitous decline in population numbers in recent decades, which makes its presence in a landscape of that scale so much harder to detect.

The regent honeyeater wasn't always so elusive. John Gould, author of *The Birds of Australia* and the first Western ornithologist to explore the country when he visited in the late 1830s, described it as being abundant in New South Wales. 'Gould said they were the most pugnacious bird he ever saw,' said Ross. 'That they absolutely dominated flowering trees in their preferred areas and would just chase off all the other smaller songbirds. They basically roamed the landscape in these immense flocks, often containing hundreds or even thousands of birds.' Gould, however, made no mention of where these nomadic journeys took the regent honeyeater outside the nesting period. 'They basically disappear,' admitted Ross. 'They vanish into the hills or wherever they go at the end of the breeding season. They could be literally anywhere; we just don't know.' That such mystery can still exist in an age when so much of the world and its workings seems so thoroughly mapped, quantified and defined is itself a kind of wonder. A sign of how stunningly wild the world can still be.

Some vanishings don't evoke wonder, however, but telegraph instead a greater disappearance. Until the 1930s, the regent honeyeater was frequently observed in the suburbs of Melbourne and Sydney; even as late as 2008 and 2009, flocks of a hundred birds or more were still occasionally being encountered. But all of that proximity and abundance are now gone, as the regent honey-eater is largely confined to just three breeding territories in the Blue Mountains west of Sydney and the tablelands of New South Wales. 'To put it bluntly,' said Ross, 'there's a very good chance that they're going to go extinct in the very near future. These were very common birds. And now there's less than three hundred of them left in the world.'

This dwindling is directly traceable to the undoing of the bird's shelter, as the woodlands on which the regent honeyeater depends have been largely destroyed for residential developments, agriculture, mining and logging. Known as Box-Gum or Box-Ironbark woodlands, these forests of varied eucalyptus species host the bird's favourite flowering trees, including yellow box, white box, mugga ironbark and the red gums. It's believed that as much as 85 per cent of these woodlands have been cleared in total, making it one of Australia's most threatened ecosystems. And the little of it that still exists is frequently found on less fertile soils, or is badly fragmented into tiny plots, so that what might once have been marginal habitat for the regent honeyeater has become, over time, its only habitat.

'The woodlands of Australia', said Ross, when I asked him to describe for me what these forests were once like,

are quite different from how you might imagine them if you haven't been here. They're not tall, dense, closed canopies; the woodlands are generally much more sparsely treed, but with bigger trees, with bigger crowns. And the thing that gets me is that when yellow box is in flower, which is the regent honeyeater's favourite food tree, you can smell the honey from far away. You can smell the blossom before you see it. Imagine if you had entire valley floors covered in yellow box trees all flowering at the

same time, then the sound of all those nectar-feeders in
the trees would have been amazing. We see it now with
individual trees, but if you had entire landscapes flowering
like that it'd be a pretty astonishing spectacle.

While the loss of such spectacles was to be expected with the
uprooting, what Ross wasn't prepared for was the consequent
changes to the bird's music. While he and his fellow researchers
hadn't originally set out to study the regent honeyeater's song,
it soon became their aim when they realised they were hearing
honeyeaters mimicking the voices of other birds. Traditional mim-
icry – the intentional replication of another species' vocalisations
in order to make a bird more appealing to potential mates or to
defend territory more successfully – appeared in the scientific literature about the species, but as Ross and his team soon discovered,
in one of those sudden moments of clarity that pulls you away from
theory and into the stream of surrounding lives in all their messy
complexity, there is no gain from this behaviour for the regent
honeyeaters, only loss. Because regent honeyeaters aren't copying
other birds in order to benefit from the adoption of their voices;
they're copying them because they're forgetting their own songs.

Both Julia and I had concrete plans about what we would do after
settling in Prespa. I intended to focus on writing, something I'd
tinkered around with for years without any real degree of commitment. Julia, having spent much of her professional career until
then as a theatre technician in London, wanted to follow a path
into the conservation field, hence carrying all those textbooks
with us in our packs during the long summer of our arrival. In a
sense, these were the two foundation stones we'd built the entire
journey on, writing and conservation. But it was years before we

would turn our attention to either of them because we decided to become organic farmers instead.

Farming might be too bold a term for the makeshift agricultural enterprise we initiated in a set of five fields we'd rented at the foot of the mountains that rose to the ridgeline border with North Macedonia, but market gardening seems too intimate a description for the expanse of earth we set to work on. Having saved enough money in London to carry us through only until the following summer, we spent our first winter in Prespa circling around the question of what came next. As snow piled up outside the house and we fed beech logs without break into the single wood stove that heated one of its rooms and only half of a second one, we carefully tallied the drachmas of our bills and other outgoings, quickly realising that those two foundation stones would have to be pushed to one side if we were to stand any chance of staying put. And on the ridiculously flimsy basis that we'd successfully grown cherry tomatoes in growbags on our London balcony and that I'd learned how to repot and care for seedlings in the greenhouses at Hyde Park, the idea that we could work the land gained strength. All winter we pored over seed catalogues and gardening books; we delved into the complicated process for organic certification and explored ways of drying herbs for sale; and, together with Vassilis, we looked at potential fields to rent until signing the contract for that suite of five. And that spring, as the meltwater memory of winter snow riffled through the river at the foot of our plots on its way to the lake, we sowed our first seeds in the earth. In their rooting, we hoped to find our own.

Not long afterwards, Vassilis needed some work doing on his truck. Taking the morning off from fieldwork, we bunched up with him on the front seat and drove to Kastoria, a fur-trading town 50 kilometres to the south of Prespa that rides into the waters of Lake Orestiada on the back of a limestone peninsula. His friend's garage was perched above the lake, set on the shoulder of

a hill between the town's last low-rise apartments and a military
base. Pulling into a lot stained with spilled oil and the rainbow
sheen of leaked petrol, we unfolded ourselves from the pick-up.
The mechanic greeted us graciously, wiping his hands on his overalls before warmly pressing them into ours in a way so common
in this country, immediately extending friendship to the friends of
friends. Vassilis explained that we'd begun cultivating organic herbs
and other aromatic plants in the fields of Prespa. Already, the seedlings of thyme, lavender, chamomile and sage were showing above
the earth – small but defiantly there. There were daily challenges
to their survival: goats were getting in through holes in the fence
that we were struggling to fix properly; bears passed through and
occasionally stomped on some of them; and irrigation sometimes
proved problematic because one of the farmers along the channel
didn't like sticking to the joint agreement about allocated hours
and days for watering. But the appearance of those seedlings lent
solidity to our decision. Despite knowing that other obstacles and
uncertainties lay ahead, the seams of green in the furrows of the
fields gave us confidence that we could make this place home.

At the mention of herbs, the mechanic immediately turned
and called his father out from the family house built over the service bay and car pit, explaining that his knowledge of traditional
medicinal plants was both broad and deep. A man in his late sixties
or early seventies stepped through the door in grey suit trousers
and a matching jacket, dressed just the same for the café as for a
wedding, as the men of a certain generation still do in Greece. As
Vassilis and his friend went off to talk about car repairs and parts,
the mechanic's father took us on a tour.

Our journey with him that day lasted no more than half an
hour and covered a physical space not much greater than the foot-
print of a terraced house. But the depth of that journey exceeded
anything I could have imagined for such a small and unprepos-
sessing place unless it concerned the maintenance of vehicles.

He began with a slow and deliberate examination of the fissures in the lot, where greenery had surged through gaps in the asphalt forced open by the seesawing seasons of heat and cold. One by one, the man pointed to some part of a plant and told a story about its medicinal properties. It was still too early in our learning of the language to know the names of the plants or the specific uses he referred to, but as we proceeded across the cracked parking lot to its edge, where rusting cars and tyres too worn to be reused bedded down in a spill of billowing vegetation, we landed on a simple method of interpretation. The mechanic's father would pluck a piece of a plant and hold it out to us; he would then direct it to the appropriate place of use on his body, keeping it as close as a poultice. In this way, each element of greenery created associations between plant and ailment, a rudimentary but successful rendering of the far more complex connections underpinning this knowledge. This is how we learned from him that a particular serrated leaf was effective against liver conditions. The hollow stem of another helped the heart. A knot of slim roots eased the intense pressure of migraines. And a clutch of flowers the colour of the summer sea could calm an upset stomach. With each detached fragment he bore upwards to us, memory and practice fitted together into a mosaic of rich cultural meaning.

That small world he introduced us to could never be rendered with any degree of accuracy on a map because this wasn't just about scale in relation to the landscape or about identifying specific species, but rather reflected the internalised traditions of composite living systems. The patterns that maps miss. The mechanic's father surveyed with an eye for forms, colours and characteristics, recognising in their presence a deeper significance. This terrain held stories of such unsung complexity, earned over centuries of interplay between people and plants and place, that he could read a whole relationship of entwinement on the forecourt of his son's garage, elaborating on a wild pharmacy in what

I would have said was the unlikeliest of spots for it. But then it was unlikely only because I lacked the cultural experience of these species and an understanding of their powerful properties. I was missing the key to unlocking their songs.

When we talk about culture, we're nearly always talking about people. It's a concept that's become synonymous with human civilisation and its accompanying spectrum of socially transmitted phenomena, encompassing a wide range of material expressions, including architecture, food, technologies and clothing, as well as intangible cultural heritage such as traditions, customs, science, literature, philosophy and myths. It includes the music we make and the songs we sing, as well as the communal knowledge of medicinal plants bursting from the asphalt of a garage. But the disappearance of the regent honeyeater's song is a cultural issue, too. For far too long the notion of culture, outside of Indigenous societies at least, has excluded the non-human world. It has set us apart, isolating us from other forms of life, despite there being species as varied as octopuses, elephants, parrots, whales, chimpanzees and meerkats, among many others, that inhabit distinctively rich and intelligent cultures as reliant on forms of social transmission as humanity. Because the real key to culture is that it flows; it passes between individuals within societies and from generation to generation through time. That's what lends culture its intricate layers of meaning – its accumulated movement. And that's how past and present, both for us and others, shapes the future to come.

Like many songbirds, the regent honeyeater learns to communicate by copying the voices of other members of its own species. Through association, its world expands into sociability. As with human children, whose early engagement with language and communication is closely tethered to the presence of family members, relatives and friends to learn from and interact with, regent honeyeaters rely on social continuity and cohesion for the transmission of cultural traits. Traditionally, they've gathered in loose congregations to nest, favouring river oaks beside running water. At the end of the breeding season, the scattered groups of an area would convene in an immense flock to ride out over the hills into those unknown places of their mysterious passage. And on these nomadic journeys, juveniles would mix with adults from other groupings and learn the songs they needed for their own eventual breeding efforts in the river oaks, too. But with the destruction of those sheltering woodlands, the bird's population has been sunk like a torpedoed boat. And as the population slips further beneath the surface, juveniles find fewer and fewer adults to travel with. 'They just don't get the chance to hang around with other honeyeaters and learn what they're supposed to sound like,' explained Ross.

Imagine a child in complete isolation just at the point that she should be establishing vocalisation as a means to communicate. She'd have no way of learning from others; no opportunity for picking up the words, utterances, ideas and meanings that constitute her culture's language and modes of expression. Now imagine that same child not in isolation but adopted at birth by a family from a different country and culture. The girl's first language will change in response to the altered social environment of her upbringing, because mother tongues, despite their name, are cultural rather than biological inheritances. Which is essentially what is happening to regent honeyeaters. Instead of their own songs, some birds are now learning the songs of other species in their shared landscape due to an absence of regent honeyeaters, so that they sound like little wattlebirds, noisy friarbirds and black-faced cuckooshrikes. But unlike that adopted child, who will develop and grow within the larger family of human languages, adopting a different song as a bird because it's forgotten its own is likely to

result in a catastrophic inability to communicate with others of
its own kind. Scientifically known as the Allee effect, this decline
in the fitness of individuals when a species reaches a low population density or size reflects the incapacity of a species to sustain
its essential dynamics once it assumes a critical mass. Eroded are
the fundamental elements of a species' lifeline. 'Our research,' said
Ross, 'shows that 12 per cent of the male population of regent
honeyeaters has entirely lost its song culture.'

This disappearance is especially poignant given that Australia
is the cradle of song culture in birds. It's where the music that
conjures the enchantment of a dawn chorus in the juniper woods
of Prespa or on a misty Sussex heath first originated some 24 million years ago, before spreading around the planet. From those
ancient Australian beginnings, the extended family of songbirds
now accounts for around half of the world's roughly 10,000 bird
species, including great tits like Wheezy in our garden in Greece.
And now one of those songs is slipping away.

'We think about species being on the brink of extinction,' said
Ross, 'but we don't think about species on the brink of extinction
being unable to communicate with one another. If you map the
trajectory of a species' decline from really abundant to extinct,
you might only be able to detect loss of song culture in a really
narrow window between being on the brink of extinction and a
species going extinct.'

Language is a communal shelter. It houses the histories, practices,
perspectives, ethics and beliefs of societies large and small, making communication, interaction and exchange between people
within them possible. And yet language is profoundly personal,
too. Each of us dwells in a house of language all our own (many,
for that matter, reside in more than one). The ability to formulate

and transmit our needs, ideas and desires – to understand and share in the world around us – through a set of established but continuously evolving codes, whether written, oral or signed, is an essential aspect of self-grounding within a collective framework. It's the furnace where personality is forged.

During our early years of learning Greek, Julia and I frequently confessed to one another that the most frustrating aspect of not having command over the language was being unable to express our personalities completely. There was a part of us missing while in Greek company, or else it was a part clumsily disclosed, sounding simplified and vague to any listeners. We didn't feel entirely whole because we lacked the linguistic foundation for fully declaring the nuances of personal and cultural identity. But ours was a choice to take on the challenges of dwelling within a different house of language. For many, that choice was never theirs to make.

The harrowing discovery of hundreds of unmarked children's graves in the grounds of residential schools in Canada in 2021 cast a stark light on that country's grievous historic relationship with Indigenous peoples. I grew up in Canada, spending nearly my entire childhood, adolescence and early adulthood in the nation's educational system. In all that time, I don't recall ever hearing about these residential schools. Belgian colonialism in Africa? *Yes*. German treatment of Jews in the 1930s and the ensuing Holocaust? *Yes*. But the nearby violence – both physical and cultural – against the people on whose lands we lived? That went unspoken. In part because the last residential school (in Rankin Inlet, in what is now Nunavut but was then the Northwest Territories) didn't close until 1997, eight years after I graduated from high school in southern Ontario. This was history not as past but present, ongoing and still traumatic for those who'd survived the system. And the silence surrounding it at the time further affirmed the original intent and purpose of the policy by denying the voices, experiences and histories of First Nations, Inuit and Métis peoples. Funded by the Canadian government and administered by various Christian churches, the Indian residential school system, which was in reality a mandatory boarding school system, saw 150,000 children in attendance over the course of its history. And it was a system specifically set up to undo the bonds between Indigenous children and their parent cultures; to separate them physically, emotionally and psychologically from their mother tongues and customs by banning the speaking of native languages. As Nicholas Flood Davin, one of the architects of the residential school system, wrote regarding its fundamental aims in his 'Report on Industrial Schools for Indians and Half-Breeds' in 1879, 'If anything is to be done with the Indian, we must catch him very young. The children must be constantly within the circle of civilised conditions.'

This assimilation was often cruelly enforced. Corporal punishment was frequent; physical, sexual and mental abuse common. While specific treatments varied from school to school, punishments for children who spoke their own language included the withdrawal of meals, forced isolation and the washing of a child's mouth with soap. In extreme examples, electric shocks were administered or needles pushed into children's tongues in order to create mental associations between the enunciation of their native language and agonising pain. In Canada, as in other parts of the world where local languages and historic linguistic patterns were overwhelmed by the arrival of outsiders, the colonial language of English, and to a lesser extent French, unified a nation not through consensus but through the violent erasure of difference. Tearing people from their language is akin to pulling down their homes.

This state-sanctioned policy of language suppression has led to a haunting generational phenomenon known as the silent speakers, in which some Indigenous people are unable to vocalise their own language because of the trauma they experienced at residential schools and the cultural stigma attached to speaking 'Indian'.

It is most common in those who emerged from the residential school system with some of their mother tongue still intact but who can't share that language or its songs with their own children out of an innate desire to protect them from the harmful and humiliating experiences they endured when speaking it. And so the language goes unspoken, a reverberating silence. Of the seventy Indigenous languages still found in Canada today, more than two-thirds of them are threatened with extinction. The rest are considered vulnerable.

While linguistic erosion undoes the sheltering bonds of community and personal identity, language loss also ripples outwards through the more-than-human world. Numerous studies have shown a positive correspondence between language diversity and biodiversity. Where multiple languages have existed in a given region, the spectrum of wild species and organisms supported there has often been simultaneously high. This has been particularly true in some of the great biodiversity hotspots of the world, such as the island of New Guinea, the Himalayan flood plain of northeast India and the Amazon basin, where, many linguists and anthropologists believe, natural barriers enabled a profusion of languages and organisms to emerge and evolve in isolation from one another. But this also means that the opposite is true. Although the evolutionary mechanism is still poorly understood, where languages have been lost, so too have the number and range of wild species generally declined. Much of this loss, both linguistic and biological, revolves around the consolidation of colonial enterprises around the globe. As empires expanded – British, Spanish, Portuguese – the linguistic systems and extractive economic practices they imposed on newly conquered territories frequently destroyed or overwhelmed local languages, economies and patterns of land use that had previously supported diverse communities of people and wildlife. In Australia, home of the disappearing regent honeyeater, Professor Ghil'ad Zuckermann,

Chair of Linguistics and Endangered Languages at the University
of Adelaide, believes there are only thirteen Indigenous languages
that can still be considered living in the sense of being socially
transmitted to children, in comparison with the 330 that were in
existence prior to British colonisation in 1788.

This pattern is being replicated across the planet. As the natural barriers that led to linguistic profusion are broken down – not
uncommonly accompanied by violence – through colonialism,
globalisation, extractive industries, slash-and-burn agriculture, displacement and migration to urban centres, the languages that have
fitted with those landscapes for sometimes thousands of years are
stretched as thin as a moth's wings. Today, hundreds of languages
are entirely dependent on just hundreds of speakers for their survival, while 40 per cent of the world's 8 billion people speak
one of only eight languages between them. Of the 7,400 languages found throughout the world, more than a quarter of them
are currently threatened with extinction. And with so many of
the world's known species also at risk from extinction, a positive
feedback loop of increasing decline spins ever faster around the
mutually linked poles of cultural and biological diversity. With
each revolution, the dizzyingly varied and inventive expressions
of life on the planet are irrevocably simplified and reduced.

Languages are an invitation to see the world through another lens.
Even though we live with golden orioles glimmering all summer
long between the willows and poplars of our valley, it took a visit
to a lowland lake in late August one year for the specificity of their
Greek name, *sikofagos*, to be finally understood. There, the birds
became the fig-eaters that they're called in this country, feasting
on fruit that is too heat-needy ever to ripen in the far cooler
highlands of Prespa. And when we moved here, the enormous and

glorious raptor that I'd long known from the *Collins Guide to the Birds of Europe* by the stingy English name of short-toed eagle was completely transformed in my understanding to *fidaetos* in Greek, as I watched these snake eagles hunt over the dry hills above our house and carry off their spiralling prey across the sky. It's for this reason – the careful attention given to the world's particularities as they exist in specific localities and surroundings – that languages can swing open the doors and windows of the house we dwell within and expose us to other views. They can relieve us of a sense of cultural centrality by expanding our understanding of unfamiliar societies and how their own experiences have shaped the way they speak.

I hear this in Prespa all the time. Despite our village holding fewer than 140 permanent residents, it's possible to encounter Greek, Macedonian, Albanian and Vlach (a Latinate language that's found in Vlach communities in various parts of the Balkans) spoken in its lanes. Across the border in Albania, several villages on the shores of Great Prespa Lake are ethnically Slavic, and so both Macedonian and Albanian are understood in their streets. While on the North Macedonian side of the lakes there exists a village where Turkish is still commonly spoken, a lifeline of language traced back to the days of the Ottoman Empire and still with us because of the region's complex political history and tangled demographic lineage.

Similarly, the topographical and cultural paths of peoples can sometimes be audibly traced through their patterns of speech. Some years ago, I was wheeled into a recovery room after a minor procedure at the hospital in Florina, the market town about an hour over the mountains that Prespa is closely tethered to for its commercial, administrative and medical needs. On the bed beside mine lay a middle-aged Roma woman surrounded by several members of her family of varying ages. Listening to them speak was a rapid-fire lesson in startling linguistic fluidity; not only did they employ several languages within their conversation but they frequently swapped from one to another within a single sentence, seamlessly shifting from Roma to Greek to Albanian to Macedonian, with two or three others mixed in for good measure. My mind boggled at how the grammar matched up.

'Excuse me,' I said in Greek, the only language common to us all. 'I'm so impressed that you're speaking several languages at the same time.'

They all smiled, including the woman in the bed as she turned towards me, her hair in long braids tied together by a red ribbon. A man about my age then laughed and said, 'We don't know many words, but we know a lot of languages!'

Languages – as was clear at the garage that day even though we couldn't understand everything the mechanic's father was sharing with us – can also illuminate an intimate sense of internalised connection and care, one that extends to our relationships with place and the natural world. Indigenous languages in particular shelter within their cultural vocabularies a repository of traditional ecological knowledge. Cumulative and wide-ranging bodies of understanding gathered and refined over hundreds and sometimes thousands of years in response to intimate interactions between people, plants, rivers, climate, lands, animals and seas within a particular place or region. As with that child learning her mother tongue, or a young regent honeyeater gleaning its song from adult birds on its voyage over the hills, these bodies of knowledge – these *lifelines* – are transmitted from generation to generation and absorbed as part of a culture's worldview. And where Indigenous cultures still flourish, the value of this traditional ecological knowledge encoded within local languages remains vigorously clear.

A 2019 study by the University of British Columbia that focused on 15,621 geographical areas in Canada, Brazil and Australia found that the total numbers of mammals, birds, reptiles and amphibians were greatest on lands either entirely managed or co-managed by Indigenous communities. Protected areas such as national parks and nature reserves, which have come to represent the zenith of nature protection for non-Indigenous societies, came a close second in the study's biodiversity rankings. Given the complex crises we face today, from the crashing population numbers of many wild species to the proliferation of devastating wildfires burning up the forest homes of countless forms of life, the ecological knowledge and experience encapsulated in many endangered language systems and the cultural perspectives and practices of Indigenous peoples across the planet is of vital and irreplaceable importance.

All of this, of course, is possible only when languages are still with us. According to the United Nations, 30 per cent of the world's languages are expected to disappear by the end of the century. And what vanishes with each extinct language is the potential practice and experience of living more lightly, more respectfully, more collegiately on the planet. 'Every language,' wrote Wade Davis in *The Wayfinders*, 'is an old-growth forest of the mind.' Gone with the last language-carriers – their living woods of words, grammar and meaning cut down to the ground – are unique perspectives on our world.

'When I hear Indigenous tongues spoken my heart swells, both for joy and sorrow,' wrote the Métis writer Chris La Tray. Alongside that joy, sorrow is still a modern reality for many, as the colonial experience of being violently stripped of cultural attributes and home places continues today. In 2019 alone, 212 land defenders and environmental activists were murdered while protecting landscapes and habitats from being ravaged by mining, logging, gas, oil and agribusiness enterprises, of whom 40 per cent were from Indigenous communities. Indigenous peoples continue to face disproportionate violence because the kind of colonial systems

that led to hundreds of unmarked graves being discovered in the
grounds of Canadian residential schools remain intact in many
parts of the world. From the Amazon and jungles of Colombia
to the mountainous heartlands of the Philippines, those systems
continue to displace and destroy native communities, languages
and lives. And in those countries where reconciliation with native
peoples is frequently held up as a core national principle, precious little political concern is given to the voices of Indigenous
communities resisting plans to run pipelines or timber operations through sacred lands and reservations – or that violate
treaty agreements between tribes and the state, as with Line 3,
the oil pipeline proposed by the petroleum company Enbridge.
Intended to deliver nearly a million barrels of diluted tar sands
every day from the bleak oilfields of Alberta in Canada – where
toxic emissions were found to have been underestimated by up
to a staggering 6,300 per cent according to a study published in
2024 – to Wisconsin in the United States, it would crash through
numerous watersheds, wetlands and the culturally significant wild
rice beds of the Anishinaabe peoples. Many of these large-scale
extractive works, under the guise of economic development and
heavily dependent on fossil-fuel subsidies and political favour, are
simply an ongoing extension of colonial assaults on the very ecosystems that underpin the health and well-being of communities
living in close relationship with the land.

Wherever we go, we pass over a tracery of layered presences.
Reminders of incalculable damage, loss and forced disappearances;
but signs, too, of stewardship, kinship, reciprocity and belonging.
And in those languages so violently and systematically suppressed
in Canada and elsewhere – Ojibway, Cree, Athabaskan, Salishan
– are stories and songs of other ways of being in the world. Ways
of being that are reclaiming ground as sovereignty over ancestral
lands is, in some places, being restored. Among other developments, the #LandBack movement has meant the transfer of the

National Bison Range in Montana to the Salish and Kootenai tribes it was originally taken from by the US government in 1908; it has meant nearly 1,200 acres of redwood forests and prairie lands being given back to the Esselen tribe, who called the Big Sur region of California home before being displaced by the Spanish; it has meant the Nimmie-Caira wetlands of New South Wales in Australia being placed under the stewardship of the Nari Nari people, who have renamed the wetlands they're seeking to rejuvenate Gayini, or 'water' in their language; and it has meant the proposed creation of the world's first Inuit-protected conservation zone, with the Canadian government working in collaboration with the Indigenous people of Nunatsiavut to safeguard the biodiversity of 15,000 square kilometres of their sub-Arctic homeland.

Such fundamental issues as Indigenous justice, land rights, endangered languages, climate change and the conservation of wild species and habitats can never be considered as separate matters because they are all linked by the same thing: the dominion of some over others. Until equality becomes the cornerstone of our cultures, our cultures will always be far less than they should and could be.

The year after Wheezy first sang in our hazel tree I stepped outside one evening to water the garden. It had been hot and dry for weeks. A welcome breeze rustled the valley as the sun dropped behind the mountains. From an old plum tree heaving with the shaggy seeds of wild clematis I heard a sudden burst of unusual music. Although fleeting, it was enough for me to recognise the singer. Wheezy had survived the winter for another season of song.

By then, we were deep into summer. I had no way of knowing whether Wheezy had successfully mated or not since I'd last heard him. But his genetic fidelity to the act of singing, just one small and single life in a dispersed lineage of songbirds spun out over millions of years from their ancient origins in Australia to wrap the hemispheres in song, made me realise more forcefully than ever that what is frequently just music to our ears is in fact a language to birds. And inside it is held their world.

After discovering the loss of song culture in regent honeyeaters, Ross and his team had changed their approach to captive-bred birds being released into the wild. Now they painstakingly teach young birds their own songs through archive recordings in the hope that the past can correct the future. It's as yet uncertain whether re-establishing the population through these releases will work, given the underlying degradation of habitat, especially as what's left of the regent honeyeater's woodlands remains at risk, but it gives that singular species a small chance of survival. It buys it some precious time in which we might change the cultures of *our* kind, because preserving the lifelines of birds, ultimately, can be done only by preserving the habitats of birds. To recognise those forests as common shelters; to understand them as homes. Otherwise, there will be songs we'll have to learn to live without as we become ever lonelier as a species: 200 native birds are currently threatened with extinction in Australia alone.

When I asked Ross why he thought this particular story had resonated so deeply, being picked up by media around the world when their paper was first published, he believed it was because it contained a simple but powerful message. 'Birds learn to sing in the same way that humans learn to speak,' he said. 'And so, people could almost empathise with the idea that if you never hung around with other humans you might never learn to speak.' Kindling the possibility of empathy for other species is one of the profound challenges we face in the midst of the biodiversity crisis. So much relies on seeing ourselves as part of a tapestry of life. To embrace the regent honeyeater as a fellow constituent of that wide weave we are simultaneously stitched into and yet also unravelling.

We may speak different languages, but that shouldn't stop us from listening closely to the songs of the world.

It had gone quiet in the plum tree. I stood watering the garden tomatoes and peppers as evening cooled around me, hoping to hear another thread of song from Wheezy before finishing up for the day. He could have been anywhere by then if he'd slipped out the back of the tree when I wasn't looking. I moved on to the courgettes, trying to keep the wild plum in my sightline as I straightened kinks in the hose. And as I did, a few notes of music slurred briefly from the leaves. A bird broke free of the tree and I turned to watch Wheezy fly further up the valley, so small in the falling summer light.

5

The Way of the River

Water sloped off the mountains, sputtering through steep gullies and spreading over tables of rock like oil in a heating pan. Unlike the limestone side of the basin, where the paths of water can sometimes feel like sworn secrets, these granite folds give up its movements easily. And in the middle of March, when the gathered snows piled on the high peaks are reshaped by sudden warmth, that water is everywhere. The whole landscape seems to be magically on the move with it, lending the meltwater season its meaning.

I pulled over at the side of the dirt road and soon after began ascending a narrow valley beside a mountain river. Above me, the sloping snowfields of Kičevo glared in the afternoon light, mirrored below by the hanging white lanterns of snowdrops on the banks by my feet. The river ran wild beside them, slapping off rocks and sloshing at the base of gnarled willows. Its deep thrum cancelled out all other sounds, so I regularly turned away from the water to scan the valley behind me, realising there was no way I would hear an approaching bear or an aggressively protective sheepdog above the din. As the river tumbled towards the lake, its sound hollowed out a channel of its own, a loud affirmation of what had begun as just the small trickles and seeps of a season in sway.

A granite boulder parted the current in the middle of the river. To either side, the water separated into horizontal as well as lateral planes. The lower of them rushed forward in a continuous white flow, as though churning against the gravel bed. Above it, however, moved another: a course much slower and more circumspect, corkscrewing on the surface like the last swirls of water in an emptying bath. I tossed a stick beyond the boulder, where the currents converged once more, and watched it shiver and flip before it was swished downstream and out of sight within seconds. What would it be like, I wondered, to exist in such turbulence, like the endemic Prespa trout that flashes upriver to spawn, or the dippers slipping into the cold rapids to fish? What would it be like for the water weeds and snails within the torrent, or the larva of caddisflies inside their self-made sleeves of sand and grit and stones? What would it be like for motion to be a home?

The ancient Greek philosopher Heraclitus famously highlighted the perpetual nature of change by saying you can never step into the same river twice, given that both you and the watercourse will have been altered in some way by the time you enter it again. In truth, as Heraclitus's disciple Cratylus pointed out in response to the philosopher's words, you can't step into the same river even once, in the sense that it's already been changed in the fraction of a second that it takes for your foot to break the surface and land on the bed. Not a single point of pure stillness exists in a moving river – and never more so than in the meltwater season. Because this river's essence, like the substance of all rivers lent force by the brimming slopes, springs and snows around them, is dynamic and continuous fluidity. Within this one flow, there are many rivers – the endless becoming of a whole watershed in motion.

All landscapes, naturally, are on the move. Evolving, shifting, growing or disappearing. Even the mountains above this river have shed enough sediment to bridge the lakes with an isthmus. But there are cultural changes that have reshaped these slopes just as intensely as any natural erosion. Gone are the agricultural terraces that once climbed nearly to the peaks of these formidable mountains. Gone too are the abundant hares that, according to the eldest villagers, thrived on the blown seeds of the upland cereals. Gone are the huge herds of goats and sheep that were so crucial to the well-being of our village that they were looked after collectively, your allotted days of shepherding them across the mountains equal to the proportion of animals you owned individually. Though, in their absence, thickets of juniper and oak are gradually recolonising the south-facing slopes that suffered the greatest pressure from grazing and woodcutting because they gathered the sun first in the year and held its warmth the longest. Even the end of movement encourages movement.

Ever since we arrived here, I've tried imagining what these mountains might have looked and sounded like back then, with their shepherds' huts not slumped in stone ruin but lived in and tended to, closed up at night with the bells of a whole herd settling down into the dark. Before the Civil War, our village held between 2,500 and 3,000 people instead of the 130 or 140 it does today; but even in the aftermath of the conflict, animal grazing remained an important economic activity because of the pastoralist Vlachs that were resettled in Prespa's villages. The area's current small numbers were cemented by later waves of migration away from the region.

It was one of these returnees – back in the old place for a month of summer in his retirement – that finally sketched some of the ordinary intimacy of these mountains for me. I never learned the man's name, and can no longer remember whether it was Toronto or Melbourne or Frankfurt he'd come back from, or any of the other places that Prespiots had spread outwards to in the 1970s, '80s and '90s, looking for work in new lands amid the economic struggles of the agricultural basin. But I remember what he said after we'd exchanged a few words about the weather while I was out walking one morning.

'I knew this path by the river so well. It was our way to Florina.'

So often it was the elder generation who spoke most intimately to us of their relationships to this place and who became our first friends in Prespa. Especially those who'd left and then returned, as though the displacement had made them more open and understanding of the journeys of others. More sympathetic to our search for a home.

'What was your way to Florina?' I'd asked the man, confused about the route he was describing, given that the road to town wound its way through the mountains some significant distance to the south of us.

'This was,' he said, lifting his head upwards in the direction of the highest mountains.

'What about the main road?' I naively asked.

'Not much use if you didn't have a car. And the village was already in the mountains, so it was easier to go over them than all the way around. We followed the way of the river, walking our animals to town on this track, climbing upwards and over, carrying sacks of grains and cereals to market.'

My map of this place was remade that day, with its paths and people and creatures moving across its surface in a different direction from what I'd previously imagined.

As the mountain cold began to flow through the valley with the falling light, I climbed up from the water and made for home. The snows might have been melting but it was still winter when the sun went down. With the river at my side, I slowed behind a herd of brown cows being guided to their stables by Thodoris and his son Zizis, cattle farmers from our village just as reliant on the water of this river as ever. You might not be able to step into the same river twice, but you can share across time the same seam of need for one.

Thodoris hung his head out of the open window, a cigarette dangling from his lips. 'Sorry,' he shouted with a smile and a shrug. 'I'll have them off the road and into the stable soon.'

'Don't worry,' I shouted back. 'I'm in no hurry.'

Thodoris slowly waved as smoke from his cigarette pooled around his door and his cows pushed on down the track. Nothing was in a rush that day except the snow-cold currents of the unwinding river.

For five years we worked beside this river, farming the fields at the foot of the mountains. While local farmers largely cultivated crops of the small and large dried beans, *plake* and *gigantes* respectively, for which Greek Prespa is renowned, we made a conscious decision to do something different, so as not to compete with existing agricultural enterprises. Which led us to growing a large range of organic fruits, vegetables and salads, in addition to those herbs that were our original idea. There was an emerging appetite for organic goods in Greece that we happened to tap into at just the right moment, eventually selling much of our produce through word of mouth to hotels in Prespa, shops in nearby towns and tavernas in Thessaloniki.

Each spring we had the fields ploughed by a friend of Vassilis and then did everything ourselves by hand. Having no vehicle in the first of those years, we wheelbarrowed to the fields each day all our tools, watering cans and the young plants we'd carefully raised from seed at home, either on a table in the living room where they tended to grow too pale and leggy by the window or, more successfully, in a set of cold frames that I built in the garden with canes left over from a neighbour's bean fields. I still have the plans and sketches we drew up during the heavy snows of winter, meticulously plotting the placement of the coming crops, the new varieties we wanted to try that year and the rotation sequence to be followed. Seeing those pages today, I'm instantly reminded of our huge hunger for the work – a desire explained in part by the fact that our aim of staying in this place was directly tethered to the success or failure of those fields, but also because the act of taking on something so completely new was simultaneously invigorating and challenging.

Being fuelled by youthful enthusiasm, however, didn't always create sufficient cover for our lack of practical agricultural experience. One morning in our first growing season, Vassilis dropped off mounds of the purple mash left over from the distilling process behind Germanos's house, saying it would be ideal to use as a soil conditioner. Without a vehicle, we had no way of conveniently spreading it across the large fields, so Julia and I took the sheet of heavy-duty plastic that we'd used to cover our woodpile that winter and loaded it by shovel with smaller quantities of mash. One of us then dragged the sheet behind them as though pulling a child on a sled, while the other raked spent grapes from it onto the fields. I can still hear the roar of laughter in the taverna that night when someone asked us whether this was how all farmers in England worked the land. Despite our thirst for the work, we never really adapted to sensible farming hours either, frequently setting out after a night in the village bar when the morning sun was already hot and high. We'd drive through the baked dust of the dirt road in a used pick-up truck that we bought in our second season and pass local farmers coming from the other direction, who would wave from the sun-cracked seats of their tractors as they returned from work for lunch and a well-earned siesta just as we were getting started in the fierce heat.

Even with our odd hours and somewhat unorthodox methods, though, we remained deeply committed to putting down roots through the physical act of raising plants in the fields. And over time, we became pretty good at it, tending to dozens of different varieties of tomatoes, peppers, cucumbers, brassicas and salad leaves. We coaxed lush rows of sage, basil and thyme from the stony soil. We devoted half a field to chamomile, so that by early

summer the plants were waist high and heavy with fragrant white
flowers, which we harvested by using our fingers like rakes, letting
the flowerheads fall into the baskets looped to our belts. Each June
we'd transplant over a thousand leeks by hand, digging them up
from the garden where we'd sown them as seed and taking them
up to the evening fields. There, we'd mound and smooth the soil
in parallel ridges and make deep holes in the rows with a dibber.
As one of us dropped seedlings into the hollow slots, the other
followed with a watering can to puddle them in. And every week,
for about seven months of the year, we harvested crates of fresh
produce that was on diners' tables the following day.

Those fields are where we grew into this place. They
immersed us in the living landscapes of the region's history, as
when we held in our hands Ottoman coins that we'd dug from
the earth while planting our crops. Dating from an age when that
empire held sway over these mountainous lands, I imagined them
having fallen through a hole in the pocket of a farmer working
the same fields that we were tending all those years later. On other
days we'd tease hollow gun cartridges from the soil after hearing
the distinctive clink of metal against metal when hoeing; in all
likelihood, ours were the first hands to have held them since those
that had pulled the trigger during the Second World War or the
ensuing Greek Civil War. In those same fields we encountered
electric green lizards, hibernating dormice and a horn-nosed viper
that had taken shelter beneath the stone I was just about to pick
up when I saw the dark gleam of its eyes at the last second. And
while we worked, mysterious birds sometimes passed through on
migration, seeming like cryptic signals sent from distant lands, as
when a flock of rose-coloured starlings made an apple tree one
murky morning look as if it had been strung for Christmas with
glowing pink lights.

Even more importantly, those fields enabled us to build a
set of friendships with fellow residents that endure to this day.

I look back now and realise, with the long view made possible by hindsight, that turning our hands to the land was the best thing we could possibly have done here. Although we raised crops that differed greatly from those of Prespa farmers, and our approach to farming was comically inefficient in comparison with local standards, we were bound to this place in the same elemental ways as others. Together we were connected by soil, seeds, harvests and storms. We shared the strains and uncertainty of working the earth at a time when climate change began noticeably affecting weather patterns in the basin. And we were, throughout the hot and dry summers, joined by our reliance on the river.

Unlike farmers on the plain, who drew water directly from the lakes via a pumping station, those of us with plots in this upper valley irrigated our crops from the river. The same river whose meltwater season is a lesson in the interconnected tendencies of watersheds. Although it swept right past the foot of our fields, in order to divert some of its water towards our plants we had to walk higher up the valley to a point where a cement irrigation channel met the descending flow. There, when it was our turn to water, we mounded rocks in such a way that some of the river flowed into it. Once in the channel, you could stopper it beside the fields of your choice with stones and a sack and direct the water towards your crops along simple furrows in the soil. In spring and early summer, when the snowmelt and rains kept the river running high, all of this was fairly simple. By August, as the river began to wane, you had to mound your stones painstakingly in such a manner that water couldn't leak beneath them if you wanted a decent volume to reach the channel. Come September, however, it was anyone's guess as to the work ahead of you as you walked up to the river from your plot. As the dry season lingered and the river receded, you'd have to stride out further and further over the exposed stones of the riverbed if you were to have any hope of patching some of the narrowing seam through to your fields.

But no matter how shallow and slow it might be, the river never stopped flowing. It was the lifeline we all relied on.

People sing of remembered rivers, those sinuous oxbows, meanders and braids tracing the earth in shades of jade, silver, brown and blue. They eulogise chalk streams and trout streams; celebrate wild burns, brooks and becks. They learn by heart the names of the great waterways: the Amazon, Indus, Danube, Yangtze, Thames and Nile. Rivers run right through us, from the water of which our bodies are largely made to the trading cultures that water has long shaped, connecting us to other people and places around the world. So much of human history – of livelihood, agriculture, urbanisation, food cultures, transport, borders, wars and migrations – has been built on the backs of rivers. And in those many moving waters, confluences of the human and more-than-human worlds, exist countless forms of life just as reliant on them as us.

A few years ago, Julia and I were sitting in a narrow wooden skiff in the northeast Indian state of Assam when a line of motion broke the smooth skin of a river. Something brushing against the surface from below, creating wakes and shallow waves. Causing the water to tilt inwards, so that a furrow was cut into the river like a tunnel being bored by machine. Then the movement slackened and stopped, and the boat oared onwards through stillness.

We'd arrived at this small tributary after asking Jaydev Mandal, an Assamese ornithologist with an enormous and infectious love of the wild world, whether Gangetic dolphins could be seen in the Brahmaputra river that we were staying beside. For days Julia and I had watched the river's milky-brown sheen shift beautifully before our eyes. So wide and sinuous, the Brahmaputra shelves off the Tibetan plateau and carries glacial water and snowmelt from the Himalayas in swirling braids through Arunachal Pradesh and Assam in India before winding through Bangladesh and empty-ing into the Bay of Bengal, supporting innumerable communities of people and wildlife along its length. But we hadn't seen in its mercurial waters the thing that we'd hoped to glimpse.

'There *are* Gangetic dolphins in the Brahmaputra,' said Jaydev, 'but to be honest they're not easy to see in such a big river.' His eyes lit up with the flicker of an idea as he smiled. 'But I know a quiet little river where we might find them.'

The next morning, Jaydev took us to the backwater tributary he'd had in mind, guiding the taxi driver through a patchwork landscape of scattered villages, small agricultural plots and orchards. The river was slow-moving and opaque when we reached our destination. Where the Brahmaputra was epic in shape and span, travelling around 4,700 kilometres from source to sea, this water-way was reflective, companionable and discrete. It was so intimate a setting that I didn't really believe it was possible to see dolphins here. While I looked doubtfully at the narrow water from the bank, Jaydev arranged for two boatmen from the neighbouring village to take us out on the river.

In common with several other river dolphin species, the Gangetic dolphin exhibits distinct physical differences from the majority of its oceanic kin. Firstly, its snout is far longer, thinner and flatter. Lined with sharp teeth on both the upper and lower jaw, it is ideally shaped for snaring crustaceans and small fish from the riverbed. Having unfused vertebrae in its neck means it's also able to twist its head while hunting, making it particularly agile in moving water. And its skull, with its noticeably pronounced fore-head, contains an especially large melon, the tissue mass common to all toothed whales that's responsible for sound communication and echolocation. The melon of the Gangetic dolphin, like that of the Indus river dolphin (long considered to be the same species as the Gangetic but which was taxonomically separated in 2021 owing to genetic divergence and differences in skull structure), is appreciatively large in relation to its overall size because the animal is effectively blind. Having evolved to live in such clouded environments as the Ganges and Brahmaputra rivers, which carry in their water columns vast cargoes of drifting sand and silt washed off the hills and plains, Gangetic dolphins have little use for true eyes. Those they do have are small and lensless, able to detect merely the presence or absence of light. But this circumscribed vision is compensated for by an acute sensitivity to sound through the acoustic medium of the melon, enabling these freshwater dwellers to read the world of the river by way of echolocation.

We set off across the surface of that world. A day of grey skies and quiet as the two boatmen rowed us into the channel and away from the village to a point where the river branched around a small island of trees. We sat there in silence, waiting. There wasn't even a ripple on the water until there was, as though a torpedo had been set free from a submarine, rocketing below the boat and out the other side. The dolphin didn't surface for even a moment but pressed water upwards like a sudden swelling beneath skin. It turned in a wide arc and circled us in a quicksilver flash, electrically at home in the river. It was as though the dolphin was at once everywhere and yet nowhere at all. A hush fell over the boat, even from the men guiding us, who'd lived with dolphins their entire lives. And when they finally spoke, they whispered their sparse words. 'We can feel them near us when we're bathing,' said one of them. 'These dolphins are just a part of the river,' added the other.

Gangetic dolphins once swam in their tens of thousands through the river systems of northern India, Nepal and Bangladesh. Today, they are largely absent from much of that formerly extensive range, and it is believed that there could be as few as just 2,000 of them. This diminishing has been primarily caused by the destruction and fragmentation of river habitat through dam construction, industrial activity, pollution, water traffic and extractive processes.

And as the dolphin arrowed for a final time beneath the boat and sleeked away beyond the island of trees, Jaydev noticed something new on the river since he'd last visited it. Several of the village men were standing chest deep in the water at its edge, reaching down with small canvas bags until their heads nearly slipped from view. When the sacks were hauled upwards, they were passed into the hands of others above the water, who tipped the open ends until a small fall of sand landed on the banks beside them.

After water, sand is the most exploited natural resource on the planet. And the vast majority of what is mined from rivers, seas, estuaries and beaches is used by the construction industry, either in the production of cement or in the manufacture of glass for windows. As a result of human population growth and rapidly increasing urbanisation throughout the world, that construction industry is booming. Sand mining has tripled in the past two decades, and the cement industry now produces around 8 per cent of global carbon emissions. By 2019, demand for sand had reached 50 billion tonnes a year, an amount, according to the United Nations Environment Programme (UNEP), sufficient to build a wall 27 metres wide and 27 metres high around the equator. This staggering volume of sand is being removed from its native places far faster than it can be replenished by natural processes, given that the transformation of stone to sand can take hundreds of thousands of years. As sand mining in many parts of the world is largely unregulated, this stripping of a communal resource carries considerable environmental and social costs, even when it potentially provides a livelihood for local people.

In *Lost World*, Kalyanee Mam's intimate and powerful documentary of what sand mining does to coastal and river communities in Cambodia, a young fisherwoman, Vy Phalla, sees for the first time where the sand underpinning the health of her people's mangroves, islands and fishing grounds ends up. 'Wow,' she exclaims, surrounded by mountains of pale grains in a Singapore storage site. 'The size of this country's sand facility is almost like a chunk of Cambodia. They've shipped over all our land.' Between 2007 and 2018, Singapore transferred over 80 million tonnes of sand from Cambodia alone in order to expand the city state's territory artificially through infill. 'They're dredging everything, all the coastlines and estuaries,' says Vy of the mining around her home place. 'The law has given us all kinds of freedoms, but here we only have the right to sit, shed tears and witness the destruction of our grandchildren's home, our village and our way of life.'

In Sri Lanka, sand mining has reversed the flow of one of the country's rivers, allowing sea water to move inland and bring saltwater crocodiles with it. The delta of the Mekong river in Vietnam is gradually sinking because of sand removal, resulting in the salinisation of fields that had previously been fertile. And in one of the Brahmaputra's major tributaries, sand mining – which had been local and small scale to begin with, much like on the backwater we visited with Jaydev – led to a sharp decline in the river's Gangetic dolphin population when it became an intensive industrial operation resulting in a drastically reduced water flow.

I bring up sand mining not because it's necessarily the worst of the many ills that plague rivers but because of what it tells us about our larger relationship to waterways and the living world. According to the United States Geological Survey (USGS), the scientific wing of the Department of the Interior, lifelines are defined as 'structures that are important or critical for a community to function, such as roadways, pipelines, powerlines, sewers, communications, and port facilities'. This narrowly anthropocentric and technological perspective means that sand stripped from a river that is then used in the construction of any of this infrastructure is considered a constituent element of a lifeline, while neither the sand in the river nor the river itself is accorded the same significance. And yet what rampant and unregulated sand mining does – what our elevation of the human over the more-than-human in fact nearly always does – is undermine or destroy other vital lifelines, ones that are just as essential for people as they are for wild species. Because those damaged or destroyed rivers and their native sands are critical to flood protection and slowing storm surges, too; they're critical for water filtration, irrigation and drinking-water supplies; they're critical for aquatic plants that act as food sources and carbon sinks; and they're critical to the flourishing of fish and other marine species relied on by communities like Vy Phalla's.

You'd be hard-pressed to guess that rivers are lifelines from the way they are frequently mistreated. They suffer the abuse of chemically dependent industries, indifferent or ideologically uninterested governments, intensive agricultural systems and privatised water companies prioritising profit at the expense of common goods. Rather than lifelines, rivers are often conveniently seen as dumping grounds, as has become depressingly clear with the dismal state of rivers in the UK in recent years. In 2021 alone, raw sewage was discharged into English rivers by water corporations 375,000 times. And between 2020 and 2023, the privatised utility company Thames Water dumped at least 72 billion litres of sewage into the River Thames. Such is the level of contamination – amounting to a 'chemical cocktail' according to a parliamentary report – that the renowned naturalist and broadcaster David Attenborough referenced the issue in his documentary series *Wild Isles*, saying, '[I]n England, every single river is polluted.' And pollution, like sand mining, is just another of the many cumulative pressures faced by rivers rather than the only one they must endure.

*

In late 2022, just a few hours' drive south of Prespa, an upper stretch of the Louros river was wrecked by the Regional Authority of Epirus. Images of the invasive works that emerged afterwards were painful to see. There were uprooted trees and boulders bulldozed to the edges of a watercourse that had been scraped, flattened and rearranged, its natural banks heaped with substrate clawed from the riverbed. When the destruction became public, the authorities defended their actions and lack of relevant licences by claiming that what they did would prevent downstream flooding. A notion that Anthi Oikonomou, a freshwater ecologist at the governmental Institute of Marine Biological Resources and Inland Waters, quickly dismissed when I spoke to her.

'It's a mountain stream and the water isn't much higher than my ankles most of the time, and I'm really short!' laughed Anthi, who not only grew up near the Louros but made this river the subject of her PhD. 'People have never seen the water there higher than a metre, but now all of those pebbles and sands that have been shifted will more easily be swept downstream, where settlements *could* have a bigger risk of flooding if they build up.'

Interventions such as these aren't uncommon in Greece, whether in rivers or at the side of roads, where well-developed vegetation and topsoil are sometimes scraped away by machine to assist with the dispersal of rainwater when a better job of it is often already being done by the living sponge of earth, roots, grasses and trees. This approach stems, in part, from a sense that being seen to be doing something is better than largely invisible natural solutions because it demonstrates to voters that their concerns are being taken seriously. Which is why the dredging, straightening and canalising of rivers – the *unrivering* of rivers, you might say – remain the political response of choice to the question of flooding, even when the science tells us that in many cases they're misguided options at best and can potentially make the situation far worse, particularly when nature-based alternatives so often exist, from respecting flood plains in the first place by not building on them to restoring wetlands that slowly release water and enabling trees to reclaim the uplands where deforestation has led to faster rates of runoff. And what is so often neglected, forgotten or dismissed when it comes to these mechanised incursions are the knock-on ramifications for wildlife.

Living in the Louros is a fish found nowhere else in the world. That endemic trout, *Salmo lourosensis*, inhabits the cold upper span of the river and is entirely dependent on a set of specific circumstances existing within its solitary home world. Relationships that might have been permanently damaged or even completely undone by the illegal alterations made to the river.

'What I saw there is that all of the plane trees had been cut, or almost all of them,' said Anthi when I asked her about the extent of interconnectedness underpinning the presence of the Louros trout. 'If we had, let's say, a thousand of them, now there are only fifty. This trout species hides, feeds and reproduces under the roots of trees that are next to the water, so its shelter has been destroyed. This trout also needs water temperatures that are less than 15°C. Without the shade of big trees covering the river, the water might now reach 20°C in the spring and summer when it used to be between 10°C and 15°C. And the trout doesn't have anywhere cooler to go, because it's already in the upper reaches of the river.'

I asked Anthi what other damage had been done to the river's habitats and what it might mean for the future. 'When you widen the main course by bulldozing it, you lose the diversity of habitats because you no longer have small ponds and sandbars and islands and slopes. Everything is flat. And trout like different velocities of water, which this stretch of the river will no longer have. So again, they'll try to go further upstream to find what they're missing, but the very highest reaches are largely dry in the summer, so there'll be nothing for them there. This was also the breeding season of the trout, so by cutting the water flow and then sweeping the bottom with machines they've destroyed not only the eggs and fry but also the whole community on which the trout feeds, every small insect, egg and larva. If we change the food supply of the trout, we can't predict what might happen to it. It's the worst thing you can do to a species that lives in just 30 kilometres of a river and nowhere else in the world.'

Come winter, the river that flowed past the foot of our fields would crust at the edges, its scattered spray turning to sheets of ice. Even with all that movement, the cold took hold, just as it did inside our water pipes in the house by the square when they froze solid on three separate occasions. The first time was because we'd been out late in the village bar one winter night and forgotten to leave the tap running when we got home and crashed into bed. A rookie mistake that we lived with for a couple of weeks before the water returned on a sun-warmed day. The second time, a friend staying in our house while we were away opened the taps only a tiny crack as she was conscious of wasting water. The third time, however, I was sure I'd done everything right. I'd insulated the pipe as best I could and opened the indoor taps at night. But what I hadn't considered was that the pipes might freeze during the day. At four o'clock on a sunlit yet cold afternoon, I turned the tap to make tea and there was nothing there to catch in the pan. Just a weak sputter of air that soon ran dry as well. I rushed outside and quickly set to work doing the only thing that was still an option at that late stage in the game, which was to light a fire under the external pipe.

Our friend Haris had showed me how to do it the last time this had happened, so I chipped at the frozen soil with a pickaxe until I'd exposed the copper cylinder and trowelled clear a shallow groove beneath it. I then scooped coals from the wood stove that smoked like a censer as I carried them outdoors in a metal tray, thinly spreading them in the furrow to avoid scorching the pipe. By then it was beginning to darken, the winter day clocking off after another short shift. With no sign of the water's return, I rang Haris. Together we checked everything he could think of until he finally nodded towards the stone wall at the edge of the garden.

'Under there?' I asked, even though I already knew the answer.

'There's nothing else I can think of,' he said. 'Your pipe must go under the wall to join the water mains on the road above.'

This wasn't good news. Any pipe threaded under the stone wall would be buried metres deep beneath the adjacent plot. Haris and I walked up through the heavy snow, kicking our heels at the frozen soil where we'd scuffed away its white covering. 'I think you'll have to wait until spring,' he said, with the kind of equanimity and poise that makes Haris the first person I usually call when any kind of problem around the house arises. Not only is he far more adept at solving practical problems than me but he's also more gracious at accepting there's sometimes nothing to be done about them but simply practise patience. After he said goodbye, I returned to sit beside the last of the smoking coals, a few embers still glowing in the dark as night took hold of the high mountain world.

What is the weight of water?

It's a question that I'd never given much thought to before we moved to Prespa. During my comfortable suburban upbringing in Canada, and then later again when I moved to the UK after finishing university, water was always there with a simple turn of the tap. A steady and reliable flow dependent on a system of reservoirs, treatment plants and pipes that the US Geological Survey is absolutely right to consider a lifeline in that together they convey water directly to people. And having grown used to that immediate presence, it rarely occurred to me what the weight of water might be when something threatened that easy accessibility. But Prespa changed that for me.

When our pipes froze for that third and final time, it was one of the harshest winters we've known here. Ice slicked the streets for weeks on end and new snow just hardened on top of it, like layers and layers of double glazing. Lesser Prespa Lake froze to a grey shield solid enough to cross on foot. At the time, the nearest inhabited house to ours was lived in by Chris, the friend that I ran the camera trap with when we caught the mother bear and her cub playing with the device. Each morning Julia and I loaded our wheelbarrow with several 5-litre glass or plastic jugs leftover from making wine and *tsipouro* in Germanos's distillery and rattled up the icy road with them to his place. After filling them from his kitchen tap, we'd slide home and crunch over the snow left at the foot of our drive by the plough and haul them up the path and into the house.

It didn't take long to understand something about the weight of water that winter. About a litre and a half was needed to make a big pot of tea, or almost a third of one of those jugs. There was another litre for coffee and several others just for drinking. A few more for boiling pasta or making soup, while the washing-up required several litres to do well. To flush the toilet, which we vowed never to do if we were only taking a pee, took a whole jug on its own. As for a shower, I had no idea, because I washed by heating a litre of water in a pan and pouring it into a plastic bowl. I then squatted in the tub and lathered, washed and rinsed by eking it out with a measuring jug. Even after minimising our use, by evening we'd have to load up the wheelbarrow with empties and once more make our way through the frozen streets.

Forty-six days after our pipes froze, the kitchen tap suddenly gurgled into life during the spring thaw. As water spattered and hissed into the sink we did a small dance of joy and relief. Not having running water in the house for nearly seven weeks made clear to us our frequently profligate use of it here in Europe (in the UK, for example, individuals use on average 140 litres per day for cooking, washing and drinking, or twenty-eight of those jugs in the wheelbarrow). Which also brought into clearer focus the daily challenges, difficulties and risks faced by others.

Around 2 billion people across the planet lack access to safe drinking water, while as much as a quarter of the world's population experiences water stress for at least a month each year. And that weight of water, that *burden*, is carried disproportionately by women, who often have to travel considerable distances to gather water from rivers, springs and wells to be shared out between family members, household needs and domestic animals. Not only do women face considerable physical risks in trying to access fresh water in often remote locations, including sexual violence and attacks by wild animals, but valuable opportunities for education, livelihood, leisure, family time and child care are dramatically reduced as well. Across the world, women and girls spend 200 million hours each and every day collecting water. 'Just imagine: 200 million hours is 8.3 million days, or over 22,800 years,' said UNICEF's global head of water, sanitation and hygiene, Sanjay Wijesekera, in response to the figure. 'It would be as if a woman started with her empty bucket in the Stone Age and didn't arrive home with water until 2016 . . . Think how much women could have achieved in that time.'

As rivers recede and springs disappear in response to a heating world, that burden placed by men onto women continues to grow. And water conflicts – a weight that water has been made to bear because of human disagreements – are also on the rise, leading to increased discord, fear and volatility in communities. When our field neighbour ignored the agreement that all of us on the channel had made as to the days and times we would irrigate our crops from the river, I began to understand what can happen when any order established over the communal use of water breaks down. You could be mid-shift in the relentless heat when the water in the channel would suddenly trickle to nothing. To this day, I can still hear the angry outbursts as tempers frayed in the fields, farmers ranging upwards through the rows of beans in search of the person responsible for cutting the flow when they were giving the crops they relied on the water they needed. It was an inkling of the fractures already appearing on a far greater scale at a time when water, as Jaideep Saikia wrote in 2022 about threats to the Brahmaputra river, is 'becoming a weapon of geopolitics'.

The Brahmaputra, where the endangered Gangetic dolphin still swims despite diminishing numbers, flows through three states: China, India and Bangladesh. But in the same way that our field neighbour was able to cut the water because they were upstream of everyone else but one, so China has a tactical geographical advantage, which meant it was able to announce unilaterally in 2020 its intention to build five hydro-electric dams on the Brahmaputra (called the Yarlung Tsangpo in Chinese-occupied Tibet) close to the border with India. Concerned about what these dams would entail for downstream flow, several Indian officials proposed building dams on their section of the river in order to meet the country's needs should China ever decide to divert water to other regions or to hold it back for punitive reasons. Given the absence of a water-sharing agreement between the three countries, this would leave Bangladesh, the final downstream neighbour, as the most seriously affected state, faced with potentially dramatic challenges for irrigation and other water needs but with little practical recourse to upstream decisions given the military and economic clout of its neighbours. And caught up alongside the Gangetic dolphin and other wild river species affected by any potential geopolitical water conflict over shared resources, borders and disputed territories would be the 140 million people who rely daily on the lifeline of the Brahmaputra as it journeys from source to sea.

One of the rivers that most amazes me is little more than a sputter of spring water that drains from the foot of the mountains to the sea of reeds beside Lesser Prespa Lake. It took us eight years of living here even to see this watercourse, despite it having existed alongside us all that time, like the neighbour a few doors down from you to whom you've never said a word. The truth is, we often passed this river on our way to somewhere else, skirting it while out walking near the lake, or keeping our eyes on the road and the staggered rise of mountains while driving by, not paying any attention to the dense ribbon of trees cleaving the agricultural plain and what it might mean.

The river corridor is what Julia and I have come to call this narrow strip of life, a name as lacking in imagination as the outward appearance of the course it describes. It holds none of the beautiful bends that distinguish other flows and is too slight to produce any of the sounds we associate with wilder currents. Nor is there a shimmering expanse of delta or estuary at its end. In fact, there's little to see of the water's slow progress at times, wrapped inside a dark kingdom of alders, willows, wild roses and vines. That water – what there is of it – runs for little more than a kilometre in a straight and deliberate line that was cut into the earth in the 1970s as a drainage channel after the marshes and wet meadows that had once spread across the eastern side of Lesser Prespa Lake were remade into agricultural acreage. But, over time, the river corridor has become what I can only describe as a line of wild surprise – a potent reminder of the vitality of all rivers.

When I spoke with Anthi about the Louros river and its endemic trout, she identified two perspectives on rivers that remain stubbornly common in Greece. First, she said, is the perception of rivers solely as something to extract resources from, such as fish and water. Secondly, she continued, is seeing rivers as places to dispose of our rubbish. 'I was by a river once,' she went on to say, 'when a guy threw a fridge into it. *Why did you do that?* I asked him. *It will disappear down to the sea*, he said. It's just so common here to think of rivers as having some kind of auto-clean setting.'

These twin perspectives are premised on the underlying notion that rivers are inanimate instead of alive. Dismissed, disregarded, damaged and destroyed, they are far too often kept downstream in our thinking rather than seen as life sources and living shelters. And yet in the years I've walked the short track beside the river corridor I've felt a billow of bearded reedlings blow past my face on a winter's afternoon and watched snipe spear into a passing storm. I've seen badgers squeeze at dusk from their riverbank sett and hen harriers ghost the sloping edge. I've watched fox cubs fumble through the spring grasses and seen penduline tits stitch together their downy nest-pouches, looping them like baskets from the willow branches. I've found fresh snow spattered by the bright blood and feathers of a water rail snatched by a wildcat and heard the haunting cry of a black woodpecker in an alder above me. I've scattered roe deer from the undergrowth and seen a pere-grine spook mistle thrush from the trees. And I've walked in the steps of bears at its sodden edge.

This trickle of water, like so many other watercourses across the planet, could just as easily have been corralled inside con-crete once the channel had been cut, but instead it was left alone. And in landscapes like this one on the lake plain, where inten-sive agriculture leaves little room for wild creatures to exist and move unseen or undisturbed, that has resulted in the river corridor becoming a vital lifeline for so much more than I could ever have imagined. A compressed memory of the old wetlands once there. Perhaps the most hidden of our places are the ones right out in the open – those made invisible by that lack of inner vision.

One afternoon, Julia and I were nearing the end of the river corridor when rasping alarm calls scattered through the trees.

We guessed that a wildcat had been slinking low through the undergrowth and surprised a mixed flock of songbirds in the branches. As the goldfinches, great tits and chaffinches reassembled in other trees, we heard the sound of water being furrowed, the slap and splash of an animal in its element that made us doubt that it was a wildcat. We edged closer, sneaking beneath a tangle of vines to find a vantage point on the patch of water down the slope from us. There was another splash from the channel and then a tight squeeze of my arm.

'Oh my god,' whispered Julia. 'It's an otter.'

Julia had a slightly different angle to me in that crouch space beneath the trees. All I could see was the ridged skin of willows and a downed branch bridging the narrow slip of water. Then a rising brown plume spoiled the surface, circles of silty water spreading outwards in swift ripples. A sleek arrow of wave sped away and then the sound of splashing again. A moment later, the otter's head broke the surface only a few metres from where we were kneeling in that cloister of dense trees. Its slicked-back fur appeared both wet and dry at the same time, as if in acknowledgment of its fluid ease between elements. The otter held steady in the water, floating on the deft flicker of its tail, its round dark eyes open to our own.

The moment was magical and magnetic, but also deeply revealing. I'd spent hours looking for otters along the bigger rivers and shores of the basin without success, only to encounter one in an unsung and easily dismissed stretch of water. Whatever expectations we have of places, those cultural preconceptions of their value and validity, will nearly always be upended by surprise if we allow others – human or wild – to be our compass and guide.

The otter broke the stillness and began swimming towards us, gliding silently across the dark channel. It kept narrowing the space until I was sure it would slide from the water and run up the bank like a dog returning a ball to its thrower. But at the muddy edge it instantly vanished, going under and away with a lash of its tail. Only the waves on the water suggested it had ever been there at all.

I still walk past our old fields from time to time. After five years of farming, we had to give them up when I was hospitalised with spondylolisthesis in my lower back and my doctor warned me that carrying on working in that way could lead to serious mobility issues later in life. The fields don't look quite the same, as the farmers who took over from us felled several of the tall trees that had provided us with shade while we worked, saying they were keeping too much sunlight from their crops. I've long been saddened by that loss because of how much those fields meant to us in our early years in Prespa, grounding us in the community and placing us in close relationship with the wildlife we shared the land with. But even if the trees and the shade they cast were there as before, the fields would still look different to us, because, just as with a river, you can never step twice into the same moment of a lifeline. Both you and the world will have changed in so many ways.

Yet change doesn't necessarily equate to a lack of constancy, either in the landscape or our lives. When I glimpse trout in the winter river beneath those old fields I can't help but think of their durable fidelity, fighting upwards against the current every year at the urging of their biological lifeline. A motion repeated and relied on, despite all the changes this landscape has witnessed, since the beginning of their kind. And when I look back at our farming years, two things in particular stand out for me. First, the intense labour and love we devoted to the land, something that we've simply redirected towards different fields of work, transferring our care and commitment for the plants we grew to other aspects of the living world. Second is the presence of the river – its sheer, animate immediacy. Its resonance, proximity and personality. For hours each day we lived with its sound inside us, whether from the booming rapids at the bottom of the fields, the bubbling gush of the irrigation channel or the quiet rippling in the furrowed earth where our crops grew. We worked with water as much as we worked with soil and seeds. Part of a watershed linking mountains, farmers, otters, plants and lakes; part of a living world in endless, replenishing motion.

'We followed the way of the river,' said the old man I'd met on the path that morning. And so did we, I now realise. So did we.

6

Higher Ground

Old photographs were being passed between hands at a table beneath trees in the lakeside village of Psaradhes. It was mid-summer, when late afternoon hung so heavily about the leaves that it looked as though they'd been painted with thick brushstrokes. Swallows and house martins chattered about the stone houses and a few tourists wandered the narrow lanes, stopping for carp at one of the tavernas along the front, Prespa's freshwater speciality. Others followed boatmen down to the pier to ride out on the lake and see up close the remarkable hermitages and chapels nested inside the cliffs of the peninsula. A line of birds flared from the white rocks each time a boat cut the water near the coast.

'In the 1970s, before they built the road to Psaradhes,' said Alexandra, holding a photograph of the village in which the hills behind it were so much sparser of trees than they are today, 'I used to rise at three in the morning and walk for three hours over these mountains and then across the isthmus to get the bus to Florina on market day. And then in the afternoon, I would walk back for three hours to get home with the shopping.'

'And when the road was first built in the mid-seventies,' added Alexandra's husband, Germanos, 'it was so narrow that only a single vehicle could pass over the mountain. You had to phone to a booth on the other side and ask if a vehicle had already been through. If they said yes, you had to wait until it arrived before you could set off.' There was a smile and a shine in his watery eyes

when he spoke. 'It was such a different age!' he exclaimed, digging
another photograph from a worn cardboard box.

Sitting there that afternoon, in the company of a couple who
had always greeted us as though part of an extended family since
we were first introduced by a mutual friend, I realised just how many
different ages and journeys Germanos and Alexandra had experienced between them. As a young woman, Alexandra had emigrated
from Psaradhes to Toronto, eventually returning to Prespa with
her and Germanos's young children. And Germanos – this one a
fisherman rather than a distiller, though both their lives had been
equally reshaped by the Civil War – was only a young boy when
he was taken from Psaradhes and out of the country in what is
referred to in Greece as the *paidomazoma*, or the gathering of the
children. It's believed that some 20,000 children were taken across
the borders by Communist forces in the last years of the war, many
of them routed through Prespa, where they walked the shore just
south of our village into what was then Yugoslavia or over the
western hills into Albania. The gathering (or the *paidosozoma*,
the saving of the children, as a friend recently heard it referred to
in a Communist café in a nearby town) was, according to leftist
leaders, carried out in order to usher children to safety and away
from hostilities and strife. There, in countries with sympathetic
ideological leanings, they would have access to education, medical attention, cultural activities and plentiful food. But there was
a less heralded military purpose to the removals, too: the absence
of children freed more men and even greater numbers of women
to take up arms or enlist for support duties for the Democratic
Army's cause, especially at a time when government forces, buoyed
by steadfast US and British support, were beginning to show their
tactical superiority. Which is how Germanos ended up spending his childhood in a state-run institution near Lake Balaton in
Hungary, another of the many exiles whose stories span the borders of socio-political divides.

'Look at this,' said Germanos, holding a photo of a Psaradhes family celebrating their saint's day festival in suits and dresses while standing in a narrow dug-out boat on the lake in the 1960s. Alexandra leaned in to have a look and smiled, whispering *po, po*. This resonant Greek word is capable of reflecting a range of feelings when voiced twice, and that day it seemed to express a nostalgic disbelief in the passage of time. I'd seen these images before, but on this occasion it felt as if they'd accrued an added layer of tenderness. A year and a half earlier, in 2021, Germanos had survived a massive stroke and a successful seven-hour operation to remove a blood clot from his brain before a lengthy period in a recovery facility enabled him to return home. Given that he was nearly eighty at the time, and that the hospital he was rushed to was several hours from Prespa, things hadn't looked good. But as testament to his formidable strength and grit, Germanos was already back in his boat and expanding on this place of his to tourists in several different languages. And that afternoon, under trees ripe with summer light, he and Alexandra spoke about their lives in a way that was even more open and intimate than usual, as though they were making the most of that near miss.

Another photo was handed to me. This one was of a small, whitewashed house, its half-enclosed wooden balcony held up by three simple columns. On the roof of the house stood a large cormorant, which was easy to miss at first glance because it wasn't even close to being the most striking feature of the image. Far more noticeable was the wooden boat carrying three passengers at the foot of the external staircase leading to the second floor. Knee deep in water, a man was pressed against the stone wall of the house at the stern of the boat. *Po, po*, said Alexandra, but without the nostalgia this time, leaving just the disbelief. I watched her turn towards the building shown in the picture, still standing six decades after the photographer released the shutter from what must have been the vantage point of a boat. But on that

midsummer's afternoon in 2023, sitting in the square as a hot wind
rustled the trees, there was no water anywhere near us.

With lakes as old as these, flux is a fact of life. Over millions of
years of existence, they've experienced periods of rising and receding water. Near the village of Tuminec, on the Albanian side of
Great Prespa Lake, archaeologists have uncovered stone axes, bone
ornaments and ceramic figurines from a Neolithic settlement built
9,000 years ago when lake levels were considerably lower than
they've been in recent centuries, during which time the site would
have been entirely beneath water.

'The high point was around 1960,' said Germanos, looking at
another image of water lapping at the front of a house. 'In just a
couple of years, the lake level rose really quickly until one day you
could just step out of your door and into your boat.'

'When I left for Canada,' said Alexandra, 'my father had to
take me out from the upper storey at the back of our house, as it
was the only place still dry.'

After this modern peak in the 1960s, Great Prespa Lake
embarked on a slow retreat. And while that gradual decline has
lasted for roughly half a century now, the loss of water rapidly
picked up pace in the 1990s. Since then, its level has fallen by a
full 9 metres. What is the weight of water when it concerns not
the use of it in a house but a lake that covers nearly 250 square
kilometres? According to satellite imagery analysed by NASA,
Great Prespa Lake has lost about 7 per cent of its surface area since
the 1970s; between 1984 and 2020, it has shed half its volume. As
Lesser Prespa Lake sits slightly higher than its far larger relative,
the water of the former moves to the latter through gravity and
sub-surface seepage. This transfer is meant to be controlled by a
sluice gate in Greece to maintain adequate levels for nesting wetland birds and agricultural irrigation, but that gate has remained

unopened for several years now because of insufficient quantity. From Great Prespa Lake the water then filters into Lake Ohrid in neighbouring North Macedonia and Albania through subterranean channels in the limestone half of the basin. In light of a significant earthquake that struck Prespa in the mid-1990s, it was reasonably assumed for a long period of time that this seismic disturbance had either enlarged the existing channels or created entirely new ones that water was now pouring through in far greater volumes. And it was a theory that made sense to most of us until a hydrological researcher was asked to study the lake's fortunes. His assessment of the long-term data laid to rest the notion of subterranean shifts: what was largely responsible for the shrinking of the lake was a pronounced reduction in precipitation due to a changing climate, a situation compounded by water abstraction. As our rains and snows falter, so too does this ancient lake dramatically change.

'We used to say that the lake went through these twenty-year cycles when it would rise and fall,' said Alexandra, as we looked towards the blue summer water further off in the bay, 'but it's been a lot longer than twenty years now.' She was silent for a moment or two. 'It's not coming back, is it?' she asked, though it didn't really sound like a question at all.

What happens when the world shifts around us is of course dependent on the scale and severity of change. The speed of the transformation. Several years ago, I climbed a volcano in Bali with a local guide called Karak, whose family farmed lush rows of onions, tomatoes and chillies in the fertile powder worn down from old lava flows on its flanks. Nearly a quarter of a century younger than me, Karak jigged up the weathered slopes of Mount Batur with ease. Reaching the crater's lip shortly after sunrise, we were wrapped in freezing sleeves of cloud that left us a circumference of visibility so small that Karak appeared as a spectre in the scrolling white world despite being only a few metres ahead of me on the path. I had to rely on his intimate knowledge to guide us safely along the wind-harried rim until a well of strange orange light poured over us. The obscuring clouds had thinned enough for stunted trees to resolve into stark silhouettes as the sun burned through the haze like flame through paper. And then the volcano clarified out of the mists, a cratering dark maw and one of the Ring of Fire's numerous active cones.

Indonesia straddles the western arc of the Ring of Fire, a roughly horseshoe-shaped belt of seismic and volcanic activity produced by the extensive movements of tectonic plates. The vast majority of the planet's earthquakes and eruptions occur inside this zone, including the colossal detonation of Krakatoa in 1883, a volcanic mount rising from the Sunda Strait between the islands of Java and Sumatra. Forty thousand people perished in the lava flows and ensuing tsunamis, and the cataclysmic power of that eruption was equal to 13,000 times the yield of the atomic bomb that obliterated Hiroshima in 1945. In an 1890 update to his book *The Malay Archipelago*, Alfred Russel Wallace wrote that the sound of the Krakatoa eruption could be heard as far away as Sri Lanka and Western Australia, noting that the 'atmospheric disturbance was so great that air-waves passed three and a quarter times around the globe, and the finer particles floating in the higher parts of the atmosphere produced remarkable colours in the sky at sunset for more than two years afterwards and in all parts of the world.'

Winds suddenly whisked open the last curtain of clouds as Karak and I stood on the rim of the crater, revealing a pair of enormous calderas encircling the volcano. Mount Batur was already some 500,000 years old when it erupted with such transfiguring power 30,000 years ago that the molten surge collapsed its ancient mass, creating the first of these concentric depressions. Nowhere near finished its work, the volcano produced a second caldera roughly 10,000 years later, when the piling up of magma stoked to between 700° to 1,200°C led to another collapse of the volcanic cone, sinking within the perimeter of the first. Since 1800 alone, Mount Batur has erupted more than twenty times, caving in new craters and seeding sibling cones on the slopes of the primary mass.

We peered inside the volcano. Scalding steam vented from fissures in the steep interior walls, like winter smoke rising from village chimneys. These seams of escaping heat – hot enough to boil eggs within seconds, said Karak – are the visible signs that the volcano hasn't yet been silenced by time. But it wasn't until Karak and I had nearly completed our circuit of the crater that I began to understand the impact of its violent spasms. From the southwest of the volcanic mount spread an immense acreage of solidified black lava. Its flow pattern could be clearly discerned, sliding from a lower cone and pouring inexorably downhill. Stone that once moved, flared and fired. Stone once the colour of hot coals, boiling and blistering as it crept with incandescent heat, scorching everything in its path.

'It was in 1963,' said Karak, anticipating my next question. In over half a century almost nothing had colonised the lava field since the last major eruption on that side of the volcano. It was entirely barren save for a solitary patch of green. A small island of trees marooned in the black desert.

'What's that green hill in the middle of the lava field?' I asked.

'That's the *lucky place*,' said Karak. 'It's the only thing that survived the eruption.'

In the summer of 2021, 16.8 million salmon hatchlings were carried by truck from fish hatcheries in California's Central Valley – many of which had been set up to mitigate the impacts of dam construction on the fish's natural spawning habitat – to coastal sites around the bays of San Pablo, San Francisco, Half Moon and Monterey. As back-to-back years of drought had left rivers too low and too warm for the salmon to travel downstream on their own, it took 146 truckloads to get them to the sea instead. Earlier that same year, hundreds of black abalone, a beautiful but endangered marine bivalve, sometimes stunningly blue in hue and occasionally containing a prized pearl inside, were moved by biologists from the coast of Big Sur in California after winter storms battered the scorched earth following the horrific Dolan wildfire, triggering landslides that either buried the abalone alive or threatened their habitat through sedimentation and debris flow. Although the Dolan fire was set by an arsonist, its devastation was compounded by the unprecedented dry conditions California has faced in recent years due to climate change. Those abalone that could still be saved were placed in intertidal zones where related snails are found. Also in 2021, black-footed albatross eggs and chicks were conveyed 6,000 kilometres by commercial jet from Midway Atoll northwest of Hawaii to Guadalupe Island, a bio-reserve 260 kilometres off the coast of Mexico. As the albatrosses of Midway nest on low-lying islands at risk of being inundated by rising waters, this complex transnational relocation to higher ground gives the species a chance at survival.

Waterless rivers. Rising seas. Raging infernos. Vanishing lakes. Stories like these have an inescapably biblical ring to them. Not just in the scale of their transfiguring elemental components but in the invention of a new narrative of arks; because these are rescue operations that are being carried out – a search for the *lucky places* of the world. As the physicality of the planet's climate transforms out of all proportion from what we've known in a relatively stable condition for roughly the past 12,000 years, we are confronting the stark reality that many species we live alongside simply lack the time to adapt in any meaningful way to this altered state. While

Earth's modern history is steeped in natural calamities and devastating upheavals, these have tended to be isolated incidents rather than connected episodes of an ongoing and unfolding plot. And like the eruption of Krakatoa in 1883, or Mount Batur in 1963, such natural disasters have been almost impossible to predict, which means little can ever be done about them in advance. They are considered to be − as some insurance policies still state to this day − acts of God. But the industrial exploitation of ancient sunlight and plants in the form of fossil fuels and the subsequent carbon emissions their burning has shed into our encircling atmosphere over the past three centuries has created a template for permanent emergency, when natural disasters (which aren't nearly so natural any more) are not only more frequent but also more foreseeable. Record droughts and soaring temperatures will inevitably result in worsening seasons of wildfire and heating oceans; for many wild species, such changes to the planet's chemistry are too sudden and convulsive to be fully registered and responded to at an evolutionary level yet.

Such was the case in the summer of 2021, when a heat dome of unparalleled ferocity hovered over British Columbia and the Pacific Northwest for five days. In that time, as temperatures soared to nearly 50°C along the rocky shores, more than a billion sea creatures were cooked alive in their shells. Barnacles, clams, oysters, crabs, mussels, snails. Whole coasts stank of death from the wreckage of empty shelters. There are no conceivable arks for such numbers of lives. And like high-altitude plants simply running out of mountain when seeking to escape overheating habitats, there may be no *lucky places* left for some forms of life.

Even when arks for the future are prepared in advance, our understanding of the speed and trajectory of climate change is being leapfrogged in real time. In 2017, the Global Seed Vault on the Norwegian island of Spitsbergen, intended as an impregnable shelter for the world's most important agricultural seed varieties,

landraces and wild plants, a refuge built to outlive global disasters and ensure humanity's ability to feed itself in a future world
marked by catastrophe, was partially flooded when spiralling winter temperatures melted the permafrost into which the vault is
sunk. The Spitsbergen site had been chosen precisely *because* of
its permafrost, but we have reached the stage of change when
even our language needs to be reconsidered. There is nothing
permanent about permafrost any more, as its great, sagging thaw
in Siberia has shown. Recently released from its embrace near
the Semyuelyakh River above the Arctic Circle was the perfectly
preserved body of a cave lion cub, still sleeved in soft fur and with
each of her whiskers clearly visible 28,000 years after she died. The
images of it are poignant, in part because being in ice has kept it
looking nearly alive and partially because of the lion cub's resemblance to a child's stuffed toy, crumpled from so much loving. So
well preserved is it that the internal organs remain completely
intact and traces of her mother's milk are thought possibly to linger
inside. A mother's milk given to her offspring long before the last
ice age wiped out her species in its entirety.

This is the world's past crashing through to the present, rising like the magma rupturing the surface of Mount Batur. What
was once locked up in frozen earth and ice is now surfacing, so
that the stories of exhumed cave lions co-exist with the stories of
translocated albatrosses and black abalones. A bestiary of species,
including the living and the extinct, the fragile and the fallen,
pushed out of their shelters by the same thing. Even that biblical
ark of old couldn't hold such disparate worlds together.

Years ago, on a winter's afternoon in the house by the square,
I rose from my desk and saw nothing but smoke through the
window. I yelled Julia's name and swung open the front door to

dark clouds pouring from the house as panic pulsed through me.
Looking up, I saw that our chimney was on fire, flames lancing
high above the roof.

I quickly grabbed the hose from the shed, thinking it a small
mercy that our pipes hadn't frozen that year. But after fitting it
to the outdoor tap, I didn't know what to do next. If I dragged
the hose up the stairs through the house, I wouldn't be able to
reach the fire; and I couldn't pass the hose to Julia on the balcony
because she was dousing the logs in the wood stove downstairs,
whose fierce heat had ignited the chimney in the first place. Today,
all these years later, what I remember most clearly of that moment
is freezing with fear. That and the billowing smoke, which made it
almost impossible to see. But suddenly there were people running
through the smoke, spilling into the garden like water from a burst
dam and speaking to me. Urgent words and phrases that built and
built until the fearful stillness couldn't hold and everything snapped
forward into motion. I ran up the stairs to the balcony and the
village taxi driver cast the hose up to me. It took several attempts
and the smashing of the pistol against the wall when he swung it
short but at least I could pour water down the chimney through
a vent in an upper-storey room. Others rushed upwards with pails
of water from the kitchen. Some helped Julia in the living room
with the wood stove. Seeing flames still blazing above the house,
someone clambered up into the roof in case the fire had spread
to the timber frame. Twice he slipped up there and put his foot
through our bedroom ceiling, his leg dangling in mid-air before
yelling down that the fire was still contained inside the chimney.
Over the next hour, and with the help of so many, we finally
managed to extinguish the blaze.

That night, when everyone had left, Julia and I sat in silence
in our living room. The whole house stank of wet ash and coals.
And it was miserably cold. The wood stove was our only source
of heat but we'd been advised not to light it again until the entire

chimney could be checked for problems. Our friend, Fanis, an
Albanian labourer who'd moved across the border with his family in the same year that we arrived in Prespa, said we'd have to
wait until morning before he could have a look at it. The president of the village, a sheep farmer called Yiannis, stopped by to
check in on us. We drank *tsipouro* with him for a while, grateful
for the warmth as much as the numbness it brought. When he'd
left, we felt drained. Shaken by the whole, horrifying ordeal, but
thankful there were people so near who came to our aid. That, in
the end, was our *lucky place*: a community in action. And while
it was easily one of the most frightening experiences of my life,
it was nothing in comparison with the fires that so many are
having to face.

It's getting harder to savour summer. Even the word itself – so
redolent of buoyant pleasures, so steeped in days of long and lingering light – tastes different than it once did. Sharper and more bitter
on the tongue. In the summer of 2021, as I began writing this
chapter, Greece's forests were burning. Beautiful, Mediterranean
woodlands of pine and fir in flames north of Athens, on the island
of Evia and near ancient Olympia. And all that those forests held
turning to ash by the hour, their residents and tourists escaping
the infernos by ferry, in cars, on scooters and by foot, or desperately staying behind to douse homes from garden hoses and tamp
down the leading edge of flames with branches and brooms. While
everything that couldn't flee fast enough – beech martens, bees,
tortoises, sheep, hedgehogs, lizards, badgers, snakes – was finished
by smoke and heat and fear.

Fire, of course, isn't new to these southern European forests;
it's a natural and integral component of Mediterranean ecosystems.
What is new, however, is their intensity: the sheer combustive *force*

of the flames. In a summer when heat records were once again shattered across the planet, Turkey's forests burned and Albania's forests burned. The forests of Siberia, Italy and California turned to smoke as well that same year. In Europe, Sicily broke the continent's highest ever recorded temperature when it reached 48.8°C. That summer, the mountain town of Lytton in British Columbia smashed Canada's heat record when it soared to 46.1°C on Sunday, 27 June. On Monday, 28 June, Lytton broke its own milestone from the previous day, peaking at 47.5°C. On the Tuesday, the temperature there rose even higher, spiking to 49.6°C. On Wednesday, just three days after first breaking the country's heat record, a large portion of Lytton was destroyed by wildfire.

It's getting harder to savour summer because summer's becoming a season of ash.

Or it's becoming a season of floods. While southern Europe burned in 2021, northern Europe drowned. One of the complications of climate change is learning to hold these jarringly contradictory images within a single frame. Although on the surface they appear at odds with each other, both phenomena are the result of our climate's stability breaking down; both are the volatile expressions of an atmosphere supercharged by carbon emissions reacting to the specificities of topography, latitude, watersheds, local weather patterns, soil profiles and microclimates. In some lands these combined conditions result in aridity and fire; in others, they resolve into rain. For Germany, Austria and Belgium that meant torrential quantities of summer stormwater churning through rivers and streams so swiftly that they overloaded and spilled out, surging, as water invariably does, into paths of least resistance. As urban and suburban streets filled with water, numerous homes, cars and buses were swept away in catastrophic floods that cost more than 200 people their lives. Visiting the ruined town of Adenau, Angela Merkel, the then Chancellor, said, 'The German language can barely describe the devastation.'

With languages unprepared for this era, the word *unprecedented* has quickly stood in as a fallback linguistic position for politicians and media when events such as 2021's fires and floods overwhelm television reports and the front pages of newspapers. And, of course, these events *are* unprecedented. Between 2008 and 2020, Greece lost on average 2,750 hectares of land per year to wildfires; in just fifteen days in the summer of 2021, however, 100,000 hectares of land went up in smoke. But we've known for some considerable time now that this is where our world was headed unless a drastic drawdown of carbon emissions was enacted. You'd need to have been wilfully oblivious or ideologically blind to the work of the world's scientists not to see that these climate events are simply the physical manifestations of what they've been saying for a long while now. These are the messages finally catching up with the messengers. And given this foreknowledge, *unprecedented* begins to sound less like a term of description for these recurring and worsening phenomena than an outsourcing of responsibility for them. To make them seem as beyond our control as those acts of God on insurance policies.

During those summer floods in Germany, a resident of a deluged town stood in shock while surveying the ruins around her, brown water swilling through the streets where she lived. 'There's so many people dead,' she said to a television reporter. 'You don't expect people to die in a flood in Germany. You expect it maybe in poor countries, but you don't expect it here.' I've often wondered whether the gap in wealth and technologies between the Global North and the Global South has encouraged a subconscious myth in the former that it could insulate itself from the worst of the climate crisis, an internalised narrative that has ultimately enabled its politicians and governments to conveniently pay lip service to the emergency. That through its economic and industrial power it could somehow stay just far enough ahead to avoid being swept away, like storm chasers in tornado country outgunning the whirling tempest. Why else would you, just hours after the Intergovernmental Panel on Climate Change (IPCC) published its 2021 report on the severity of the climate crisis, in which the world's leading scientific body on the subject declared this moment in history as 'code red for humanity', state that you needed to keep burning fossil fuels in order to raise revenue to battle climate change, unless you believed you were at least partially immune to the worst of its expressions? Because that's exactly what Canada's Minister of Environment and Climate Change, Jonathan Wilkinson, did when asked a question about the government's controversial purchase of the Trans Mountain oil pipeline from Kinder Morgan for $4.5 billion. 'Canada,' Wilkinson said, 'needs to ensure that in the context of that transition [to sustainable energy], it's extracting full value for its resources and using that money to push forward in terms of reducing emissions.' It's almost as though Wilkinson had forgotten what happened to the Canadian town of Lytton little more than a month before his pronouncement.

The cumulative carbon emissions that have brought us to this point in time are unequivocally clear about historic responsibility. Even without considering the outsourcing of emissions when regions such as Europe and North America satisfy consumer demand by purchasing goods produced in China and elsewhere, the figures are revealing. According to Our World in Data, carbon emissions from 1751 to 2017 show that the United States produced 399 billion tonnes, or 25 per cent of the world's total. The EU was responsible for 353 billion tonnes in that time, or 22 per cent. China was responsible for 12.7 per cent and Russia 6 per cent. But Africa, a continent of around one billion inhabitants, an eighth of the world's total, produced only 43 billion tonnes of carbon emissions in that 266-year period, or 2.73 per cent.

The electricity use of computer gamers in California alone is greater than the overall electricity consumption of such individual African nations as Ghana, Kenya and Ethiopia; while California's televisions require more electricity than either Senegal or Niger use across their entire networks. The same goes for the Golden State's hot tubs and pools. And yet the change to the African continent as a result of global emissions – the change to the lives that are lived there – will be transfiguring. While we share the shelter of the world, we don't share it equally, as the greater burden of extreme climate experiences will fall on young people and lower-income communities and countries, a burden for which they hold little responsibility. Vanessa Nakate, a young Ugandan climate activist, articulated the scale of this new reality with penetrating clarity at a speech during the pre-COP26 Youth4Climate conference in Milan:

> You cannot adapt to lost cultures. You cannot adapt to lost traditions. You cannot adapt to lost history. You cannot adapt to starvation. And you cannot adapt to extinction. The climate crisis is pushing many communities beyond their ability to adapt.

If there is anything to be gained from the harrowing tragedies of 2021, when wealthy as well as less advantaged countries were ravaged by extreme weather events, it may stem from a frank acknowledgement that nowhere is safe from the climate crisis. That we are collectively, if unequally, vulnerable. Seattle, a city renowned for its wet, misty and temperate climate, where the Crane brothers regularly stepped through the door wearing expensive raincoats regardless of the season on the set of *Frasier*, recorded temperatures over 37.7°C three times in the summer of 2021, which equalled the number of days the city experienced such temperatures throughout the entirety of the twentieth century. While the Global North may be better placed to ameliorate some of the coming damage through costly climate adaptations, there is – as residents of Greek villages, British Columbian mountain towns and German riverside communities will tell you – nowhere to hide when the fires and floods arrive. None of us is immune, regardless of whether we live comfortable lives or not, because the climate crisis touches everything. And without action to reduce radically the use of fossil fuels that were, according to the International Monetary Fund in 2022, subsidised by governments across the planet to the tune of $13 million *every single minute*, nothing will be spared from some kind of harm. Because the extreme climate events of 2021 weren't an end point or dramatic note of resolution to the emergency – a smouldering-out of its limited and exhausted energies – but simply one more wave crashing into shore, with other waves, far wilder and higher, piled up behind it into the distance.

It's getting harder to savour summer because summer isn't the same any more.

One of the origin myths of the name Prespa concerns snow. In the book that first brought us to the region, Giorgos Catsadorakis shares the story of an elderly man in a fishing village who told him that the place name had Slavic roots related to snow, drifting snow or an area covered by snow. The man goes on to say that the older generation of the basin used to tell the tale of a traveller from the north who arrived in a Prespa village in winter, asking the inhabitants why they complained of being poor when they lived beside such a broad plain that could easily be cultivated.

'What plain?' the villagers asked the man. 'That flat ground you walked across when you came here isn't a plain. It's a frozen lake with snow covering the ice.'

Perception can be deceptive, especially when it concerns lakes as magnetic and mercurial as these. They shapeshift with the weather to reveal a range of inner moods. What had seemed a plain to the traveller of old can sometimes resemble the sea, as when winter waves rise high and the far shores are vanished by mists, or when its blue surface is stirred by summer light, leaving you feeling as if you're standing at the edge of the Aegean. At other times these lakes feel so pondlike that dropping a stone into the stillness shatters the sky. And when the basin is pooled by heat haze, so that pelicans in the distance never seem to get any closer but just fold in on themselves in an endlessly looped illusion or mirage, it's easy to be unsure about what you're seeing here. *Is that fishing boat tied up a little further away than last time, or am I just imagining it? Was this stretch of sand here on my last visit?* And that, in a wider sense, is the problem we face in trying to internalise incremental environmental changes, whether it's one less song heard each spring or a sliver of land stripped away from a beloved place for development, in that the gradations of difference amplified and made cumulative by time – *all those lost songs, those vanished lands* – can be fully appreciated only when you're able to compare them side by side. Which is why the shoreline of Great Prespa Lake in particular is such an invaluable archive.

For well over twenty years now I've followed the same route to reach the big lake, crossing the sandy isthmus on a path marked by the tracks of snakes and tortoises and then slipping through stands of alders and willows to the water. At the edge of the lake, I can turn around and clearly see how I've descended over old shorelines, curving coasts that were once lake bed rather than exposed land. They're distinguished from one another by subtle differences in colour, consistency and vegetation, each telling a story of its origins as distinctive as the rings of a tree that has lived through years of drought and fullness and fire. Each year, newly uncovered lines are being added to the archive. The waters of this ancient lake have withdrawn so dramatically in the time that we've lived here that I sometimes joke with visiting friends that they should think about carrying their passports with them if they want to go swimming.

While the smaller of the two lakes still occasionally freezes hard enough to walk across, it's difficult to imagine a scene in which a visitor could believe the lake was a plain when it rarely snows that much these days. And yet I remember our first winters here, when snow piled up so deeply one year that the post office with its row of swallow nests shut its doors for several days right before Christmas because the delivery van from town couldn't make it over the mountains. And I remember, too, the annual autumn rains – so persistent that October and November were one long season of saturation. Spans of the year that simply aren't like that any more. The winter of 2023/24, for example, was the warmest in recorded Greek history, in which the north of the country experienced an average maximum temperature that was 2–3°C higher than during the period 1991–2020.

Variations in weather patterns aren't unusual of course, making direct associations between individual weather events and climate change a far from simple process, but the long-term trend in Prespa is clear. For three years running recently, I had to water my bone-dry strawberry beds at the end of November just to keep the plants alive – something that was unimaginable when we first moved here. But then that traveller of old, when he'd learned that he'd been walking across a body of water and not a plain, could never have imagined that bombs from a civil war still far in the future would later reappear when a warming climate began radically shrinking the lake surfaces. And the rapid dwindling of an ancient lake that's been around for several million years seems unimaginable too, except that the higher ground of those old shorelines, curving in the same graceful arc as the water of today, doesn't lie. They're visible markers of movement, like a contrast dye used in medical imaging, allowing us to visualise the current condition of the lakes as clearly as in those old photographs being passed around a table by Germanos and Alexandra.

Climate change is fundamentally affecting the things that people rely on around these shared waters. The lake has receded so much that none of the waterfront tavernas in the village of Psaradhes (the village name itself literally means 'fishermen') can truly claim to be on the water any more, while the jetties for the community's boats have already been moved once in the time we've lived here to keep pace with the retreating edge and will almost certainly need to be moved again in the coming years. Though the question remains of how far you can meaningfully keep going in pursuit of something that's disappearing. In North Macedonia, boardwalks, piers, lifeguard stations and outdoor cafés and bars were erected a few years ago to encourage tourism to the struggling lakeside village of Stenje, but the infrastructure is no longer anywhere near water, surreally stranded on higher ground instead. And in the Albanian village of Pustec, pipes that draw water up into a small patchwork of subsistence fields are having to be extended further and further each year, snaking across mudflats that weren't even there when I first visited that side of the basin.

It's not just the quantity and regularity of precipitation that has been compromised by climate change, threatening agricultural and fishing livelihoods on all sides of the basin and placing increased stress on communities of wild species reliant on the watershed's rivers, seasonal pools, damp soil and wet meadows, but the complexion of the weather that passes through. Hail is always a worry in the mountains, but its formerly infrequent appearance meant it wasn't something we were overly concerned about, even when we were still farming. In recent years, however, right across the basin, from the apple orchards of North Macedonia and the cereal plots of Albania to the bean fields of Greece, it's on many farmers' minds when storms begin to brew above the mountains. I've seen it smash car windows and roof tiles; I watched it shred every last growing thing in our vegetable plot one August afternoon, when the weight of gathered hail and water also took down a three-metre stone retaining wall in the garden that collapsed with a thundering crash into the adjacent stream; and, in 2022, for the only time in all the years we've lived here, it fell on three separate occasions in Prespa. On the last of those, near midnight on 1 October, hail the size of walnuts battered the southern end of the basin. By morning, it looked as though a tornado had swept through. Farmers woke to destroyed crops just days before a season's worth of beans that are dried on the stem were meant to be harvested and sold.

For an area already contending with an ageing population and the flight of young people to urban centres, climate change places an additional pressure on those making decisions about whether to leave or stay. After the hailstorm, friends told me of a desperate farmer drinking himself into a stupor, inconsolable about not having anything left in his fields to repay the loan he'd taken out to plant his crops. I saw an old woman by the side of the road desperately trying to gather in her hands what she could from her shattered plants. And a friend that I ran into in town shortly afterwards said he wasn't very well when I asked.

'I'm one of the people who lost their bean crop,' he said. 'Most of it, anyways. Some are even worse off because they lost everything. They won't even have bean seeds to start again with next year. We'll have two economies in Prespa – a wealthier one where the hail didn't hit and a poorer one where it did.'

These, too, are the stories of the place I love; this small part of the planet, where, on ground already higher than most, climate change is reshaping realities.

When we'd descended from the rim of Mount Batur on Bali, Karak showed me the place that he and his family loved – the small corner of the world that *they* held close. We circled the volcano on his motorbike, passing the shining golds and greens of village temples and kids kicking footballs across the cracked earth. Eventually, we reached the *lucky place*. Up close, that hill of green islanded in old lava that we'd seen from the edge of the crater was even more remarkable than from a distance, as the radiance of its trees and bushes contrasted so sharply with its surroundings. It felt as though all the colour drained from the land by the eruption had been absorbed by this one prominence, so that in its meagre acres it held the light of the entire highland, as saturated as old, colourised photos.

At the edge of the hill stood a temple, its scarlet banners waving in the warm breeze. Stone lions watched from carved plinths as Karak placed a clutch of flowers by the steps, whispering a short prayer as he bowed. We were all alone there, silence pooling around the black, volcanic barrens. Known as a cinder cone, this hill is the smallest type of volcano in existence. It was formed aeons ago during a brief eruption, when fragments of molten rock were squeezed through a small, solitary vent. Lacking the quantity and momentum needed to create a cone anywhere near the size of the main crater, the lava oozed over the surface but quickly cooled and hardened into a distinctive eminence on the volcano's lower slope. And over the course of thousands of years it had slowly seeded with trees, until, in 1963, when Mount Batur erupted on this side of its cone once more, that small hill became shelter.

Relatives of Karak had survived that night of fires, he said, though no sign of their settlement could still be seen. Before it was consumed by lava, some of the village's residents managed to reach this hill of trees, clambering aboard it like a rescue ship in a storm. It's hard to conceive of the seething panic and combusting lands they would have experienced that night; the relentless, shaking fear as the small cinder cone rose above the molten rivers. There – on the green hill, ringed by the burning world – they'd found higher ground.

In the days after the eruption, each of the survivors was airlifted out of the wreckage, eventually settling in villages nearby. Years later, the temple was built on the dark and hardened vista to honour their saving grace. It was raised to remember the *lucky place*.

What are the *lucky places* of the world when the planet is on fire and flooding, not just from natural causes, as with Karak's home place on the slopes of Mount Batur, but from a human-triggered and industrial transformation of the climate? Beyond the migrations of people to higher ground that are already well under way, from regions of thawing permafrost in Alaska and low-lying, river-braided Bangladesh to the island nation of Fiji, which keeps an official record of all the villages at risk of having to be moved within the next five to ten years (forty-eight as of 2022), it's a question perhaps best understood by simply going outside and looking up. Because wherever you happen to be – on a city pavement or in a village square, high on a mountain ridge or deep in an ancient wood – you're looking at the luckiest place of all: our encircling atmosphere. Given the extraordinary rarity of the thin envelope of gases that wraps this planet, it is without question our ultimate shelter. Our most vital lifeline. It's what keeps us insulated from the obliterating conditions of outer space and the caustic pummelling of solar radiation and UV rays. It's what regulates temperatures and prevents this planet from having the unendurable extremes of others. It's what vivifies the profoundly complex ecological processes and climatic patterns that underpin the functioning of the ecosystems we rely on. It's what acts as a medium for the conduction of water, oxygen and carbon dioxide, all of which are required by life on this planet to survive. And it is, to the best of our current knowledge, unique. As Martin Rees, the British Astronomer Royal, once wrote, 'Nowhere in our solar system offers an environment even as clement as the Antarctic or the top of Everest.'

That thin breathable shell above our heads right now, so startling when sharp winter light cuts through it or when cloudless nights allow stars to pour into the darkness, is all that stands between being here and not being here. And while the air might look just the same today as it did last week or last year or a decade ago, its fundamental properties are being substantially altered. The very lifeline of the planet is being changed, both in the sense of its own geological future, imprinted as it will be with the dizzying physical scale of the Anthropocene, and in its ability to shelter us safely in an external expanse otherwise hostile to life. Without that *lucky place*, without that enveloping atmosphere we move through and live our lives within each day, we simply wouldn't exist.

In fact, none of this would exist. Because in a shared world, where everything is connected at multiple points to everything else, that atmosphere above our heads shelters blue whales surfacing through fathoms of blue water; it shelters the lights of fireflies sparking in the midnight dark; it shelters our love in all its tenderness and fervour; it shelters dung beetles navigating by the celestial spacing of the Milky Way; it shelters the sway of prairie grasses on hot summer winds; it shelters our living histories and songs and traditions; it shelters the bioluminescence of marine creatures trailing light through the sea; it shelters a mother bear and her curious cub on a limestone ridge studded with junipers; it shelters redwoods so tall that they hold forests of other tree species in their spires; it shelters our families and friends, our lives and longings;

it shelters pelicans passing between a pair of ancient lakes set high in a bowl of mountains; it shelters everyone that's ever mattered to us and the only world we all know as home.

It's getting harder to savour summer. In 2023, as I was nearing the end of writing this chapter, Greece's forests were burning once again. Beautiful, Mediterranean woodlands of pine and fir in flames north of Athens, on iconic Mount Pantokratoras at the northern end of Corfu and on the slopes of Mount Helicon near ancient Delphi. Not the same forests that were burning two years previously when I began this chapter, but others. Forests such as those of the Dadia National Park in northeastern Greece near the border with Turkey, in which thirty-six of Europe's thirty-eight birds of prey can be found, making it one of the continent's most important havens for raptors. The flames that raged for nearly three weeks across the rolling hills of oak and pine in Dadia and the adjacent region of Evros burned up over a thousand square kilometres of wooded lands, making it the largest recorded fire in European history. So much of that remarkable wild shelter – the only place in the Balkans where black vultures nest and one of the few sites in Greece where the endangered Egyptian vulture clings on – was turned to smoke and ash and emptiness, undoing hundreds of years of ecological entwinement in a matter of days during a summer believed to be the hottest in human history. And after the fires came the floods.

Earlier, I wrote that one of the great challenges presented by the climate emergency is trying to keep such seemingly contradictory images as summer floods and summer fires together in a single frame. What I hadn't considered in 2021 when writing that sentence, however, was that they could be near simultaneous phenomena in the same country. But in 2023, as the fires in the

Dadia forest were gradually coming under control, Storm Daniel swept over Greece, dropping, in places, a year's worth of rainwater within a few catastrophic hours. Coastal houses on the Pelion peninsula were swept out to sea, while the plain of Thessaly, Greece's agricultural breadbasket, became a vast liquid expanse covering around 700 square kilometres, or nearly three times the size of Great Prespa Lake. As water levels in Prespa recede, the country's plains are turning to lakes. In some of the worst-affected villages, only the roofs of houses were visible in aerial footage, as the bulk of the buildings were entirely concealed by a murky brown stew. It's hard to describe, let alone comprehend, the destruction these floodwaters brought. The lost human lives and devastated families, rail lines bent into bewildering new shapes, roads and bridges fallen away, metre-long catfish swept out of swollen rivers and later found in wheatfields, and tens of thousands of dead domestic animals rotting in the hot sun that followed the rains. And in the aftermath of it all, the overwhelming and scary uncertainty for agricultural communities coming to terms with the fact that it could take years before soils now burdened by silt, leached oils and hazardous chemicals are suitable for sowing crops in again. The climate crisis isn't just the fires and floods, but also what is gone, what remains, what is irrevocably changed.

'I have never seen anything like it in my life,' said local resident Stavroula Brazioti, aged a hundred and four. 'We've gone through wars, hardship, hunger, but we haven't drowned.' In an age of immense change, the unfamiliar could well become the most frighteningly familiar thing of all.

'I haven't even begun to absorb or process the floods,' said my friend Matina Galati when we spoke while Thessaly was underwater. 'I'm still mourning the destroyed forests of Dadia,' she added, summing up the psychological impact of internalising successive climatic crises in any meaningful kind of way. 'But then I realise that we don't have time to grieve properly because we've already moved on to the next disaster. And soon the news will move on to something else as well.'

She was right, of course. In 2021, I'd seen just how quickly that summer of wildfires had become history. Unless you'd been directly affected by them, life carried on largely as it had before. But in the process of moving on, as we inevitably will from the catastrophes of 2023 and whatever other ones follow, it's critical that we never normalise the conflagrations that are being made more likely and devastating by climate change. It's vital that we never normalise the summer floods. Or the increased prevalence of droughts, hurricanes and hail. Because the second we do, the moment we begin to normalise extreme climate events psychologically, we accept there is nothing to be done about a rapidly changing climate. And in doing so, we help validate an ideological position that a degree of damage is the price to be paid to retain our overarching economic model, even if that system foreshortens or makes miserable the lives of others. Adapting to our new climate reality is absolutely essential, of course, something we're already witnessing in Prespa as the ancient lakes recede, triggering a need to rethink irrigation techniques, tourism approaches, fishing methods and cross-border water management, but that's a fundamentally different matter from the normalisation of that new climate reality. And the reason for this is simple: while a dimension of planetary change is now irreversible, as increased temperatures have already baked into humanity's long-term future such consequences as glacial melt and sea-level rises, there exists a vast gap between the best and worst possible outcomes. Particularly given that global temperatures will almost immediately stop rising once carbon emissions reach net zero and the climate will then gradually stabilise, clarifying not only the urgency of the situation but, just as critically, our fundamental agency.

According to a paper published in *Science* in 2021, children born in 2020 will have to live with thirty heatwaves in their lifetimes even if emissions pledges made under the Paris Agreement in 2015 ideally to limit the rise in global temperatures to 1.5°C are met, compared to just four heatwaves experienced in the lifetimes of those born in 1960. Examining six major climate events – heatwaves, crop failures, droughts, wildfires, river flooding and tropical cyclones – the researchers noted that today's youth will live an 'unprecedented life' (to borrow that same word again when language falls short), facing 'conditions which older generations have never experienced'. The authors also openly admit that their work is a conservative estimate of the long-term effects of climate change, because it considers only the future *frequency* of those six phenomena, not their *intensity*. In time, summers such as those of 2021 and 2023 might be remembered as kind.

To galvanise concerted climate action with sufficient strength to shift policy and legislation requires widespread solidarity between communities across the world, especially given the forces invested in maintaining the damaging status quo, as we saw at the COP28 climate talks in the United Arab Emirates in 2023. Presided over by Sultan Al Jaber, the president of the country's national oil company, who claimed there was 'no science' indicating a phase-out of fossil fuels was needed to restrict global warming to 1.5°C, the climate talks were attended by at least 2,456 fossil-fuel lobbyists, far exceeding the combined 1,609 delegates that received passes from the ten countries most vulnerable to climate change.

But climate action requires solidarity *within* communities as well as *between* them, something I'm reminded of whenever I think of the fire that caught in our chimney that winter afternoon in the house by the square. Because helping out in our home that day were people who wouldn't speak to each other outside of it due to enduring family feuds. There were people who had become our friends and people who had little, if anything, to do with us. And there were people whose politics spanned the ideological spectrum, representing seams of radical difference that were openly and sometimes vitriolically exposed during local elections and at times of other polarising issues. My abiding memory of that day, beyond the fear we'd experienced from the moment we first saw the smoke, will always be of how people, despite the many and considerable differences that exist in communities the world over, came together with a singularly fierce desire to put out a fire. A focused and protective instinct to save a home.

The key to solidarity is that it has the capacity to embrace difference when it draws others into its wider circle of care and concern – and maybe that's what makes it a kind of *lucky place* too, its ability to harness shared energies at times of crisis, so that it rises like a hill of green trees above a burning slope. And it's a solidarity that needs, ultimately, to be extended into the future we'll never know, given that it's the world that's on fire and not just a single house; a solidarity extended to those as yet unborn generations of human and more-than-human communities, who'll inherit a world radically different to the one we now know. A world as different as we decide to make it today.

7

A Shrinking World

It felt strange moving beyond the circumference of our valley at the end of the first pandemic lockdown in Greece, but heart-lifting, too. After forty-two days of strict restrictions on movement, my appreciation of passing through open space, of being somewhere other than our village and its near surroundings, was overwhelming in its lightness. Even if all I was doing was soaking up the sun and watching birds for a few hours. Contained within those simple acts was a sense of possibility regained. Like many others, I'd journeyed through memory more frequently than ever during lockdown, travelling across landscapes already known in search of a remembered thread of connection or commonality of experience that made sense of that particular moment in time. But with the lifting of restrictions, being able to return to the familiar hills, meadows and woods of my wider home was a way of physically reaffirming the network of relationships that holds me in place. And on that day when horizons briefly widened, oblivious to the fact that we would be constrained by an even stricter lockdown only a few months later, I decided to see if bee-eaters were with us again in Prespa.

Seeing bee-eaters at their nests is like witnessing a magician's trick. What appears at first to be a bank of bare earth suddenly erupts into astonishing colour, a feathered blend of turquoise, cinnamon, lemon and green shooting through air. The birds seem to materialise out of nowhere, as if rabbits pulled from a hat. But like all magic shows, there's a secret to the illusion – some sleight of hand or trick of the eye – which is when you begin noticing the scattered holes in the earthen bank, each roughly the size of a tennis ball. It's from these nesting tunnels that the birds have emerged, sliding from darkness into light. A startling glint of the tropics here in temperate Europe. Tracking a single bird as it circles towards its burrow, you watch it fold its extravagant colours back into the earth. And maybe that's when the real magic occurs: in the afterimage held by the eye; knowing, even when there's nothing to see, what beauty is inside.

If they've remained stable and free of vegetation, old nesting sites will frequently be reused by European bee-eaters, the birds journeying together in small migratory groups and gathering colonially on those bare vertical surfaces where the substrate has proved sufficiently soft to enable tunnelling but solid enough to withstand subsidence and collapse. It was to one of these summer shelters that I was headed. The road wound through the rolling hills until the oak woods parted, where an open valley studded with small cereal fields and sheepfolds fenced by latticed juniper branches was islanded between trees. Leaving the car, I climbed a grassy rise above the road, near the border with Albania. A pair of turtle doves hummed through the heating air. Across the stony grasslands to the north sounded the gravelly staccato of a wryneck. On the crest of the rise, I found a row of Turkey oaks greening into leaf to sit beneath. Unseen above me, a golden oriole poured its liquid song through new leaves.

Time suddenly felt different to me. Throughout lockdown, it had appeared to stall, as though suspended by its own uncertainty. Everyone I spoke to at the time said the same thing: that March and April in the first year of the pandemic had seemed the longest months of their lives. Months that spawned a decade's worth of memes. But that day, beneath oaks surging with sap as birds regained their songs after a long winter, time expanded, gaining buoyancy and lift.

On the other side of the empty road, above the bank of earth I'd come to see, stood a wild plum tree. Its blossom had already fallen and it was still too early for fruit, but it held something else that day: the brilliant chromatic light of some thirty bee-eaters in its branches. Others circled above them, their singular flight note hanging in the still air. Now and then, birds would exchange places, taking off as others landed, or swapping positions where they perched. Around the nesting burrows, however, it was quiet – which seemed odd to me, unless this migratory group belonged elsewhere and had paused its journey here only by coincidence. But that all changed about an hour later, when some of the bee-eaters broke from the branches, circling over the road and then lowering to the wall of red soil. Already sorted into pairs, each couple positioned itself by a tunnel entrance. As one of the bee-eaters kept watch from outside, the bird's partner entered the burrow, its rainbow sheen swallowed up by soil.

It's hard to believe something so resplendent and made for light can exist in such a dark, excluding chamber, in the same way that common kingfishers slip their brilliant blues into the mud of a riverbank nest. Seeing them squeeze into the tunnels reminded me of being in Fez, that astonishing medieval city in central Morocco, where the plain and windowless exteriors of homes in the medina frequently mask courtyards of trellised flowers, beautifully tiled floors and ornate wooden screens carved with the dizzying geometry of Islamic patterns. Beyond the door, the beauty of the interior – like bee-eaters inside their burrows. Birds that now began cleaning the chambers as I watched from the oaks, deploying their sharp curving beaks to reshape the two-metre-long tunnel in which up to five eggs would be laid, flicking any fallen earth and winter debris overboard with their feet, renovating a space that would become home to hatchling birds for three weeks before they'd fledge and feel light on their feathers for the first time. These bee-eaters, which had journeyed from subtropical

Africa on migration, had arrived in Prespa just as our lockdown was lifted. And I remembered then, on a day when time felt so expansive that it seemed to spool around an extended luminous moment, how these same tunnels were plugged one summer by a person jamming lengths of wood inside them, purposely sealing them shut. Reminding me that pandemic lockdowns were just one way of experiencing constricted shelters and a shrinking world.

Shelter takes many forms.

Years ago, when living in north London, I met a middle-aged man sitting on a bench outside Highgate underground station on a summer's evening. He had with him a rudimentary folding telescope to observe the stars, saying he liked to come up on cloudless nights as leaves otherwise obscured his view of them. Asking him where he was coming up from, we descended into the wooded ravine to the side of the station, where he showed me the shack he'd assembled from skip-salvaged timber after he'd lost his job and found himself homeless in the city, the canopy of trees hiding the stars above.

Years later, in that ancient heart of Fez, I met a rap musician and poet living with just his dog and a collection of 1970s rock'n'roll records in the crumbling palace where his father had been a trusted servant and confidant. The owner of the palace had left the edifice to the musician's father when he died; when the musician's father had passed on as well, it had come to his son. But there was no money to maintain the palace, so its fountains no longer fountained, its high-ceilinged rooms were empty of everything but echoes, the ornate plaster frescoes in the horse stables peeled away and fell to the floral tiles and the opulent open courtyards once shaded by orange trees and lemons were filmed in deepening grey dust. But it was the only home he'd ever had or known, the rapper said, as he sat smoking in his turquoise robes in a frayed emerald armchair, the Rolling Stones' *Sticky Fingers* playing on the turntable beside him while he scribbled lyrics on a sheet of paper as the sun burned up the summer air of the courtyard.

Three and a half thousand years ago, a monumental tholos tomb was constructed on the southwest slopes of the citadel at Mycenae in Greece to house an unknown ruler or other person of high status after death. Three and a half thousand years later, with its elite beneficiary and their grave goods long looted and gone, the tomb is missing its vaulted roof, so that its vast circular walls are open to the sky. Inside, a pair of rock nuthatches has fashioned a shelter for the living, fastening to the arched interior an exquisite mud nest. They have beaked the wet earth into a shape strangely similar to the tomb and decorated its surface with crushed leaf beetles, the nest speckled with the red pigments of their wing cases as it hangs there in the hard stony light of the Peloponnese in the place where Agamemnon was murdered on his return from Troy.

On 19 September 2021, the Cumbre Vieja volcano erupted on the Spanish island of La Palma, destroying thousands of houses and making more than 7,000 people homeless. Fifty days later, a beekeeper discovered five of his hives buried beneath thick volcanic ash in which the Canary black bees inside were still alive. The bees had used propolis, a resin-like mixture of saliva, beeswax and the gathered sap of tree buds, to seal themselves away from the poisonous gases and heat of the volcano, surviving in their shelter on stores of self-made honey until they were unearthed from the ash.

In 1914, a man was taken from his home in the coastal city of Sunderland in the northeast of England. Forced to leave behind his wife and children, who were then placed under curfew and prohibited from owning a wireless or from moving beyond a 12-mile radius of their house, he was transported across the Irish Sea. By then, Charles Hoffmann had been living in England for fifteen years, but his German citizenship meant he was considered an enemy alien by the British government. As a result, he was interned for the duration of the First World War at Camp Knockaloe on the Isle of Man, locked down in a shelter that wasn't his own 300 kilometres from his family home.

There are considerable gaps in my ancestral lifeline, as there are for anyone who tries to piece together the past as it relates to them personally. Especially as the most valuable and telling stories are always the ones that fall between place names and dates; those that slip into the fathomless cracks and unknown interiors where all lives are ultimately made. The ones behind those plain and windowless walls, with their courtyards and lemon trees and wooden screens. My mother, however, has done a remarkable job of piecing together the fragments we have. Only a couple of photos of Charles Hoffmann still exist. Beyond his marriage and death certificates, there are almost no documents to which to refer. And we have little in the way of shared stories to sift through beyond a handful of sparse remembrances passed down the generational line. There are just too few details and intimate particulars to be able to raise sails over the rigging of my great-grandfather's life. Despite this, I found myself frequently thinking of him during our pandemic lockdowns in Greece, as the contraction they entailed highlighted for me something of his own experience over a century ago.

Few would disagree with me when I say that we'd prefer not to live in lockdown. The global experience of reduced freedoms and restricted movement during the pandemic was, and continues to be for many immuno-suppressed and other vulnerable groups of people, an enormous personal, public and economic challenge.

While lockdowns largely honoured the greater good by slowing the circulation of the virus and, just as importantly, shielding
overloaded health systems at a critical juncture, particularly in the
earliest stages of the crisis in 2020 when effective treatments and
vaccines were still non-existent, the restrictions nonetheless had
a deleterious impact on individuals, families and communities at
the psychological, emotional and educational level. Which is easy
enough to understand, because the underlying epidemiological
reason for implementing lockdowns is our sociability as a species.
Nothing accelerates aerosol-based disease transmission rates more
than the thing that makes us who we are. We're hardwired for
contact with others right across the spheres of human relationship,
from lovers and family to friends, colleagues and strangers. We rel-
ish physical touch and social connection. We seek out others so as
not to be alone. We invite people into our lives for the pure pleasure of fellow company. And many of our most cherished customs
are communal in nature. In addition to this, we value autonomy,
freedom, movement and choice. All of which made lockdowns
feel so stark to so many, even when, at least to some degree, they
were acknowledged and accepted as ultimately necessary because
of the wider duty of care they encompassed.

My great-grandfather's internment during the First World War
was of an entirely different order to pandemic lockdowns, but on
one fundamental matter they were aligned: both radically reduced
the range of human lives. Charles's story of shifting shelters began
in the Prussian city of Stettin, where he was born in 1876, and
which, after the redrawing of European maps at the close of the
Second World War, is now the Polish city of Szczecin. Spanning
the banks of the Oder river, Stettin was a major port city, directly
linked by its winding northward route to the Baltic. And it was
from there that my great-grandfather went to sea when he joined
the German merchant navy and a fleet of vessels that would have
sailed throughout the Baltic and the North Sea. In all likelihood,

he would have journeyed up the Thames, the Neva, the Elbe and the Humber, all those pale-blue lines that I've traced with my finger on maps when considering his life. One thing we're absolutely certain about, however, is where his last route with the German merchant fleet took him, because that voyage marked both an end and a beginning for him in the late 1890s when, presumably on a routine journey with goods in the hold, perhaps grain or timber or coal, he jumped ship in South Shields at the mouth of the River Tyne in northeast England.

I have no way of knowing what compelled his decision that day, but like so many people across the planet who are in motion this very minute, changing places out of hope, fear, desire or desperation, my great-grandfather would have been spurred on by the same impulse that has been part of the human condition ever since we first spread out of Africa, leaving home to make a new one despite all the struggles it entails. My parents were no different when they emigrated from England to Canada when I was a child, and Julia and I were no different when departing for Greece. When I'm asked why we decided to set out on this journey of ours, I say that we wanted to change our lives. Which is completely true, of course, but it's only partially complete as a reason. Because what that answer doesn't contain is our unhappiness at the place we'd found ourselves in back then, and by that I don't mean just a physical location. Our greater struggle was with who we were becoming in that place, drained of desire and so tired of the patterns of retreat we kept repeating, shrinking further and further away from how we wanted to live in the world. Our journey wasn't just a way of reaching a new place but a way of reaching out to ourselves, to find on the other side – or so we hoped – something we'd lost along the way. I'd like to think that my great-grandfather's decision to jump ship – when he re-rooted a cutting of our family tree in another country – helped narrow the distance between his reality and his desires.

After signing on with the merchant navy in his new country, my great-grandfather married an English herbalist from South Shields called Mary Hannah Ross. Charles and Mary would have six children together (the double N in Hoffmann lost with the birth of my grandfather – their fifth child – the result, as far as we can tell, of a registrar's error on the birth certificate), but after their daughter, Hannah, died in a house fire in 1906, my great-grandfather gave up the sea in order to be closer to home. But home, like shelter, also has many meanings, and as far as the British state was concerned, Charles Hoffmann was a long way from his own when the First World War erupted on the continent. All his years in England, alongside his marriage, children and employment, counted for nothing in his rapidly diminishing world when he was taken from his family and encircled by barbed wire.

Discovering the sealed bee-eater tunnels in Prespa one summer morning, a local conservationist swiftly removed the wooden posts. Any birds not inside the burrows had abandoned the colony and gone, but there was no way of knowing what, if anything, was still inside them. Bee-eaters are among the very last of our breeding birds to arrive each summer, so there's every chance that young were still in the nests at the time. Whoever was responsible was never found, or not officially at least. Given the species' fondness for bees, as its English name plainly if unimaginatively spells out, it wouldn't surprise me to learn that it was a bee-keeper who had corked the tunnels, seeing the birds as a direct threat to livelihood. It was Aristotle after all, one of Ancient Greece's most attentive chroniclers of the natural world, who, writing in his *History of Animals* in 350 BC, said that bee-keepers were known to destroy the nests of bee-eaters when found close to hives. What was true then could still easily be true today.

As shocking as the sealing of the tunnels was, this is what we do to wild creatures and organisms all the time. Not necessarily with the same raw immediacy as trapping birds inside their shelters, leaving them inevitably to perish in the airless dark, but with no less damaging an impact on their lives. We do this through deforestation, through unrestrained hedge-flailing and through shearing our lawns and municipal verges to the bone. We do this through the straightening, damming and polluting of rivers. We do this through the drainage of wetlands, the grubbing up of scrub and the paving over of gardens. We do this through the toxic spread of insecticides and the introduction of neonicotinoids into the food chain of agricultural landscapes. We do this all the time, in just about every major society on the planet, at the collective, corporate, institutional and industrial level. And this persistent pressure on habitat, this cumulative burden on the wild shelters of the world and the inevitable fragmentation and spoiling of homes that follows, reduces the ability of wild animals and other life forms to exist unimpeded as surely as blocking the nesting burrows of birds. And in doing so, we shrink their worlds – just like my great-grandfather's world was shrunk on that island in the Irish Sea.

A University of Cambridge study published in 2020 showed that birds, mammals and amphibians across the planet have, on average, lost almost a fifth of their natural range in just the past 300 years. Nearly 17,000 species were studied on all the major continents, with researchers sifting through the observations and records of naturalists going back to 1700 to compile a map of shrinking ranges and freedom curtailed. By the end of our current century, it's expected that the average amount of lost territory will have grown to a quarter. And what these figures mask, of course, is how certain species have been affected to a far greater extent. The jaguar, for instance, has experienced a 21 per cent contraction of its native range in the past three centuries; the cheetah, 28 per cent; and the black rhinoceros, 53 per cent. Such staggering reductions in the totality of a species' homeland, the result of land conversion to agriculture and the expansion of urban areas alongside multiple other pressures, places a considerable number of species at risk of disappearing altogether.

A version of those lockdowns that so radically reduced the horizon of our personal and collective worlds during the pandemic is what a great deal of wildlife constantly endures. Each time another piece of the planet is retooled for largely human use, further restrictions on movement are imposed, making wild shelters smaller and more constrictive, locking animals, birds, insects and plants into increasingly limited and less viable spaces. As the climate journalist Tim Radford wrote in response to the University of Cambridge paper, 'Even those charismatic creatures slow in movement and static of habitat have felt the confinement. The panda has 11 per cent less freedom. The koala's range has been reduced by 22 per cent.' In February 2022, less than two years after the publication of the paper, the Australian government officially listed the koala as endangered, its dramatic decline in numbers largely the result of persistent habitat loss and the increasingly cataclysmic intensity of climate-change phenomena such as wildfires and droughts. The span of its world shrinking each day, until, finally, what's left of a home completely disappears.

Home takes many forms.

Stavros and Eleni had no house to return to in Prespa, having sold theirs years earlier when they'd emigrated to Australia in search of work and opportunities. But after several decades in Melbourne, a city with one of the largest Greek-speaking populations in the world outside Greece, and with several children and grandchildren living nearby, they finally acknowledged that the city, irrespective of all they'd gained from moving there, had never truly felt like home. Not in the way that Prespa had.

'When you feel a home inside you, you can't just ignore it,' said Stavros as we stood by an outdoor table where he pottered about assembling wooden toys. 'This is where we're from.' There was a lovely lightness to the way Stavros spoke, each line lilting upwards at its end, nudging you towards optimism regardless of the subject of conversation.

Eleni descended the stairs, her hands full of empty pails. 'Come on, you,' she said abruptly. 'Why are you just standing around when we have work to do?' She shook her head and dropped some of the pails by his feet.

'That's my signal,' said Stavros, turning towards me. That lilt at the end again, with a cheeky smile added this time.

Their long relationship had settled into a comfortable groove that presented Stavros as the convivial but hapless one and Eleni as the practical yet stern one. While there was an element of truth to the portrayal, it also hid the tender bonds between the pair, and ignored just how inseparable they were, completely reliant on one another and their differing strengths as they set about remaking a home. And even though Stavros was eighty-five and Eleni was in her late seventies when we first met them, there was absolutely nothing you could say to get either of them to slow down. On that they were in complete agreement. All you could really do was lend a hand – which, depending on her mood, Eleni might grudgingly accept.

I picked up a couple of the buckets and descended a steep bank to fill them from a narrow stream. Eleni was already in the water, her shoes slipped off to one side as she dunked her pail, passing it up to her husband on the bank when it was full. The house they were squatting in had no water supply, so this was their sole source, using the stream for drinking, for washing, for cooking, for cleaning. I filled my pails and hauled them upwards, and together we carried six buckets between us into the house. It was a house left empty by the Civil War and the depopulation of later decades, a house that nobody owned, or, if they did, they were living elsewhere and lacked the papers to sell it legally. Only partial panes of glass filled the window frames, so Eleni had cut fabric to patch up the holes, taping over the edges to create an imperfect seal. On winter days, winds followed you through the rooms like phantoms. The house was heated by a single wood stove that Stavros and Eleni fed with found wood, the two of them roaming the village each afternoon for discarded pieces or fallen branches. As there was no electricity, they lit their evenings with candles and cooked on the wood stove. Mice ran through the rooms at will, but neither Stavros nor Eleni paid them much attention, especially when Stavros played his violin, which he liked to do whenever we stopped by, reading sheet music of Vivaldi, Mozart and Bach from a stand. As a bottle of *tsipouro* from Germanos's distillery inevitably began to flow, Eleni would pull us upwards to dance, twirling her patterned headscarf in her hands as we clinked glasses, smiling the widest of smiles as the room and the music and the mice spun around us. At moments like these, it might have felt to them as if they'd never left home in the first place.

One weekend, Stavros and Eleni travelled by bus to visit relatives elsewhere in the country and left a friend looking after the squatted house. While the friend was working in the fields, the fire he'd set in the stove spilled out and spread quickly, burning up the wooden floors and beams and sending smoke upwards into a plume above the village. There was nothing left by the time Stavros and Eleni returned except a wooden sign that I managed to salvage from the wreckage. Stavros had chiselled *The Cottage* into a flat piece of wood and blackened each letter so that it stood out against the grain. And then he'd hung the sign, and all the longing it held, above their door.

Nothing was the same for them afterwards. No matter how hard they looked, Stavros and Eleni couldn't find another house in our village to live in. Eventually, they found somewhere outside the basin, but the energy and drive to be back in Prespa bled away. That upwards lilt at the end of Stavros's sentences became less noticeable. Occasionally I would look out of the window from my desk onto the schoolyard behind our house by the square and see them sitting on a bench in a small wooden gazebo, sharing a packed lunch on the one day a week that a local bus connected our villages. They would catch it in the morning just to spend a few hours in this place of theirs before taking it back in the afternoon to somewhere that was so close but simply not home.

There's a tree in a corner of the Indian city of Guwahati that I'll always remember. I never managed to learn what kind of tree it was, just how it was used. It stood on a busy intersection where buses, cars, scooters, rickshaws and pedestrians bustled past and cricket matches were played on a pitch to one side of it. But it was the action in the tree that fascinated me most, because at dawn and dusk each day a change of residency took place there, like shift workers keeping costs down by sharing the same room. As the sky began to dim, dozens of Brahminy kites that had been hunting along the city's edge or circling over the Brahmaputra river convened at the tree, jostling for night-time roosting places that had been occupied by fruit bats during the day. The bats, known as Indian flying foxes because of their uncanny facial resemblance to the fleet-footed ground mammal, would rouse themselves with all the enthusiasm of a child on the first morning of school after the Christmas holidays. They hung there in their dozens: heads down, wings folded to the side, gradually stirring. The Brahminy kites circled incessantly as the flying foxes began their evening stretches, lengthening out wings whose span can reach a metre and a half when fully extended. There they slowly twirled, eyes suddenly wide and flickering, until dusk reached its optimal degree of

darkness. And then they left the tree to the kites, fanning upwards
to join other fruit bats in quickening aerial rivers, overhanging the
busy city in a great trembling mass, where they spread out beneath
thundercloud or stars to find night trees in flower and fruit to feed
from. When the sky eventually lightened at dawn, they poured
back into the same tree, and the Brahminy kites replaced their
moving shapes in the air over the city.

Just as certain trees like this one in Guwahati hold significance as
shelter for wild species, sometimes so do whole forests. But what
if, like Stavros and Eleni on the other side of the world from where
they were born and raised, another place can't make up for it as
home? What if, as the elderly couple experienced after visiting
relatives for a weekend, you return to it and find it destroyed?

I'd never heard of the Kasanka National Park in Zambia until
its swamp forests of waterberries, red mahoganies and quinine
trees showed up in my Twitter feed in a forty-four-second video
of straw-coloured fruit bats. The sheer extraordinariness of the
spectacle captured by Doris Kofi with a handheld camera or phone
was transporting. If it wasn't for the trees lending scale to the bats,
you might imagine the footage was a close-up of swarming midges
in the Scottish Highlands. That's how dense they were: swirling,
wavering, massing. The camera struggles to focus, because the
aggregate of bats is composed of so many focal bands that there's
nothing to hold on to. Or, more precisely, there's simply too
much to hold on to. The whole scene is stupendous and scarcely
believable, but then that's what certain wild wonders of the world
amount to, something bordering on the unfathomable from a
human perspective, whether it's the migration of monarch butterflies across staggering distances to places they've never before
been or the blurring speed of a stooping peregrine as it falls from
the sky onto its prey. But this particular wonder is of a different

kind entirely, because it relates to numbers. The movement of 10 million straw-coloured fruit bats to Kasanka National Park between October and December each year is the largest migration of any mammal on the planet. And having arrived, they make those singular swamp forests their home before dispersing again a few months later.

Given that there's nowhere else in all of the world in which such extraordinary assemblies of fruit bats occur you might think that the protection of the Kasanka National Park would be sacrosanct. But as with so many other unique places across the planet that should be off-limits to ruinous developments, Kasanka is at risk of being seriously degraded by a plan put forward by Lake Agro Industries and Gulf Adventures to clear 7,000 hectares of buffer forest surrounding the core of the park. The project, which would see an agribusiness enterprise sow the cleared land with wheat, soya and maize, would eradicate a vast expanse of richly wooded habitat while extracting water from the nearby Luwombwa river for large-scale irrigation, a watercourse essential to both local communities and wildlife as it winds through the park and its encircling buffer forest.

Park officials have described the proposal as an 'existential threat' to Kasanka, putting in jeopardy the annual presence of those 10 million bats. In response to a challenge by the Kasanka Trust and two local community groups against the proposals, the Zambian High Court issued an interim injunction in 2022 temporarily preventing any commercial agriculture and deforestation on the edge of the park, but not before the companies responsible for the proposal had carried out preliminary works, levelling hundreds of hectares of forest, constructing roads and permanent dwellings, diverting rivers and laying an airstrip. While awaiting a definitive legal resolution, James Mwanza of the Kasanka Trust warned that if the plan were given approval it could have 'irreversible' and 'catastrophic' impacts on the park, potentially opening the door to more commercial activities within its borders. His colleague, Richard Peel, said that the migration of straw-coloured bats 'depends on healthy and intact forest within and around the park'. The bats, he went on to say, 'utilise more than ten times the size of the national park, which highlights the importance of protecting these areas.'

We don't know precisely why straw-coloured fruit bats gather in this particular place, but the consequences of its degradation are easy enough to understand. Our own keening for home gives us guidance. I remember just how deflated and drained of energy Stavros and Eleni were once their house in Prespa was destroyed. How undone they were by its loss. I can imagine, too, just how bereft my great-grandfather must have felt when separated from his home and family. In cultures that have long emphasised the differences between humans and the more-than-human world in order to underscore the presumed exceptionalism of the former, the prevailing perspective is to dismiss the commonalities we share. But as David Abram has written about such forced distinctions, humans aren't '*uniquely* unique' when it comes to relationships with the wider world. And the need for shelter, or the pull towards home, is but one of our affinities. The destruction of Kasanka's buffer forests or the fragmentation of the park itself would in all likelihood force the straw-coloured bats out of a place that could well be irreplaceable to them, or it would concentrate them in an increasingly smaller space, locking them down in a way that would put unsustainable pressure on the very habitat that makes Kasanka so vital, eventually eroding its life-support systems entirely. And if left without these anchoring forests to dwell in, if pushed out beyond a forested place considered home by this species, there's no way of knowing whether another could ever be found.

While few details of my great-grandfather's life either before or after his internment are known, he left something behind from his lockdown on the Isle of Man that's survived to this day. Something that still speaks of his longings more than a century after his imprisonment. Although for years I'd heard about the bone-carvings he'd made at Camp Knockaloe I didn't see any of the objects until 2016, when four of the carved bones were sent to my father in Canada by a cousin of his in England, two of which I now have here with me in Greece. I suppose I'd always imagined them to be simple affairs, naive artefacts whose amateur artistic merit wouldn't diminish the fact that they'd helped pass the interminable time during the long years that Charles Hoffmann was locked away from his family and home. And so I was completely unprepared for their luminous and beautiful grace when I finally held them. Or the way in which my great-grandfather had shaped a life with his hands, creating gifts from cleaned and bleached cow bones salvaged from the camp's kitchens, devoting countless days and painstaking care to shoring up the unexpected fractures in his world when the two countries he'd known – one that he'd left, the other that he'd arrived in – were suddenly at war.

Thirty thousand men, nearly all of them Germans living in the UK, were interned as enemy aliens at Camp Knockaloe during the First World War. Among them, I picture a stout and slightly stooped figure, now using his seafarer's hands that had once worked ropes and pulleys to whittle, pare and carve with extraordinary precision. There, behind barbed-wire fences, he embarked on a project of devotion, teasing out delicate, filigreed flowers and elegant bouquets that are not only embossed on the bone but raised free from the smoothed surfaces, anchored at key points but otherwise floating on slender seams of air that have been hollowed out from behind by the deftest of blades. From the no-man's-land of the internment camp – where he was neither civilian nor soldier; not truly British nor entirely German any more – Charles Hoffmann carved a landscape of longing, entwining the roses, flowers and leaves of his beloved garden at home, dedicating a birthday wish to his distant wife and fashioning napkin holders and vases for the family table in his absence. He transformed ordinary cow bones into objects of great beauty – tender summations of time and desire. If 'a place in the landscape corresponds to a place in the heart', as the Czech writer Václav Cílek has suggested, then my great-grandfather endured his lockdown by grafting both onto bone, trying with each snick of the blade and smooth draw of a file to keep that connection alive within his shrinking world.

More than a century after he'd shaped them, I found myself holding these bones in the early days of the Covid-19 pandemic. Something about their weight and solidity – the poignancy of them having been worked by a man so in the dark as to when his imprisonment might end that he'd carved *Souvenir of the Great War 1914–1916* into the reverse of one of them – confirmed for me just how radically and swiftly our worlds can close around us, just as it had for Germanos when he'd returned to Greece from exile in Tashkent only to be imprisoned on a rocky island in the Aegean. They were like a message whose meaning gained further relevancy with time, because I began to understand then, as constrictive measures took hold of human societies across the planet, that we, like the wild world, have long been in a kind of lockdown alongside it. Because *our* worlds have been shrinking, too.

Pandemic restrictions on movement and activity were revealing on multiple levels, perhaps no more so than in the response of a great many citizens to the natural world, particularly in the first wave of Covid-19. Across the northern hemisphere in spring 2020, as so much human motion came to a halt, one of the noticeable points of connection between people was the sudden clarity of birdsong. It was remarked on in newspaper articles and on social media, in family conversations and on television chat shows. It was like a new frequency had been tuned into, a register lost or never known because of the dense constancy of human sounds in urban and suburban spaces. But with the silencing of aircraft, vehicles and industries, another soundscape came appreciably within range. As Steven Lovatt remarked in his book *Birdsong in a Time of Silence*, the 'spring of 2020 might be remembered differently – as the time when we first heard the birds and, hearing them, began to recover an appreciation of something universal we had somehow mislaid.' And when those songs faded once more with the renewal of activity, it became painfully clear just how many walls we've built around us. Because all lockdown restrictions did was reveal what is already there; there was no sudden boom in the populations of songbirds making themselves volubly known; there was no rapid infilling of the spaces temporarily ceded by humans. Just a rearrangement in the hierarchy of voices and an opportunity to clearly see, to *hear* so richly when those walls were briefly lowered, how our lives are already bordered and restricted when it comes to the greater world we're held within.

A shrinking world brings so much to an end. Earlier in this book I wrote that our lifelines aren't solely our own, given that the possibilities open to us at any moment are the compound reflection of the paths already taken by family, ancestors, strangers and societies. We are always connected to far more than we'll ever know. And this is true too for wild lives and our frequently invisible relationships with them. Although scientists don't know precisely where the 10 million straw-coloured fruit bats go when they depart the Kasanka forests, preliminary studies using radio-tracked bats suggest they spread out in multiple directions and cross huge expanses of Africa, breaking into countless smaller groups that are attached to other forests on the continent. And in migrating as they do, they act as affirming lifelines for trees, carrying with them forest seeds that they broadcast as they fly and feed, sowing the possibility of new life and helping maintain genetic diversity across an extensive topographical span. Simultaneously, they pollinate isolated trees and connect arboreal species in landscapes that are often fragmented, establishing corridors between them, tying in the loose strands that weave together our lives with the wild and replenishing a shared terrain with fruiting trees of incalculable benefit not only to bats but to people and other creatures as well. We can no more say that the disappearance of a wild species leaves the larger web of interconnected lives unaffected than we can say that the death of a person leaves their family and network of friends and colleagues untouched.

Already, the rapid unravelling of insect populations as a result of habitat loss and pesticides threatens the pollination of human food crops. The levelling of old-growth forests destroys ancient trees and their irreplaceable ecosystems as well as potentially vital medicinal compounds for human use before they're even discovered. The bleaching of coral reefs because of increasingly acidic and overheating seas jeopardises countless marine species together with the livelihoods of millions of coastal residents who are dependent on thriving fish populations. The disappearance of swallows and swifts thins the skies of wild agency while simultaneously lessening the scope of human joy, further curtailing the potential mental and emotional benefits of contact with nature. There's no point in making shelter for ourselves if the wild world goes unhoused, because that's our world, too. And unless greater bonds are established between humanity and the more-than-human, recognising the fundamental affinities between us and actively remaking this planet into a shared sphere, then our descendants might reasonably ask why we placed barriers between ourselves and our potential, reducing the viability of the earth's living systems and its spectrum of wild species so drastically that the world kept shrinking about us. They'll wonder why we made our lives smaller, more restricted and locked down by the day.

I remember how connective in quality my great-grandfather's carvings felt during the pandemic, the lifelines scored on my palms meeting his when I held them. They were beautifully reassuring despite the poignancy of their story. Each inscribed message a reminder of my paternal family's lifeline as it shifted from one country to another; each delicate detail a suspended moment in time during those years of internment. Like those bee-eaters that might still have been inside their burrows on the day their tunnels were plugged, Charles Hoffmann had no choice about the imprisonment he endured on the Isle of Man. All he could do was reach out to his family by rendering some essence of the home he yearned for through the flowers and leaves he engraved onto bone, celebrating what was on the other side of the barbed wire. By remembering, like those songs heard in the silence of lockdown, the things that made him whole.

WRENS III

I'm washing the dishes when I hear what I think are wrens by the front of the house – that sharp, insistent clicking of theirs, as though they want to be let inside. I slot a plate into the drying rack and wipe my hands on a tea towel as I walk quietly towards the door. A whole spring, summer and autumn have come and gone since the wrens last gathered in the empty swallow's nest. And nearly all of a winter, too. I press my ear against the wood of the door, unsure if it was just a bird or two passing through that I heard or the start of something bigger. But it's all gone quiet in the garden again.

I haven't given much thought to the wrens returning after that first winter, believing their time with us had been a wondrous one-off, a serendipitous crossing of paths when the nest above our door had coincided with the lifeline of a bird who'd softened its interior with lichens and mosses in spring. And it's now so late into the following winter that any remaining link to those freezing nights when we shared the house live on solely in memory, sparked into sharp focus on those days when for some reason or another I find myself looking up at the cup of moulded mud, still amazed by what it had once held. But this has been a strange winter so far, even more so than usual of late – a season of warm light and little snow, when lizards unfold themselves from hollows in the garden wall to bask on the sun-struck stones. When bears pattern the valley with paw prints.

I quickly pull on a jacket and unlock the back door. Outside, the air is cooling but not cold. Late light floods the mountains, where the grey spires of the leafless beeches are split by an ever-green seam of silver firs. All crisply edged by the sinking sun. I move forward beside the wall of the house, hearing those same sharp clickings above the ripplings of the stream. Peeking around the corner, I see four small brown birds fluttering by the front door. As I watch, another arrows in from the meadow and clings to the rim of the empty nest. Then it slips inside.

It appears that wrens are with us again.

It's an hour before sunrise. A week has passed since the wrens gathered for the first time in the old swallow's nest this second winter. Crusted snow shines in the moonlight and the cold of the stream passes right through me where I'm sitting at the edge of the garden. I've been out here each morning, rising before the light to witness the emptying of the nest. But the wrens aren't always there. I've come to realise these past few days that their presence is determined by an internal thermal gauge; so sensitively attuned are they to fluctuating temperatures that only on the nights of greatest risk from the cold do they assemble. On that clear-skied evening of their return, when I'd stepped out in just a light jacket, they foresaw a shift in the weather that I'd been completely oblivious to, filing into the nest hours before the temperature in the valley suddenly plummeted to minus ten. Since then, the ice and snow we woke to the following morning has thawed and refrozen several times, but if our thermometer registers even a degree or two increase in the overnight temperature the wrens stay away from the nest, with not a single bird taking shelter there. And if it then dips by a degree or two, they knowingly arrive and crowd inside for warmth. They're aware of the need to convene.

Right now, it's perishing. The cold feels as if it's been ham-mered into place, fitted as close as metal armour. With each breath it catches in my throat. Even as the winter dark gradually lifts, there's no sense that anything warmer will take its place. I lift my binoculars to my eyes, and through the fog that forms on the lenses I can just make out some movement around the nest. A small, waking fire is being kindled inside, the first stretches and wing-shakes of birds that have endured the night, a head briefly raised above the parapet. And now the wrens flow outwards and into flight, leaving the feathered warmth to forage alone in the ice and snow during daylight. It takes little more than a minute for a total of twelve of them to stream into the valley. The night before I'd counted zero; and the night before that there were eleven. All week I've witnessed the same numerical consistency: roughly a dozen or none.

I don't think wrens have ever been considered a sentinel species, one of those life forms that humans have used to guard against environmental dangers, like canaries sent deep into the earth ahead of miners because of their sensitivity to poisonous gases underground. But as daylight deepens across the valley and I crunch over the snow back to the house, it occurs to me that they should be, because there are valuable things to be learned from our wild kin beyond simply the presence of environmental hazards. Especially when the ability to detect danger is a quality that we share too, given that the signs are as easy for us to read as the coming cold is for these birds – the floods, the fires, the extinctions. But by gathering in this empty cup of mud, a shelter perfectly protected from winds and snow by the overhang of the balcony, these wrens reveal not only a subtle understanding of the degrees of risk the cold represents but, crucially, a capability to respond in ways that keep themselves safe from the danger. What we need aren't more canaries to warn us of the risks ahead, but more wrens to remind us that the whole point of sentinels is found in the act of taking heed.

III

THE SHARED WORLD

8

In the Eyes of a Bear

The sharp scent of junipers was baked hard into the August heat. It wasn't even mid-morning and already the sun pressed down on the rocky hillside like a weight. I gently scraped at a small patch of red earth. Once I'd loosened enough soil, I scooped it with my trowel and slowly tipped it into a plastic fruit crate that was acting as a sieve. When the crate was full, we each took turns shaking it from side to side to see what fell through the holes and what stayed behind. It was a form of archaeology we were effectively engaged in – the scraping, the sieving, the sifting – but rather than the long-buried artefacts of human civilisation we were instead bringing to the surface the skeleton of a European brown bear, lifting it piece by piece into the late summer glare. Unearthing it as a way of remembering.

The bear had been found in April 2012 between patches of juniper and box only metres above a lonely road on the other side of the bay from the village of Psaradhes. Decomposition had given it away, a stench that even the snow-chilled air couldn't seal. The images from that day are hard to look at for any length of time, in the way that all scenes of suffering are difficult to confront, serving as a visceral reminder of the brutality humans are capable of inflicting on others. Because this bear, a large male weighing around 300 kilograms, hadn't died from natural causes at the end of a long life in the basin but was killed by the laying of poisoned bait.

The bait had been deliberately placed inside a dead cow on the outskirts of the village and left there. While wolves were the most likely target, the poison – as poison nearly always does – killed whatever came into contact with it, indiscriminately taking out dogs, foxes and cats, along with the brown bear that we would exhume eight years later in the fierce, August heat. The use of illegal poison remains far too common in Greece, deployed not only to kill apex predators but sometimes used against village strays and in feuds between hunters and shepherds that come at the expense of their respective dogs. The photographs from that April day are unsettling not just because of the blood and exposed bone of the poisoned bear, where foxes or dogs had wrenched loose a back foot and stolen it away, but because of the stark vulnerability seen in the animal's slumped stance – a helplessness so at odds with its formidable strength and size. The bear had almost certainly been trying to reach the lake after it began spasming and froth-ing at the mouth, instinctively seeking water to cleanse whatever was making it so violently ill – but it never got that far. Instead, it collapsed face forward to the rocky ground and died just a short distance from where it had fed on what must have seemed at the time like a welcome feast.

Having been away from home on the first day of the excava-tion, I turned up the following morning. What I'd missed was the removal of the largest pieces of the bear's skeleton. Before we got started I'd held its skull in my hands, lifting it from a beige formica table in the building in Psaradhes that was our base. The dense helmet of bone was smooth and stained reddish-brown. From the cranium, where it arched above the enormous eye sock-ets, it sloped to the sharp canine teeth at the tapered end of the upper mandible. While cradling it, I couldn't help but think of the beautiful intelligence it had once held and protected. After returning the skull to the table, I joined the others for the next day of work, where we would be labouring deeper inside the hollow that the bear had created through its own weight. As the hillside was too rocky to dig a deep enough hole to bury the body, and the animal was too heavy to easily transport elsewhere, the bear had been covered with thick tarp and then mounded over with a layer of stones. And there, over time, it had sunk under the force of gravity until, having elaborated its own grave, it was held inside the earth.

The exhumation of the bear's skeleton with the eventual aim of restoring it as a public memorial was largely the vision of Yannis Ziogas, an artist and professor of art at the University of Western Macedonia in nearby Florina. Yannis has developed a deep attachment to Prespa since his first visit in 2006 when the art school opened. Letting the university administrators know that he wouldn't be contained by the walls of the institution, he's put into practice a form of collective engagement with the landscape by walking across the mountains from Florina to Prespa with his students over four or five days each academic year. For Yannis, walking is art. It's beauty, perception and self-expression. But walking is also political for him, a movement into activism and community. A way of not only cultivating attention to the complex histories of a place – traumatic as they can sometimes be in the case of Prespa with its memories of the Civil War – but establishing solidarity with the people and wild species at home there. Several of his students from the Department of Visual and Fine Arts were helping document the excavation that morning as part of a larger project called the Art March to Prespa.

When I next eased my trowel into the earth I felt resistance. I thumbed away soil from a flat, kidney-shaped segment that resembled a slice of dried orange hooked on the rim of a cocktail glass. We all gathered close, eventually agreeing that it must be a vertebral disk. Other disks were soon salvaged and added to the box after they'd been brushed clean of debris. At some point they would be reunited with the corresponding vertebrae gathered the day before and made whole once more. As none of us was intimately familiar with the skeletal structure of a bear, we had no real way of knowing what might still be missing as we dug. So we worked on in the blazing dry heat, slowly enlarging the space and sifting through it as carefully as we could.

As well as Yannis's students, my friends Sinéad and Angelos – an Irish-Greek couple living in Prespa at the time – were with us that day. Sinéad had previously worked with Yannis on a walking symposium that has now become a biennial event here, attracting as many as 140 people from nearly two dozen countries to a week of walkshops, panel discussions, lectures and art installations on the many meanings and ways of walking.

'I think I have something here,' said Sinéad, carefully brushing an earthen ledge over a slab of limestone. 'Wow, look at these.'

Four pale claws embedded in the red soil. They were so closely spaced that it was clear one of the bear's front paws had come to a final rest there. An unspoken moment filled our shared space, when the silence felt like a reckoning. I don't know why the claws affected us differently from the disks and smaller bones we'd been exhuming all morning, but they definitely did. There was something especially poignant and transportive about seeing them like that, flush with the earth as though the vivid strokes of an ancient cave painting. They carried the power and potency of another life in their lines: the settled memory of sentience.

About an hour later, with the sun now directly above us, we gathered our tools and walked back to the village, having collected everything we could find of the skeleton. 'When the bear was spread out on the ground it would have been huge,' said Yannis, remembering the images from the day it had been covered with tarp and stones, 'and now it's just a few bones in some boxes. Its whole life is in here.'

One summer morning in our second farming season – the first after expanding our production from just herbs to a whole array of vegetables and salads – I made my regular call to the restaurant in Thessaloniki that was our biggest buyer, only to be told by the owner that they didn't need anything that week. 'The restaurant is so much quieter,' he explained, 'because people have started escaping the city for the sea on their holidays.' It had never occurred to us while sowing seeds in spring that there might be a summer lull, so when the owner then suggested we start up again in the autumn I felt a sudden spasm of panic.

'What's the matter?' asked Julia when I got off the phone.

'The restaurant doesn't want anything until September.'

'But the fields are full. Everything's ripe and ready, what are we going to do?'

'I have no idea. The only thing I can think of at the moment is that we'd better try preserving whatever we can to use ourselves.'

And so we did, dipping into recipe books and online food forums, linking up what sounded tasty with whatever glut was current in the fields. All of which gradually led us to building up a business making homemade jams, preserves, pickles, chutneys and dried teas from the ingredients in our plots. By the end of our farming years, this side shoot of the original seedling was responsible for the majority of our income, as we supplied a number of local tourist shops in Prespa and businesses in several Greek cities with the products we made. After giving up the fields, we had to think carefully about what to grow in the garden for the business and what high-quality fruit and vegetables we could source locally to make up the difference, but at least we had a well-established line of items and dedicated customers that we could rely on. But within a year of the Greek financial crisis beginning in 2009, every last one of the bakeries, delicatessens, tourist centres and shops that we supplied either went under or radically cut back on stock, especially of homemade gift items such as ours. Eventually the phone stopped ringing with new orders and our jam pans hung unused in the kitchen. Which is when it dawned on us that we'd reached another crossroads in our lives.

With little work and no sign of any forthcoming on the horizon, we increasingly wondered whether we'd come to the natural end of our time here. By then, we'd spent nearly a decade in Prespa – far longer than I think either of us had ever imagined was possible when we set out on this journey. It had been an extraordinary and enlarging period for us both. Unforgettable through all that we'd experienced and learned. The shared basin, and the friendships and connections forged within its folds, had fundamentally changed us. Emotionally, it had given us the space to grow into new skins, enabling us to regain the curiosity, desire and focus that had gone missing in our last years in London. And it had introduced us to a wilder and more vital world than we'd ever before known. But despite all that we'd gained here, it suddenly felt, given the narrowing range of possibilities for keeping ourselves financially afloat, that it was time to move on again. And so, after long evenings of talking about what we would do and where we might go, we decided to emigrate to Canada, where I'd grown up and my parents and brother still live. The paperwork that needed completing, particularly for Julia as a non-Canadian citizen, was daunting. And because it was so daunting we procrastinated – as the two of us have a tendency to do even at the best of times – so that it took us far longer to tackle than we'd originally imagined. Which was just as well in the end, because partway through tracking down all the copious documents and official papers required by the Canadian immigration services everything changed for us in Prespa.

Our love of birds was well known in the area. Having seen us with binoculars on our walks, people would sometimes stop to ask about a species they'd glimpsed in their garden or a remembered bird that they hadn't seen for years. And we reported any unusual sightings from our fields to local conservationists, such as the rare black vulture that floated overhead one morning, its huge shadow darkening the soil. Although we had no formal ornithological training, our knowledge of birds and their behaviour was sufficiently broad through years of passionate birdwatching, traced right back to the early days of our relationship when we travelled together through India, that when an opportunity arose for monitoring them in the mountains of Prespa it was us who were offered the work.

The ornithological surveys we were asked to carry out over the following five years would form the basis of environmental assessments being conducted where wind turbines had either been proposed or already built, ascertaining the risk of those spinning white blades to the avian lives being lived there. From early spring through late autumn each year, we spent a considerable portion of our days in the limestone uplands or along the granite ridges surrounding these lakes, recording the flight patterns and routes of both resident and migratory species. And in tracing the living pathways of birds, a lifeline emerged for us that allowed us to stay in Prespa. A place that feels more like home than it ever has.

As the sun rose over the basin, I followed a treeless ridge that buckled into the hazy distance. Skylark song sparkled above the meadows and a warm breeze rolled over my shoulders. Julia had dropped me off on a dirt track within walking distance of my vantage point for that day's shift and then carried on to her own. Being able to work separately meant that we could monitor much more of the airspace around the thirty-four turbines strung along the Varnoundas mountains beyond the eastern edge of the Prespa National Park. It was early June by then and the alpine world was bursting at its seams, the granite bones of the highlands clothed in wildflowers and butterflies for that brief, ecstatic season. I couldn't help but hum to myself as I walked that morning, but as I neared the spot where I'd spend the coming hours scanning the skies around the wind farm something stepped into sunlight ahead of me.

The animal's appearance was so sudden and strange that for the slenderest of moments I had no idea what I was looking at, whether some giant feral dog or an unusual hybrid of creatures more common to me. Emerging from behind a rocky outcrop that had kept it hidden until the last second, it didn't fit with anything I'd ever experienced as it clambered onto a boulder and settled there. But that momentary flicker of uncertainty was eclipsed by a swift blaze of clarity, as if the scene had been suddenly floodlit and telescoped into focus: only twenty metres of alpine meadow separated me from a European brown bear, a near relative of the American grizzly. As it eyed me from its saddle of stone, the wild rushed in like a river.

In his book *Becoming Animal*, David Abram says that 'reciprocity is the very structure of perception'. To look into the eyes of a wild creature as they look into yours is to enter into relationship, an intimate exchange carried out within a shared moment of time. Peering into the reflective gleam of a frog at ease on both land and water, or to look between the wrinkled lids of a tortoise housed inside a mobile shell, is to be offered the possibility of empathy, a way of imagining a life and lineage vastly different from our own. But there in that bright meadow, looking back at the bear as its stare deepened inside me, I felt no tingle of curiosity or inquisitiveness. Awe and fear had filled me in equal measure, leaving little space for anything but the fierce immediacy of the moment – that still centre that the structure of perception is built around.

Although the sun was still low in the sky, it was rising with summer fire. The light poured over the mountains until the bear was enthroned in its glow. Its fur appeared more grizzled than brown, sleek and shimmering across the valleys of its coat, as if the tips of the hairs had been dipped in silver. Dark rings encircled its eyes and waves of muscle rolled through its shoulders. With its stout black muzzle, it tapped at the air, sifting through whatever traces of adrenalin and fear had seeped out of me. Although it stood higher than my waist even while on all fours, it appeared to be a young bear on the verge of adulthood – and it suddenly occurred to me that its mother might be near. I turned slowly in search of her, the space between the bear and me seeming even smaller than before when I considered the consequences of coming between them – all that a threat to a mother's long labour of blood and nourishing would entail – to see only an empty meadow rippling with wildflowers and wind. Knowing there was open ground behind me, I began backing up slowly into sunlight.

For as long as we've depicted animals on cave walls and shared language around fires, stories of our relationship with the wild kingdom have helped render this world sensible to human consciousness. And they've been vital guides to our survival, containing hard-earned learning warning us of dangers. But when thinking about that ridge of spilling light some days later, I finally understood something of what the philosopher Krishnamurti meant when he wrote that 'the description is not the described . . . the word is not the thing'. No intellectual or emotional understanding of our wild inheritance could prepare me for its actuality – the sudden stirring of my animal essence. From the moment the bear made its startling appearance, my skin was alive and firing, every last hair tingling with attention. My whole body felt charged with a taut, electrical pulse, as if no longer flesh but a conductor of pure and vital energy. I acted with little thought beyond a basic run-through of what I'd read and remembered about how to behave in the presence of a brown bear; beyond that, I was operating on some ancient, self-preserving level, articulating through action the same instincts that our distant human ancestors must have known so frequently and intimately. That visceral response was simply the evolutionary reaction of prey to a predator. Up there in the mountains, where we often lacked a phone signal even if I'd wanted to call Julia for help, I was no longer the dominant species; and all the assumptions about our cultural exceptionalism fell quickly away, exposing some kernel at the core of our animal beginnings, like the stripped-back mountains after summer shuts down. All that was ever wild is still within us.

The bear started. There'd been no sign of a mother in the end, so that only the two of us shared that brimming alpine world. I still don't know why it moved when it did, but perhaps it had picked up an additional scent, some pungent, primitive smell of mine that resonated with its genetic inheritance, the stories its own species carries in blood and nerve and bone. Or maybe, as I took the smallest of steps backwards and the sun behind me continued its rise, I'd edged beyond what might have been a vague and hazy glare to the bear and clarified into something solid and substantial. Something identifiable. Either way, the bear suddenly padded off the rock to hit the meadow in full flight, thumping towards me. It cut the distance between us in half before sheering away, hurtling down the slope and slipping into a pocket of mountain beeches. The echo of its run beat like a drum inside me, so that all I could do was stand still in the meadow – breathing, breathing, breathing – as skylark song fell about me like rain.

The natural borders that distinguish Prespa as a crossroads place are also partly responsible for its unique value as a biodiversity haven. Like that collision of limestone and granite that makes it possible for over 1,800 plants to dwell here, or the overlap of Mediterranean and central European biomes enabling species characteristically northern in character to share this place with those that are far more redolent of the hotter south. But the other critical factor determining the remarkable range and abundance of species found in Prespa is the diversity of habitats located within a relatively small geographical context. Between the lakes and the mountain heights exist reedbeds, islands, sandbars, marshland, mudflats, plains, rivers, riparian forest, oak woods, juniper stands, abandoned fields, burgeoning scrub, mountain beech woods, sub-alpine meadows and rocky outcrops. There's even a whole karst country of sinkholes and stony grasslands undulating across a plateau where we encountered species while bird-monitoring that we'd never seen anywhere else in the Greek part of the basin. Another of the many shelters that in their sum make Prespa so singular and irreplaceable as a home for wild creatures.

To give some idea of that biological richness, 172 of Greece's 234 species of butterfly are found in Prespa, or more than three times the total number of butterfly species found in all of the UK. Twenty-six of Europe's forty bat species exist here, some denning in those peninsular caves that were lived in long ago as monastic cells. And nine of the twenty-three fish species coursing the rivers and lakes of the basin are endemic to Prespa or the southwest Balkans, such as the trout flashing upriver past our old fields in winter. Life forms are still being found here, too. Our own limited floral knowledge has added common snowdrop and wild aquilegia to Prespa's list, largely because of our familiarity with those previously unrecorded plants from other parts of the world. But of the thousands of species that make a home here for at least part of the year, there's only one that so noticeably makes use of the whole of Prespa's vertical span, turning up in nearly every last one of the habitats that I mentioned above – and that's the brown bear.

Signs of brown bears aren't all that hard to find. There are the unmistakable prints they leave behind in snow, sand, soil and mud, large enough to make my hand look like a child's in comparison. Or the huge boulders shifted in search of ant nests and grubs. With a bit of luck, you might even see a tree that's been used as a scratching post, where pale-brown hairs sometimes snag and stand proud. Until the Greek electricity company swapped it for a new one, there was a wooden electricity pole just up the track from our house that had been used as a scratching post for years. Attached to it was a metal plaque engraved with the words ΚΙΝΔΥΝΟΣ and ΘΑΝΑΤΟΣ, meaning DANGER and DEATH. I'd like to think the bear was expressing just how little it cared about such warnings when it stood on its back legs to sharpen its claws and sliced clean through the metal sign in four ragged lines.

The other hard-to-miss sign of bear is, naturally, scat. Depending on the time of year and available food sources, bear scat comes in a variety of shapes and sizes. And it doesn't take long to start distinguishing some of the seasonal ingredients left behind in the mounds: plum stones, beetle wings, walnut shells, apple pips. The prevalence of bear scat also makes it ideal for any study examining the broader diet of these large mammals, or for genetic analysis if fresh, as happened in 2018 and 2019 in a cross-border project initiated under the auspices of PrespaNet.

PrespaNet is a transboundary alliance of environmental organisations working around the shared lakes, comprising the Society for the Protection of Prespa (SPP) in Greece, Protection and Preservation of Natural Environment in Albania (PPNEA) and the Macedonian Ecological Society (MES) in North Macedonia. By the time the bear diet and genetic study began in 2018, Julia was managing the PrespaNet project on the Greek side of the lakes. Spurred on by the bird assessment work we'd begun carrying out in the mountains in 2010, Julia had applied to do an online master's degree in environmental management and geographic information systems with the University of Ulster. Dedicating every last bit of spare time and energy she had to the course, she'd graduated with distinction and been hired by the SPP in 2012 while still completing her studies. That long-term desire of hers to work in conservation in Prespa – going right back to our decision to move here and to carry those environmental textbooks with us so hopefully in our rucksacks – finally came to fruition.

While I was thrilled to help out with the bear-diet study, using my regular walks to gather fresh scat and seal it inside clear plastic bags, recording the time, date, location and habitat type before the samples were then frozen, Julia had the far more challenging task of assisting with the analysis in winter. 'We defrosted the scats, weighed them, measured their volume and then basically washed away the scat part in cold water through a series of sieves outdoors,' she'd said, still shaking with cold when she got home and I'd asked her how the day of analysis had gone. 'It was hard and fiddly work in freezing weather with lots of cold water, wearing woolly hats and waddling around in waterproofs, but rewarding when we started finding the stones or kernels of disintegrated fruit, bits of acorns or insects, and then a tortoise leg, which was a big surprise to me and the others.'

From the diet phase of the study, the project then moved on to the genetic component, which entailed molecular analysis and DNA sequencing in a laboratory at the University of Ljubljana in Slovenia. What we eventually learned from the gathered samples is that there were at least fifty-one individual brown bears in the Prespa basin as of 2019. Due to the difficulty in accessing some of the more remote and mountainous reaches of the watershed, and the fact that many areas were visited infrequently by research-ers or volunteers, it's thought that the true population size might be somewhere in the region of sixty to seventy animals. As genetic analysis meant that the location of individual scats and the corres-ponding animals could be mapped using the geographical data we'd recorded in the field, it also confirmed with startling clarity that at least some of these brown bears were crossing the borders of the transboundary park, perhaps following the route that Chris and I had been trying to identify with our camera trap when

I'd stepped on the bomb in the sands along the shore. Zooming in on the map marked up with the individual scat sites, I can see that a male bear identified in our valley in 2018 also showed up several times on the lower slopes of the Mali i Thatë mountains on the Albanian side of the lakes before crossing into North Macedonia in 2019.

'Large carnivores like bear, wolf and lynx need large territories,' said Bledi Hoxha when I asked him about the transboundary dimension of the study. Bledi is a large carnivore expert working for PPNEA in Albania, where some 200 to 250 brown bears are estimated to exist in the whole country. Albania happens to be where I saw my first ever brown bear in the year we moved here; not a wild one as I would have hoped but rather a 'dancing' bear being led through the streets of Korçë, looking miserable with its nose ring and bells and chains. Since then, the tradition of 'dancing bears' – in which animals are tortured and trained to stand and 'dance' by being forced onto metal platforms above hot coals – has largely been eradicated in the Balkans as a result of pressure from environmental organisations and greater enforcement of the law. But Bledi told me of an ongoing threat to bears just as horrific: the illegal capture and confinement of them in cages as attractions for drinkers and diners. 'A few years ago, Four Paws [an Austrian animal welfare NGO] and Albanian institutions and organisations confiscated about fifty bears from restaurants and bars that were then transferred to bear sanctuaries in the Balkans and Europe.'

Like the many threats to rivers, these illegal captures are far from the only pressure that bears face, as Bledi went on to mention the fragmentation and destruction of habitat caused by intensive logging, road-building projects, wind parks and hydropower infrastructure in sensitive ecological sites and corridors as significant issues common to the three countries that come together around Prespa.

'Through transboundary networks like PrespaNet,' he continued, 'we can harmonise our data with the aim of understanding the status of bear populations and their threats in the Prespa basin. These cross-border initiatives bring together different people and organisations to protect biodiversity regardless of the borders of a country.'

My phone pinged in my pocket.

There's a Montagu's harrier headed your way, read the text.

Whenever we had a phone signal, Julia and I would message each other with updates while monitoring, especially if a bird was moving in the direction of the other's position. As I'd only just reached my vantage point and unpacked my gear, I called Julia straight back.

'Did you see the harrier?' she asked, before I'd had a chance to say anything else.

'No, but I've just had a really close encounter with a bear.' I could hear my voice waver when telling her.

'Seriously? Are you okay? Do you want me to come and get you and we can do the shift tomorrow instead?'

'I'm here now and feeling okay. A bit shaky, but let's carry on.'

'Okay, be careful. And just message me if you want to stop.'

Although I was meant to be watching the sky that morning, I barely looked at it. I just kept turning in a circle, thinking the bear was still there. And I jumped whenever the grasses shifted with wind.

It took several weeks for the heightened sensation of my bear encounter to release me. In that time, I would unintentionally drift back to the meadow where we'd met even while sitting at a table with friends, entirely consumed by the closeness of that day. Someone would tap me on the shoulder or say my name and I would rejoin the conversation – but only for a short time before the bear reclaimed me again. What might have appeared as vacancy or disinterest was just the outward expression of an inner link, something that held me so tight that those few minutes in the mountains pushed everything else to the side. The bear not only filled my days but I would wake at night with it already in mind. It's impossible to live with such intensity for long, or at least it was for me, and so I was quietly relieved when its hold over me gradually eased. But it will always be there, like a scar that reshapes as you and your skin gradually age.

Rarely do the paths of humans and bears cross as close as this in Prespa. Far more often the contact is distant or fleeting, if there is any encounter at all. On a bright afternoon in October 2023, I drove to the edge of Great Prespa Lake. It was my birthday that day, but as Julia still had work to finish I decided to go for a short celebratory walk on my own before friends arrived in the evening. I parked the car where I always do, beside a wide, sandy track that passes through an open landscape of grasses and brambles bordered on one side by reedbeds and on the other by a strip of forest. I locked the door and set off along the track, but after just a few metres I spun around. I turned only because I realised that I'd left my hat in the car. And I needed my hat only because the sun was still hot for October and I was another year older and my hair isn't getting any thicker with time. And there, on the path that had been behind me but was now in front, a huge mother bear was quickly but quietly shepherding her three cubs across the track and away from me. There are the gifts we find and the gifts we sometimes miss. And most of them, when it comes to top predators, pass us by entirely.

In the thousands of hours that I've walked or worked in Prespa's landscapes, I've encountered apex mammals only a handful of times. But that doesn't necessarily mean they aren't near, just that their desire to avoid altercations, after an exceedingly long and crushing history of persecution in Europe that saw them extinguished across whole parts of the continent, is highly refined. One grey December afternoon I stood at the end of the river corridor. It had been a largely uneventful walk along its banks that day, a quiet stroll on my own that led me to a vast expanse of reeds before the true beginning of the lake. I've long loved that particular spot for its atmosphere, the sense of mystery it occasions by encircling you on all sides except one with tall reeds rustling and swaying in the wind. With vision limited and the shape of the enclosure amplifying the auditory, it's a place where I enjoy being able to tune in to the sounds of the landscape: the murmuring of those reeds, warblers in song season, the cackling laugh-track of marsh frogs. But on that quiet winter's day it was a single deep growl that electrified me as I stood there. It came from just inside the edge of the reeds – long, guttural and fierce. Otherworldly in its invisible intimacy. The utterance was a warning, that much I knew, and its message was perfectly clear: *I'm here and this is my place, so best just to leave.* I walked away, turning only once to see if anything had emerged from the reeds, but all was silent and still.

That evening, a friend phoned to say he'd just seen wolves in his headlights by the river corridor where he knew I liked to walk.

It's no exaggeration to say that the wild world is infinitely wondrous and affirming. It has the extraordinary ability to inspire, captivate and transform. It can console us when we most need it and help heal us when broken. It elicits joy, pleasure, astonishment and awe. And it can, so often and for so many, lift the horizons of our lives. But the wild world should never be reduced and simplified to something that's merely positive for people and nothing more. Its intrinsic value is dependent not on humankind but its own evolutionary course and story. Made animate through agency, it exists not only alongside us but simultaneously beyond: autonomous, volitional, dynamic. And just like the human world that is no stranger to contradiction and complexity as a result of our *own* fundamental agency, nature can also be messy, difficult, unsettling and violent. And sometimes it's dangerous, too. For those of us advocating for wilder places, or who would like to see apex species reintroduced to landscapes where they've long been missing, it's critical to be honest about that in our conversations and not pretend that there's no additional risk from the presence of bears or wolves nearby.

But talking about any added risk first requires putting it into context, because as societies we've become remarkably adept at accepting significant dangers from human-related causes through the cultural, economic and political normalisation of those risks and the stubborn distinctions still made between the human and the more-than-human world. It's why deaths from shark attacks in one country frequently make the front pages in others but deaths from domestic dogs rarely do. Even when unfounded, the wild world has been made to carry a far greater burden of guilt and responsibility when it comes to threats to human life. Not a single person has died of a wolf attack in Europe in the past four decades yet air pollution is responsible for 500,000 premature deaths on the continent each year. Around the world, nearly 2,000 children under the age of five die of air pollution every single day. Between 2000 and 2015, seventy-four people in Britain were killed by domestic cows, making it the country's most dangerous large animal; of those deaths, fifty-six were of farm workers while the remaining eighteen were of people simply out for a walk in the countryside. And while only one person has lost their life to a bear attack in Greece since we arrived in the year 2000, over 27,000 people have been killed in car accidents on the country's roads in that same period.

This isn't to diminish in any way the horrific deaths and unthinkable grief that *do* sometimes result from contact with apex predators but simply to show that, in Europe at least, those risks are dwarfed by what should be far greater collective concerns.

The other essential aspect of the conversation about apex animals is considering our own role in cultivating the conditions for co-existence. Some years ago, two Italian tourists saw a pair of bear cubs in a field in Prespa. Deciding they wanted to get close enough to photograph them, the men crossed the field and approached the animals on foot. And then, just as surely as in any of those horror films in which you know something awful is about to happen because of a shadowy movement at the edge of the screen, the cubs' mother emerged from behind the stand of brambles where she'd been feeding. Luckily, the men escaped with their lives, but not before being chased by the understandably defensive mother and suffering slashes to their backs.

The more distant we become from the living world as a result of declining biodiversity, increased urbanisation and cultural and educational failures to foreground ecological connection, the easier it is to see nature as merely pleasant and inanimate scenery. In doing so, we end up placing wildlife on a pedestal of expectancy, so that our acceptance and tolerance of wild creatures becomes inevitably hinged to their behaviour as we imagine or wish it ideally to be. For apex predators, this romanticisation can be as deadly as demonisation. After the incident in the field with the Italians, several people in Prespa called for the killing of the bear, even questioning the presence of the species here altogether. 'Look at what they're doing to tourists,' said one local politician, as though the fault lay with the bear and not the visitors. Not only did the men recklessly risk their own lives for the sake of a photograph but they selfishly endangered the bears' lives as well.

*

On the advice of Vassilis, we'd built a sturdy gate for the fields in our second year of farming. Together with him we sledge-hammered iron posts deep into the ground. Then we hinged to one of them a large wooden frame we'd overlaid with metal fencing and locked it to the other post with a thick chain and padlock. One morning, Julia and I arrived for a day of work to discover the gate almost entirely flattened. The metal fencing was badly warped and the wooden frame splintered and smashed. The iron posts were bent like cheap plastic straws.

'I don't believe it,' said Julia as we pulled up at the gate.

'Shit,' I said, hopping out of the pick-up. 'Someone must have rammed it with a truck.' We stood and stared in disbelief at our ruined gate until one of us spotted something snagged on the metal fencing. We plucked the bear fur free and held the tufts in our hands, looking once more at those folded iron posts.

Co-existence isn't simply an ethical or ecological arrangement. It's also a set of choices we make within a practical framework. For us, that meant keeping a route open to bears through our fields because we quickly understood that it was a path long used by them while out foraging. Our gate had raised a border where there had never been one before. And seeing the damage done to it that morning reminded us of the respect these animals need to be accorded to live alongside them successfully. There are numerous ways of helping ensure safety in a place shared with large preda-tors: letting them know you're around by occasionally talking or making a noise while out walking; keeping your distance if you see an animal; learning how best to respond during a close encounter; making settlements unappealing by keeping food waste out of their reach. But these practices aren't enough on their own to reach a state of equilibrium when it comes to communities dependent on livestock and other animals for their economic well-being.

'We are part of nature too,' said Milica Ivovic when I asked her about the issue of co-existence in Greece, 'so you can't not consider the needs of people.' A wildlife biologist, Milica was to be responsible for restoring the skeleton of the Prespa bear that we'd exhumed in 2020. Originally from Serbia, Milica now lives in Crete, where she works for the Natural History Museum in Heraklion. When we spoke by phone on a December afternoon she was high on a Cretan mountain recording birds around a wind farm and we immediately developed a rapport over the common-ality of our monitoring experiences.

'You can't just come up to Prespa from Athens,' she contin-ued, 'and talk to Giorgos who has 300 animals and tell him to co-exist after a bear comes down the mountain and kills five of those animals. Because that same Giorgos is raising two or three kids and this is his income. If we decide that we are going to have predators and we have signed all the laws and the legislation that obliges us to do so, then we have to have the financial instruments to uphold this, and this is usually done through compensation to the farmers for animals lost. But this system doesn't work in Greece – and it's tragic.'

Greece's agricultural compensation mechanism has been criti-cised by both conservationists and farmers as being too strict in the burden of proof demanded from livestock owners (it can insist on the recovery of the heads of predated animals as evidence, an incredibly hard thing to do if a carcass has been dragged away), for being too slow in responding to incidents on the ground when preserving the signs of an attack is logistically difficult and for not paying out when the loss pertains to a single sheep or goat. Unless a compensation system functions well, and above all else is trusted to act quickly, fairly and equitably, we might see farmers return to the tools of persecution that eradicated large carnivores from most parts of Europe in the past. As their numbers rise across the con-tinent again as a result of legislative protection, improved forest cover, rural depopulation and a shift in public opinion towards safeguarding endangered species, social division around the issue is becoming increasingly heated. 'Working with tourists, I see some who think that if the farmers here disappeared, the wolves could live, and that we, the people from the villages, are superfluous,' said Sofía González Berdasco, a shepherd and tourist guide, in a recent article about what it's like living with wolves in Spain. 'And then I listen to many farmers who say that all the wolves should be killed, and it will be better for us.'

When it comes to farming communities, compensation is just one approach to the sensitive matter of co-existence. A more powerful and effective tool is a much older one – and that's traditional knowledge. Frequently lost alongside localised animal extinctions are the cultural memories and practical skills of living with wild species, so that whole regions of the continent no longer employ the traditional shepherding measures that can greatly minimise conflict between farmers and apex predators. It's like a language falling out of use – or the regent honeyeater forgetting its own songs – until we no longer know what the words mean.

According to a study carried out in northwestern Greece by wolf researcher Maria Petridou, traditional practices such as increased surveillance by shepherds, an adequate number of sheepdogs and strict confinement of a herd at night dramatically reduces wolf predation on free-ranging sheep, goats and cattle. Critical, too, is the use of native breeds as guardian animals, varieties that became far less common on the continent as large carnivore populations declined. Here in Greece, that animal is the Greek shepherd dog. Also known as the Poimenikos, it's specifically adapted to the harsh mountain conditions of the Greek mainland, retaining a generational sensitivity to the presence of predators. As Plato wrote of dogs similar in form and function in the uplands of Epirus in 800 BC, it's possible that the Poimenikos has been protecting flocks here since ancient times. Now, all these years later, it's vital that the cultural skills and tools of shepherding gained through generations of experience be restored with the financial support of European agricultural programmes wherever they've been lost, while being reaffirmed in those places where they still exist but are only partially maintained.

It's not just the old ways that can be utilised to resolve modern conflicts either, but also emerging ideas and technologies. Electric fences are now common around beehives in bear country, while Kallisto, a Greek NGO specialising in the protection of bears and wolves through research, awareness-raising and the deployment of a rapid response unit in conflict situations, is currently trialling rubbish bins equipped with pepper spray to be placed on the outskirts of villages in Greece, Albania and North Macedonia to deter brown bears from getting too close to settlements. By bringing together old and new approaches, and in seeking common ground between farmers and conservationists in ways that respect the aims and concerns of both, it's eminently possible that a balance can be reached to make co-existence with large carnivores a practical reality.

'I don't see that one side is more right than the other,' concluded Sofía González Berdasco. 'Neither side can lose everything, and the other side gain everything.'

In 2023, three years after we'd unearthed the bones of the poisoned bear from the rocky hillside and well over eleven since the animal had died, its skeleton was reassembled by Milica in the village of Psaradhes. I met Yannis on a cold December morning and together we entered the old schoolhouse being slowly restored by the university as an artistic and educational space. The skeleton was positioned on a table in a ground-floor room and supported by two metal stands, one for its body and another for its skull. Pale winter light fell over it from the windows. Depending on the angle I approached it from, the skeleton looked either enormous or oddly small, and it struck me that our perspective on a bear's proportions is entirely dependent on whether it's coming towards you or moving away. I then stood back and tried to absorb its entire form. To see it there, so carefully pieced together from the gathered fragments we'd unearthed in the blazing heat and returned to a recognisable being once more, opened my heart in an instant. It was wondrous, reflective and moving.

'The idea,' said Yannis, 'is that you'll enter what was a school and you'll see the skeleton and the photos and begin to understand the bear's story. And its story, I hope, will create a greater awareness of living alongside such creatures.'

The bear's head was tilted at an angle that suggested inquisitiveness and curiosity, turned towards something in the landscape that had gained its attention. Its front right paw was lifted off the table, creating the impression of moving through a landscape. Its powerful legs were so widely spaced that they formed an arch with its ribcage, while its thick, sharp claws left me as bewildered as ever as to how a bear can use them to gather the smallest of wild strawberries in a meadow. Despite being structure rather than life – a life that had been in its prime, as the bear was around seven or eight years old when it was killed – the skeleton gave off a sense of fullness and depth. Something beyond merely bone. And it had taken on the expressive reddish tint of the soil from the iron oxides and leaf tannins where it fell.

'I was trying to solve the technical aspects of the reconstruction but I wanted to do the bear justice too,' said Milica, adding that it had taken her eight full days to reassemble the skeleton. 'I wanted to show the beauty of this animal. And I wanted to show the ingenuity of evolution. At the same time, though, it's a big predator. Like any other conservation issue, it has many facets.'

An adult brown bear has 206 bones in its body, the exact same number as an adult human. Of those bones, we'd ended up finding somewhere in the region of 170 of them in our excavations, which meant that Milica had to work with absence as well as presence when assembling them.

'You see that one of the front feet is complete and then you look at the back one and there are no bones there, so there's this idea of the disappearing, the vanishing. As this was meant as a memorial, and wanting to accent the fact that the brown bear is an endangered species, it didn't feel right to artificially reconstruct the missing bones, so I left those spaces empty.'

From the head of the table, I peered into the deep eye sockets, the reciprocity of perception no longer a possibility. The fact that humans and bears have the same number of bones was a connective thread between us, the kinship of sharing a basic mammalian template, but being so near to the underlying form of this animal highlighted for me the far more complex issue of difference and the terrible reason it was there in the first place. I remembered a line in James Bridle's *Ways of Being* that had stayed with me since reading it earlier in the year: 'Where we start to move forward is when we learn to ask questions which are less concerned with "Are you like us?", and more interested in "What is it like to be you?"'

What were your seven or eight years like here? Crossing borders that aren't borders but just another step forward. Tracing paths through the steep beeches and rolling oaks, winding from the valley behind our house where you picked up the smoke of village chimneys on the wind and then over the isthmus at night to the snow-capped mountains on the other side of the basin. Was it you whose prints I followed on the sandy shore that morning, suddenly halting and turning to face the lake, as though glimpsing something out there on the dark water – perhaps a light, a boat, a bird? How did you get through those dry autumns of lean fruit and thankless searching; and what raw hunger brought you near in winters of snow and wind and ice? How close the crack of gunshots and the fear in the hills on hunting days? What of the lush burst of everything in spring – did you

remember which meadows brightened best with berries and under which
trees fungi first crowned? And what did you know of those last moments?
The burst belly of the cow you found and fed from after descending at
night down the path, the stumbling forward dizzy and shifting everything
blurring and hurting, falling into darkness towards the lake so near.

'It's an exploration of co-existence,' said Yannis of the memorial,
as I took a few final photos of what had once been a bear, 'in
the sense of how we respond to what is other. What is the other?
Because it's not just about bears and local residents. This otherness
is about other people as well, other nationalities, other religions,
other, other, other, other. We can't just sit with this one bear as
though it's the end, because there will be a next bear that's killed,
there will be another person who's shot, there will be another "I
can't breathe". All of these things are connected. Co-existence
is connected; power and domination disconnect us. Whenever
I now see the restored skeleton I also go to the place where the
bear died to pay my respects and to make that connection. It
has become a part of me, this bear. And even though I know
something terrible happened there, terrible things can sometimes
initiate better things.'

I said goodbye to Yannis, letting him get back to the class of
students who were with him in Prespa that weekend. I hadn't
given any thought to returning to the place where the bear had
died until he'd mentioned it, but once he had it felt like the most
natural thing in the world to do. Snow was falling over the hills
and waters as I walked the road around the bay, the winter lake
like a sheet of steel ahead of me. I left the road and found the narrow path the bear had been on that night when poison coursed
through its body. Over a decade later, I walked in its last steps.

Until we moved to Prespa, I'd never known what it meant to
share space with large carnivores. While I'd grown up in Ontario
– where such animals are far from uncommon – my experience

there had been typically suburban when young and thoroughly urban as an adult while at university in Ottawa. It wasn't until I'd completed my studies and moved to England in my mid-twenties that I developed an interest in exploring landscapes beyond the reach of towns and cities, by which time I was living in a country where apex species no longer existed. But here, in this border-land region where brown bears and wolves are keystone citizens of these shared terrains, benefiting the ecological structure of the whole basin, to walk the old fields and thickets of our valley, or to rise through the silver pillars of beeches saddling the mountains around the village, is to engage with an extraordinary and essential energy in the landscape. Something untouchable but perceptively there: transformative, resonant and enlarging. These forests and shores, these mountains and meadows – they're all charged and changed in generative ways by the presence of apex mammals. Simply put, we live alongside them, and they alongside us. In being here, part of a wider community connected to each other through the sharing of this small corner of the world, bears and wolves fundamentally help shape the essence of the basin. Without them, Prespa wouldn't be the same place that I love today. And I now struggle to imagine living in a landscape where they didn't exist.

I stopped on the path. Weather had reclaimed our excavations, so all that remained of where we'd dug was a shallow dip in the soil and a rim of stones from the weighted tarp. Waves of cold were settling over the hills and a raven sculled high overhead. Mistle thrushes clattered from the junipers as I knelt down and pressed my hand against the red soil, the snow falling and fading on my fingers.

9

The Wild Nearby

It was late summer and the sun was sliding from the sky. A kestrel glided over the rippled water and from the small municipal park rose children's laughter and the barking of dogs. Julia and I were nursing beers on a hotel balcony overlooking Lake Pamvotis in the city of Ioannina. Just a few hours south of Prespa, Ioannina is built hard against the shore. The Byzantine walls, medieval fortress and Ottoman-era mosques of its old town fill the headland where Ali Pasha notoriously ruled until he revolted against the sultan in Istanbul and was killed in 1822. The air was still cloying with heat as people took to the evening streets and the lake sparkled in silver and blue. Above the water, another kestrel swept through the sunset sky.

On the road from Prespa that morning, I'd quizzed Julia on Greek politics, geography, literature, systems of governance and historical events, including the dates of the Greek War of Independence, which began a year before Ali Pasha's death on the island in the lake that we looked out over from the balcony. Cross-checking her replies with the answers at the back of the citizenship book, I rallied her on by saying *yes!* just a little bit louder each time she was right. In the immediate aftermath of the Brexit referendum in 2016, no one knew precisely what our future status in Greece would be, as we – along with more than a million other British citizens spread across the continent – had been beneficiaries of the European Union's freedom-of-movement principle when we first moved here. That fundamental idea, the freedom to move between member states easily and legally without having to be wealthy or well connected – whether to live, to work, to love or to study – is why we'd decided to stay in Europe in the first place, discarding other potential destinations largely because of the possibilities nearby. But that all ended with the referendum – a result that was to remove from British citizens, and from young people in particular, precisely the opportunity that Julia and I had had when we moved here with little idea of what we would do next. Although our fears and anxieties about having to leave Greece were eventually eased when bilateral residency agreements were made by individual EU states with the British government, it became clear that we would lose our right to free movement. Which is why I'd been peppering Julia with questions on our journey to Ioannina that morning. 'I'm not giving up my EU rights that easily,' she'd suddenly said a couple of years after the referendum. 'I've decided to apply to become a Greek citizen.'

Another kestrel sailed over the lake, immediately followed by two more. Then a third flashed by close behind. The small and elegant raptors appeared to be using the same aerial route across the water, tracing a line that roughly cut from the mountains to the southeast of the lake towards Ioannina on the northwestern shore. Our hotel was just south of the centre, and from where we sat it looked as though they were headed straight for the historic headland. After a further four or five birds had coasted by, I fetched my binoculars from the room.

'Could they be lesser kestrels and not common kestrels?' asked Julia, looking up from a last bout of revision about Ancient Greek history before her citizenship test the following morning.

'That's what I'm wondering too,' I said, pressing the binoculars against my eyes. Although lesser kestrels are slightly smaller and more delicate than common kestrels, physical differences between the species can be difficult to distinguish at a distance. But there's a distinctive behavioural note that helps separate their identities. While common kestrels are usually solitary birds outside the pair bond and raising of chicks, lesser kestrels are colonial creatures; they pull together into communities for the breeding season, when they frequently nest on buildings in urban landscapes, and migrate in flocks between southern Europe and sub-Saharan Africa. By now, a river of birds was beginning to thicken over the water, wavering in the breeze that had suddenly picked up as the sun slipped away. With the shift in winds, birds were being pushed towards the shore, updraughting near our balcony and floating close, where we could clearly make out the bluish–grey wing panels of male lesser kestrels as they turned into the light and pressed onwards along the coast.

I pulled out my phone and messaged my friend Dimitris Vavylis, an excellent ornithologist who is often my first port of call when I have bird queries about parts of Greece that are unfamiliar to me.

We're in Ioannina and watching loads of lesser kestrels flying across the lake. Do you know if there is a roost nearby?

Yes! There is a large pre-migratory roost in the platanus [plane] *trees by the lake shore beneath the castle! Ioannina only has about thirty breeding pairs but the roost holds about 2,000 birds.*

I excitedly read the text out to Julia, who'd by then given up on ancient history to watch the lesser kestrels flow over the lake in waves. My phone pinged again and I saw that Dimitris had sent two more messages, each including a map marked by a red pin.

This is the best viewpoint to see the whole beauty of the roost, said the first, its square of attached map showing the old town and castle walls on the headland. *And from this point*, read the second, *you can have coffee and see them roosting.*

When it comes to the wild nearby, we don't always know what might be there alongside us. What *could* be there alongside us. At the back of the house, our vegetable plot slopes to a narrow stream, one of the numerous small veins that make up the circulatory system of the watershed. Marsh marigolds flood it in spring and sparrowhawks bathe in its cold pools, while its damp banks rise high into a thicket of nettles beside the garden. I try to scythe these nettles back at the beginning of June to keep their seeds from spreading, but in the first year of the pandemic, when I seemed to be late for everything despite having more free time than ever because of cancelled plans, it was almost July before I lifted my scythe from the wall in the shed.

I ran a whetstone over the blade that had been fitted and hammered into shape by Germanos two decades earlier. Working at a table outside the distillery, he'd spent a couple of hours making sure the scythe cut like a carving knife, telling me how he would sometimes spend a whole day searching for just the right piece of wood for the handle before you could buy them in shops as easily as I had mine. Each time I use the scythe I remember Germanos fondly: the way he showed me how to bend into the sweep of the blade; how to move the whetstone at an angle to keep the edge just right. And after all these years, it still cuts as if new.

Slipping the whetstone in my pocket, I swung the blade through the nettles at their base, levelling them into windrows of fallen stems that smoked with loosening seed. As I moved from left to right, I spotted some unusual dark patches on the next stand of plants. I put the scythe down to look more closely at what I could now see were caterpillars gathered in small clumps. They were jet black and stippled with fine white dots, like a clear sky at night. With the handle of the scythe, I spread open the forest of nettles to find dozens of other assemblies inside, munching through the freshest leaves. I roughly counted over a hundred individuals and suddenly became aware of how I'd been getting my timing wrong with the scything in previous years, removing a shelter for nearby wild species just when it was most needed. I went inside and pulled from a shelf our field guide to insects and quickly found the right page, where the side-by-side illustrations made clear the transformation to come. The caterpillars, which had emerged from eggs laid on the nettles I would normally have cut down by now, would soon become peacock butterflies and a blaze of stunning colour.

After Julia made the decision to become a Greek citizen, we both began thinking about the broader notion of being part of a place. For her, the original impetus to secure her EU rights had widened out into a reflection of her sense of belonging. It became more about a commitment to the country itself, in that citizenship confers responsibilities as well as rights. 'Belonging isn't passive but active,' she'd said one evening. 'It's as much about what you give to a place and community as it is about what you gain from it.' She then reminded me of when we'd just moved into the house by the square. Needing firewood for the winter, Vassilis had recommended that we do something to help the village as a way of affirming that circle of exchange. On his advice, we walked the entire route taken by the local wood lorries and tractors down from the mountains to the village, kicking every last stone off the rough dirt road so that they didn't cause problems for the vehicles' tyres, a walk that must have been 10 kilometres at least and which garnered us plenty of backslaps and beers in the bar that night, but which also made us feel part of something so much bigger than simply buying wood to keep warm in winter.

While Julia spent her evenings pushing deeper into her Greek studies, I began remembering the welcome we'd received in Prespa. In the months after the taxi driver dropped us in the

village square with our rucksacks, we were met with a remarkable generosity and spirit of kindness. Not by everyone, naturally.
There were some who gave us hard, suspicious stares and those
who had no interest or inclination to speak with us. And, as laugh-
ingly related to us by Vassilis after conversations in Prespa's cafés,
there were a few who, finding it difficult to accept that anyone
without an ulterior motive would wish to come here, believed
we were British spies, which would suggest a staggering decline
in the skill set needed for contemporary espionage if true. But by
and large – and far beyond any expectations we held when setting
out from London – we encountered gracious hospitality, friendly
curiosity (albeit often puzzled) and a sincere desire to help us make
this place our home. Fast forward a few years and I was in our village shop one morning buying some groceries and speaking to the
owner in Greek when a tourist from Athens stepped inside. After
briefly listening to our conversation, the visitor then interrupted
us, asking the owner if I was a foreigner. I was about to point out
that I was standing right there if he wanted to ask me something,
but I never got the chance. 'Yes, he's a foreigner,' said Nikos, the
owner of the shop, 'but he's our foreigner.'

I'm a big proponent of paying it forward, an idea also known as
serial reciprocity. At its simplest, it revolves around the recipient
of a good deed repaying the kindness onwards to others rather
than back to the original benefactor, so that a sequence of positive exchange is created between people. We've consciously tried
doing this when visitors turn up in Prespa, offering them help after
our own warm experience on arrival, but it occurred to me after
the appearance of the peacock butterfly caterpillars that I hadn't
been as welcoming a neighbour as I could be to the more-than-
human world. And so I began learning to let our grasses grow
long. And together with the grasses, the wild geraniums, plantago

and potentilla that rise alongside them in connected community. I began learning to let the sun-spill of spring dandelions radiate around the house. I began learning to let the great mulleins spire towards the sky in a burst of yellow buttons. I began learning, ultimately, to let the garden be a greater shelter.

I say learning because I'm born of a culture that has typically shunned such neighbourly intent. As a teenager in the suburbs of southern Ontario, my newspaper route each morning took me past a sequence of nearly identical lawns kept short and ordered by frequent mowing and even more frequent watering, fertilising and weeding. I was so used to the elevation of the lawn to a symbol of industrious perfection that those suburban swards seemed entirely natural to me; not in the sense that they were expressions of the natural world, which was a province of completely different and enlarging possibility that my brother and I keenly explored in our forays with friends down the tangled banks of streams and still undeveloped fields, but rather that they were the norm, the expected, the goal. The accepted aesthetic consensus. It wasn't until years later that I began to see the wild nearby differently. Influenced by cultural shifts that would have seemed so alien and 'unnatural' to that teenager delivering papers in the 1980s – from campaigns celebrating native plants and 'No-Mow May' to the more activist affirmations of the *sauvages de ma rue* (wild things of my street) movement, in which rebel botanists encourage nature connection by chalking the names of self-willed plants that might typically be dismissed as weeds on the residential pavements where they grow – a broader idea of community began to take shape. It wasn't just about bears and wolves, I realised, but about the presence of things far smaller and more familiar to us all. In time, I began to connect beauty not so much with a particular visual appearance but with a place's ability to sustain life.

Beyond thinking about a limited set of practicalities such as open paths and somewhere for our table and chairs, or a spot where the laundry can hang clear of vegetation (as well as cutting back the longest growth by midsummer to abide by Greece's new fire-protection regulations), I've discovered there's room in the garden for exuberance and movement. There's space for wilder patches and edges; for the teeming and tangled. There's shelter, ultimately, for more than just us. And ever since we consciously began encouraging wildlife around the house, the chorus songs of field crickets swell through the night and the coiled copper bracelets of young slow-worms appear more frequently in the longer grasses. Goldfinches tease seeds free from the pale, swaying clocks of dandelions. The extraordinary *Carabus gigas*, Europe's largest ground beetle, bosses the wilder edges in search of the snails it preys on. Moving in and making a home alongside us are metallic green mint beetles, cream-spotted tiger moths and drifts of butterflies. Lady's bedstraw, once used as stuffing in medieval mattresses, and St John's wort, long utilised as a remedy for depression, have naturally risen in different parts of the garden, reminding me of the car mechanic's father as he showed us the beneficial plants around the garage, where the living world was still there, just waiting. Community needn't always be built, but sometimes just let be.

One of the last times I saw Vassilis before he left to live in another part of the country, he was in a tree. We'd sadly drifted apart over the years as he took new arrivals under his wing after a volunteer programme drew young people from around Europe to Prespa and our network of friends expanded as our Greek improved and our fieldwork connected us to other residents. I still don't quite understand how it happened, but it did. We had learned so much from him, *shared* so much with him. He taught us that the only sure way over the mountains in a blizzard when you have to get to the city on the other side is to catch a lift with the snowplough, sweetening the deal by gifting the driver a large bottle of *tsipouro* from Germanos's distillery. Or that if your barrel of wine in the garden shed isn't fermenting because of the autumn cold, the only way to get it going again is to haul a wood stove in beside it and stay up all night feeding it logs while making sure the shed doesn't go up in flames. Or all the advice and practical skills of his that went into building the shed from scratch in the first place. There is still a huge amount of generosity to be paid forward. Vassilis's friendship, support and help were utterly invaluable; in those earliest of days, he was our community in Prespa.

I'd been woken at dawn by a chainsaw. Instantly knowing what the sound meant, I threw on some clothes and dashed out the door of the house by the square. As I did, I saw Vassilis running up the road. In a single, unbroken motion, he then jumped from the cement embankment of the river and clambered up one of the willow trees between our garden and the post office. An angry outburst erupted from the riverbed as Vassilis shimmied upwards. At the foot of the tree, the then president of our village, who had been threatening for weeks to cut down all the river willows even though he had no legal right to, pressed his chainsaw against the trunk that Vassilis was hugging higher up. I pleaded with him to stop as Vassilis yelled down at him from above. Others began joining us on the banks, including the police. But not soon enough to save the three trees brought down before any of us were even properly awake.

It wasn't long before the whole village was in the square, divided into two roughly equal camps: those who wanted to keep the trees and those who wanted rid of them. Some of those arguing against took a practical position, saying their presence could cause a flood in the village, even though the extensive root systems of the trees were actually helping mitigate flooding through slowing and absorbing any stormwater. Others, however, adopted the aesthetic perspective, claiming that self-seeded wild trees didn't

belong in a village setting as they detracted from its beauty. The
man who'd cut three of them down even went as far as to say
that if we wanted to make the village more attractive to tourists
it would be best to grub up the trees entirely, concrete the stream
bed to match the sides of the channel, embed lights to illuminate
the water and introduce ducks with clipped wings for the viewing
pleasure of visitors.

Eventually, Prespa's then mayor was called to adjudicate.
People parted in the square when his vehicle arrived, the *fors* and
the *againsts* to either side as spokespeople for each quickly stated
their case. The mayor then looked up at the long line of river
willows that we'd lived beside for years, where from the garden
we'd watch long-tailed tits, the tiny acrobats of the avian world,
twirl among the leaves and goldcrests crown their tops, and raised
his arm in their direction. 'Those,' he said, with a dismissive nod
of his head, 'they're nothing.'

It was only after a long and rancorous meeting in a village
bar that some common ground was eventually found between
the two sides, when a group of us in the *for* camp volunteered to
clean the river of fallen branches and to trim the trees to make
them look tidier.

I can't say exactly why Vassilis jumped in the tree, other than
he'd always been extremely protective of Prespa's nature, but I do
understand the sense of attachment he may have felt for those willows. In the mid-1990s, before I met Julia, I spent a couple of years
living in London after coming over from Canada, where I worked
variously as a bartender in Camden Town, a gardener in the Hyde
Park greenhouses and as a painter and decorator in various parts
of the city. I can still vividly recall the crushing, late-afternoon
commute on the underground, physically drained and spattered
with either beer suds, soil, plaster or paint. I'd arrive back at my

rented room with little hunger for anything but the pub. As I had neither a car nor enough money to explore the countryside easily, two things helped ease the weariness of work come the weekend. I would call them openings – the kind of clearings that exist not only in the built environment but which can be created internally too through contact with green and blue spaces. The first of them was Camley Street Nature Reserve, a small oasis of amber ponds and trees set in the then seedy surrounds of King's Cross railway station, where dragonflies glittered in sunlight beneath an awning of bright leaves. The second was a long ribbon of greenery that had burgeoned to each side of a disused railway line near Finsbury Park, where wildflowers, birds and people converged in secluded profusion. I don't recall ever seeing anything unusual or rare in either of those places; what made them important was the sense that they could heal over me, like sap hardening across the wound in a tree. Both were refuges in which I could let the working week fall away, but, more crucially, also find some essential space and the kind of compressed animate quiet that is common to the natural world but far less so to predominantly human landscapes. Those green clearings in the urban fabric were where I came to ease my tiredness and anxiety, and to try to work through the depression that I lived with for a period at the time. While the wild wasn't enough on its own to reach a settled equilibrium, it made it possible for me to see beyond; to lean into a world where other forms of life made me acutely aware of something other than myself. If either of those places had been threatened by chainsaws, I would most likely have ended up in a tree as well.

As countless studies have now confirmed and the pandemic dramatically showed, when nearby green and blue spaces became literal lifelines for many during lockdown, we know that such places are good for us. Particularly in urban areas where socio-economic factors are frequent obstacles to equal access to the wider countryside. But what are rightfully points of connection, beauty and replenishment for people are also critical lifelines for the more-than-human world; especially at a time when the Sixth Extinction is well under way. Across the planet, as many as 2 million wild species are currently believed to be at risk of disappearing. In Europe alone, according to a comprehensive study in 2023 led by lead researcher Axel Hochkirch from the Musée National d'Histoire Naturelle in Luxembourg, a fifth of the continent's wild organisms are being pushed towards a devastating and unnatural end by human pressures, including 27 per cent of all plants, 24 per cent of invertebrates and 18 per cent of vertebrates. As Anne Larigauderie, executive secretary of IPBES, the UN's Intergovernmental Science-Policy Platform on Biodiversity and Ecosystem Services, said of the alarming results, 'We are losing biodiversity and nature's contributions to people at rates never before seen in human history.'

But what *is* biodiversity? We've already seen what happens to the living world through the erasure of languages, when vital lifeways and perspectives forged in close relationship with the more-than-human world are forever lost, but what if the languages we use lack the language we need to strengthen our relationship with that living world? What if our words fail to convey its depth, complexity and vitality? Because biodiversity – which is simply a shortened form of biological diversity – is an incredibly distancing term for something so extraordinary, enlarging and essential. Its strange muteness in English risks leaving people unaware of its deeper and more animate meaning unless they're already attuned to it for other reasons.

Biodiversity, then, is that river of lesser kestrels crossing the evening water towards the old town of Ioannina. It's the kingfisher burning a bright-blue line along the shore of the lake. It's oak leaves unfolding in your urban park with the lengthening light of spring. It's the bear in the meadow and the skylarks above it. It's a flotilla of pelicans feeding at dawn on a vast shoal of bleak. It's the slow-worms and ground beetles and field crickets in the garden. It's the teaspoon of soil beneath your feet that can hold up to 10 billion microorganisms absolutely essential to life on the planet. But that's just the very beginning, of course, because biodiversity is the sum of *all* life and forms of life on Earth. Try remembering every wild species you've ever even fleetingly encountered – the birds, the trees, the beetles and bees – and then consider the entire sphere we inhabit and all its countless places populated by more organisms than you could possibly imagine. Everywhere threaded with life. All the seas, forests, swamps and rivers; all the meadows, mountains, estuaries and steppes. The earth beneath and the sky above. All the villages, towns and cities, too. And even then, even if it were somehow possible to grasp the totality of that biological abundance and variety, that's not really biodiversity either, because biodiversity takes its fundamental energy from the infinite interactions between all of those wild lives in relationship with each other, tangled together within supporting webs and networks and communities and ecosystems. It's not some static pattern grid-mapped onto the earth but the very stuff of life itself. All evolving and in motion and helping shape the world we share. Biodiversity, ultimately, is what makes our planet tick. And, as we all know, it's never a good thing when a clock or a watch or a heart stops ticking.

On a July evening, in the enclosing hold of what would be wrenlight if it were winter, a mass of small magpie moths swirl around the bank of nettles where the peacock butterfly caterpillars had emerged a month earlier. Dozens in a dance at dusk, a spray of black dots on white wings, their yellow heads as though they've been dusted in pollen. A whirling blur as they seek nettle leaves to entrust a new generation of eggs and future moths to. With one species having left, another is taking its place – their lifelines spooling around the same shelter.

Our time monitoring birds in the karst country left a lasting mark on us. There fell a light on that mountain plateau at the southern end of Lesser Prespa Lake that I'd never seen before, as though it were the remembered radiance of the sea that preceded the lifted limestone millions of years ago. Up there, so much closer to the sky, silence never suggested absence but merely the mystery of things we couldn't fully perceive. We followed the passage of a shepherd as he rose and fell with the swells in the land through the music of the flute he'd made by punching holes in a metal pipe. And while measuring the impact on avian life from a large set of wind turbines proposed for the area, we encountered reminders of the Civil War everywhere. On a late August morning, I met a man called Ritsos in a place where I'd never seen anyone before.

'What are you doing here?' I'd asked him, having abandoned my telescope and other gear to run down the slope as fast as I could in the hope of speaking to him before he left.

'I was born here,' he replied, pointing to a small heap of stones beside him. 'This is all that remains of the house that we left when I was five years old in 1948 during the Civil War. Make sure you tell them there are people up here as well as birds.'

And sharing the karst country with the shepherd, the light and the exile – together with the silence that wasn't really silence because so many stories were written into it – was a staggering abundance of wildlife. Butterflies pooled around patches of damp earth; snake eagles spiralled high on the hot winds; wheatears and rock nuthatches stood sentinel on stones; and storms of wildflowers flooded the summer hills in brilliance. The whole radiant place – either lived in or still longed for – trembled with a rare and remarkable energy. And we quickly came to see that the karst country was one of the most unique, sensitive and valuable parts of the entire basin.

One day, a director with the company behind the wind-park proposal came to see how we carried out our observations. While his colleague stayed behind with Julia to gain insight into her work at a static vantage point, the director followed me across stony grassland ridges as I conducted transects, recording the number of seen or heard birds within range of the proposed turbine envelope. Clearly interested, he asked plenty of pertinent questions as I led him across that luminous landscape and pointed out the blue rock thrushes, black redstarts, woodlarks and hoopoes that I was noting on the data sheet. The two of us got on extremely well, and it was obvious from our conversation that he was hopeful of finding ways to mitigate bird impacts for large species if shifting the position of a turbine would help minimise the risk. Keen to impress on me his environmental credentials, he proudly told me that his company would never clear-cut forests in order to install turbines as some energy companies in Greece were doing. He then swept his arm across the vast landscape that I'd come to love deeply and fiercely, reminding me of the way our former mayor had pointed at the willow trees that Vassilis had climbed into, and then said, 'At least here there's nothing at all. Just a bunch of rocks.'

The idea that there's nothing there, of course, isn't a new one. Sometimes it just seems like nothing because we don't know what might be there alongside us. What *could* be there alongside us. Sometimes it feels like nothing because we simply can't see it, even when it's right there in front of our eyes, like the river corridor and its otters, wildcats and water rails that we'd been blind to for nearly a decade. Sometimes it's made to seem like nothing because we've devalued the living world so efficiently against the profits extracted from it. And sometimes we think of it as nothing because to acknowledge it as something might force us to rethink our place in the world.

While the wildfires in the Dadia forest and the Evros region were incinerating one of the country's most important biodiversity hotspots in the summer of 2023, obliterating not only a significant proportion of that unique home for wild species but also the human livelihoods such as bee-keeping, shepherding and logging that relied on it, Greece's prime minister, Kyriakos Mitsotakis, travelled to Thessaloniki, where he spoke to a gathering of business leaders. At the meeting, he was reported as saying the following: 'Αν κάτι αντισταθμίζει το σκοτεινό κλίμα που υπάρχει στην κοινωνία λόγω των καταστροφικών φωτιών του Έβρου αυτό είναι η πολύ καλή απόδοση της οικονομίας μας η οποία αναπτύσσεται γρήγορα, η καλή απόδοση του τουρισμού, οι εξαγωγές και οι σημαντικές επενδύσεις που δρομολογούνται.' ('If something compensates for the dark climate that exists in society due to the devastating fires of the Evros, it is the very good performance of our economy which is growing rapidly, the good performance of tourism, exports and the important investments that are under way.')

The Greek prime minister is hardly an exception when it comes to politicians focusing on the economy when so much else that is essential to human well-being is going up in flames. But given the horrific destruction experienced in Greece and elsewhere that summer, a statement as unvarnished as this was a stark reminder of the ideological disconnect that so often dominates our thinking about the living world within a system that categorises planetary health as a subset of economic health rather than the other way around. Writing in *The New Yorker* a year before the forests of Dadia turned to ash, Sarah Miller remarked that even 'as we watch economic growth literally killing us, it is what we talk about before we talk about anything else – we are told, over and over, that we must run to it for help.'

Fortunately, this creed is beginning to be challenged by some economists, including James Meadway, who was once an economic advisor to the UK shadow chancellor and who recently said that 'we cannot simply pretend that . . . the entire ecological crisis is a separate and distinct thing from what's happening in the economy'. And if it's the economy we wish to talk about, we would do well to remember the origins of the word, because 'economy' shares a root with the word 'ecology'. That ancient Greek root, *oikos*, means 'house'. What economy refers to, then, in its original sense, is *the act of looking after one's house*, which is why it's entirely natural for ecology to share not only a linguistic affinity with it but also a wider concern for the living shelter of the world. Because there's no genuinely sustainable economy without flourishing forests, clean water and healthy soils and seas; there's no reliable and meaningful economy without thriving biodiversity. To stay true to the wisdom of its ancient roots, economy must entail looking after our larger home because this extraordinary sphere we find ourselves spinning through space on has always revolved around the relationships between all things.

Which is why the approach that Greece has taken to the climate crisis – a nation that's better placed than many to be sensitive to such ecological linkages, not only as a result of that ancestral linguistic connection but because of the extraordinary biodiversity and high number of endemic species it's been blessed by – has been so dismaying until now. While the state's decarbonisation targets are admirable, especially in light of its reliance on lignite to power its energy sector, the dirtiest coal in existence and the probable cause of increased cancer rates in the regions where it's mined and burned, the path it has chosen towards carbon neutrality is proving extremely costly in other ways. While many northern European countries have concentrated wind-energy infrastructure in lowland sites with an already significant degree of anthropogenic modification, Greece has established an investor-friendly atmosphere by opening up public land in mountainous zones with often high ecological value for nearly all of its numerous wind parks and the thousands of turbines already in the planning pipeline. The bleak, zigzagging scars on the country's mountains are visible from a great distance, as the erection of turbines on such steep gradients necessitates hundreds of kilometres of new roads being broken through largely untrammelled expanses, with hundreds and hundreds of smaller tracks widened sufficiently to facilitate the passage of turbine blades as much as 80 metres in length. According to a study carried out by the Biodiversity Conservation Lab in Ioannina, the amount of land being converted to artificial surfaces for wind parks in Greece is 3.5 times greater than the global average because of the roadless areas frequently chosen.

Land take, however, is only the beginning of the impacts. Just as Greece's 2020 environment bill (frequently referred to by opponents as the 'anti-environment bill' because of its focus on economic growth rather than ecosystem and wildlife protection) risks biodiversity degradation by legalising exploratory drilling for gas and oil within protected areas – including Natura 2000 sites specifically selected for their conservation significance – a wind-energy policy focused on mountains erodes vital habitat across a vast span of land. Once roadless areas become roaded, they open the door to increased poaching, logging and construction. Fragmentation undermines animal territories, pushing bears and wolves into places nearer humans and risking increased conflict. Turbine blades on prominent migratory corridors kill pelicans, eagles, vultures and bats. And expansive and intact ecosystems – the vital ticking heart of biodiversity protection – are made smaller, less whole and ultimately more human-centred. Irreparable damage in exchange for sometimes so little. 'If it wasn't

for the subsidies,' admitted the director of the wind-turbine company at the end of our day together in the karst country, referring
to an EU scheme for supporting renewable energy infrastructure
and a Greek one for investing in the border regions of the country,
'we would never consider building here. The wind is only right
on the threshold of viability.'

In a paper examining Greece's wind energy approach that also
provided a comprehensive set of alternative locations for turbine
expansion, the authors, led by biologist Vassiliki Kati, concluded
that 'there is no convergence of the climate and biodiversity policies', a discrepancy of associated value that 'might have serious if
not irreversible effects on species and habitats'. We are witnessing – and I say this as an ardent supporter of wind energy when
sited well, fully aware of the urgent need to shift energy production away from fossil fuels at pace – the rapid industrialisation of
some of this country's most astonishing, majestic and ecologically
alive mountains.

'The biodiversity crisis,' wrote the author and economist
John Reid on *Mongabay*, 'is arguably a good deal further along
than the climate crisis – and fully linked to it. And still, some of
us are asking whether our world, some decades hence, equipped
with sea walls, cooling centres, and windmills, may still function
as a terrarium for humans. This is a morally vapid question. It
ignores the fact that the planet is an intricate living system of
which humans are a part.'

We can't respond to one crisis without responding equally to
the other, nor can we simply replicate the patterns of extraction
and dominion that got us to this point in the first place by claiming
that there's nothing there but a bunch of rocks. If we're just going
to keep telling the same story, we shouldn't expect the ending to
be any different.

☀

On a warm summer night, fireflies float free of the garden grasses. From the banks of nettles by the stream they rise to drift like stars through the dark, the males signalling to females through a series of illuminated pulses. They're speaking a language of light, a script of glowing semaphores and sparks that's utterly magical to us. We stand there, barefoot inside a world of quiet wonder, something so beautiful and mysterious and near. Whole constellations of calling creatures, each flicker a lifeline to another.

I now look at how the grasses sway in the shimmer-hot days of early summer and wonder how I ever thought the garden was more beautiful without them. And yet I did. It was simply part of the cultural landscape that I'd grown up with and absorbed since I was a child. But one of the wonders of culture is the way in which it changes. As Lance says to Andy in an episode of *Detectorists*, that tender and thoughtful series that looks lovingly at the earth through the lens of two emotionally awkward and introverted metal detectorists: 'The idea of what is considered beautiful changes through time. Back in the Tudor period, you might have been considered really attractive. Scrawny, you know, with the beard and the hair. Stick a ruff around your neck and you could have been one of Lizzie the First's favourites.'

It's a gentle moment of humour between friends in a show that's all about the subtle ways in which emotional growth and change occur; and it's this fundamental capacity we have for shifting our perspectives on beauty – not just personally but as whole cultures that are continually being reshaped by individual as well as collective actions – that provides openings not unlike those green clearings in the urban fabric so crucial to me while living in London. Observing how our garden has become a greater shelter for other species – watching it become so vitally *alive* with butterflies, beetles, glow-worms and fireflies – has recalibrated my aesthetic sensibility so that it includes the practice of belonging. Because belonging, ultimately, isn't only a state of being but often a choice made by others. A choice that can pertain to the acceptance or exclusion of people in a place but also to the wider affiliation of life alongside us. And in those decisions, those points of potential opening, exist the opportunity to tell other stories about the world we share.

To see what one of those stories might look like, I went in search of a tree. It was a warm autumn morning when I arrived in Krivogaštani in North Macedonia and parked by the Church of St Peter. The tree – a vast and beautiful oak spreading its branches high above the church's cemetery – dominated the scene. Thought to be 500 years old, its circumference was so great that it took me thirty paces to circle it fully. Hornets droned around the trunk and collared doves called from above, while a red admiral basked on the bark. I looked up through the heavy scaffolding of branches and sunlit leaves to see the nests of hooded crows and the huge stick baskets of a heronry scattered throughout the tree. And right at the top, according to a local woman I spoke with, nested a pair of storks. Although the nests were all empty so late in the year, it wasn't hard to imagine the noisy vibrancy of the scene in spring and summer. A whole other world orbiting the oak. And beneath it, I found something just as beautiful as the tree itself. Each one of the dozens of graves in its immense shadow was covered by a simple shelter constructed of four metal posts and a sloping tin roof. In this way, said Biljana, the woman in her late thirties that I began talking to after she'd laid flowers on a family member's grave, birds can live in the tree and their droppings don't make a mess of the memorial stones. 'We love this place and we love this tree,' she said. 'It's so important to us, and the life it brings is so beautiful, that we protect it.'

The imaginative way in which local people have embraced
the sharing of such a meaningful place – paying forward their
loved ones' lives by encouraging the living presence of other kin –
reminded me of the Cameroonian philosopher Achille Mbembe's
idea that the 'political in our time must start from the imperative
to reconstruct the world in common'. In the cemetery, there was
no segregation of space between the human and the more-than-
human world; there were none of the anti-bird spikes sometimes
deployed in trees to prevent droppings from landing on cars,
deterrents as crude and callous as the hostile architecture of anti-
homeless studs in city centres. Instead, there was a communal act
of care, a reaching out to others.

There are considerable forces arrayed against the idea of
reconstructing the world in common, not least from those who
gain from keeping the world and its inequalities and diminishings
exactly as they are, which is what makes it all the more necessary
and urgent an idea. And maybe care is a good place to begin.
Because care's particular form of potency – what has always lent
connective force to the political at its most fundamental level –
stems from being able to seed and spread at any moment and from
almost anywhere: a garden or a churchyard, a neighbourhood
or city, the head or the heart. At a time when social, political,
economic and cultural divisions are widening across the planet,
caring – both for each other and for the living world – may turn
out to be one of the most radical and transformative acts of all.
And by imagining what might be there alongside us, what *could*
be there alongside us, the world is remade.

Lesser kestrels were incoming, arrowing over the water and rising
above the headland in waves. Flapping fast through a sky of dimming light. Beneath them was the whole of Ioannina's historic

centre: the tomb of Ali Pasha, the Ottoman mosques and minarets, the castle walls, stone houses and museums. Tourists licked at melting ice creams and couples caught the glow of the golden hour in selfies on their phones. There was an inescapable lightness to the end of day, a sense of things expanding, growing, letting go. And as more and more people filled the evening streets, lesser kestrels were becoming part of the same city, flowing in on that invisible river across the water.

'They spend their days on those mountains over there,' said Tasos Bounas, pointing to the alpine slopes southeast of the lake that were turning lilac with the lowering light. 'They hover a foot or two off the ground and feed on grasshoppers.'

'Amazing,' was all I seemed able to say, my eyes turned skywards as the raptors swirled around a minaret. 'Seriously?' I then said, finally processing what I'd just heard.

'Yeah,' smiled Tasos. 'They hover low over the grasslands in small groups, anywhere from two or three birds up to as many as twenty-five.'

Although we'd briefly met Tasos on a few occasions over the years, we hadn't seen him for some time. But he happened to be good friends with Dimitris, whom I'd messaged from the balcony the previous evening when we'd first seen the lesser kestrels. Not only that, but Tasos was an expert in these birds, and he'd kindly offered to show us the roost with his partner Ellie after he'd heard we were in town.

'This pre-migration gathering draws birds from all over the Balkans and they use it to feed up and prepare for their journeys. There's probably around twelve to fourteen hundred here this year, though it's been about two thousand in recent years.'

'And they'll spend the night in Ioannina?' I asked, thinking about that widening aperture of belonging when the human and more-than-human world share the shelter of a place.

'Right here in the centre,' he said. 'They only roost in the plane trees for some reason, not in the pines or the oaks. The big issue is that there's an invasive canker disease spreading through planes in Greece now and the only way to deal with it is to remove an affected tree before it spreads to the next one. All we can do is wait and see what happens here.'

'What would it mean if all these plane trees were lost?' asked Julia.

'It'll mean the city won't be as beautiful,' said Tasos. 'It'll mean that lesser kestrels might leave Ioannina and go to Albania or somewhere else.'

'Did you come here just to see the roost?' asked Ellie.

'No, we only learned about it last night,' said Julia. 'We actually came because I had my Greek citizenship test here this morning.'

'Really?' they both asked at the same time with a mixture of surprise and excitement.

'Wow,' said Ellie. 'How did it go?'

'Good, I think. I'm pretty sure I got most things right but I just have to wait for the results now.'

Everything was silhouetting against the spreading orange light – the minarets, the castle walls, the lesser kestrels. A half-moon glowed in the fainter blue reaches as Julia explained her citizenship test with its three examiners and their rapid-fire questions on politics, history and geography. How she had to sing the national anthem in front of them at the end, all of them wearing masks because of pandemic protocols. There was laughter in the near dark from Tasos and Ellie. As they talked, the sky had begun emptying of birds. It felt as if they were slipping out of orbit as one by one they broke from the whirling masses to fold themselves into the plane trees around the old town. As soon as one tree was full, its branches shifting and shaking from all the settling down for the night, the birds that were still sliding from the sky simply moved on to the next one. Finding shelter in the city together.

'Come on, drinks are on us,' said Tasos. We followed them down the castle steps. Scooters and cars sped past on the lakeshore road and music buzzed from speakers outside bars in the warren of lanes ahead of us. It was a classic summer night in a Greek city, the cane chairs and tables with checkered cloths filling with drinkers and diners beneath the beautiful canopies of the plane trees. I looked up through the rustling leaves of one of them to see in the spray of streetlight dozens of lesser kestrels perched across its branches. For a moment it felt like Christmas, with the gifts tucked inside instead of beneath the tree.

Some months later, Julia would receive her results and officially became a Greek citizen, sworn in at the municipal offices of Florina in a low-key ceremony that we toasted with a coffee in the car park, but to celebrate on that day of lesser kestrels and national anthems, Tasos and Ellie led us to their favourite local bar. After they had a quiet word with the owner inside, Julia was presented with the largest, strongest and most welcome Mai Tai ever.

10

Of Water, Mountains, Sky

The islands were mantled with dead pelicans, like a late fall of snow. In the low light of a March afternoon, I was standing above the lake on the small hill that commands clear views of the wetland and its dense reedbeds. The same hill that I'd stood on right before our first pandemic lockdown, when seeing pelicans on their nests felt like an anchor point in an uncertain world. But now, instead of the great surging clamour of the world's largest colony of rare Dalmatian pelicans, the dark water was whitened by a mass of floating carcasses. And the islets of detached reedbed on which some 1,400 pairs of this remarkable species typically breed were saddled with slack birds. They seemed strangely flat from a distance, as though life had been pressed out of them by a great, immovable weight.

When the first dead Dalmatian pelicans were discovered on Lesser Prespa Lake on 17 February 2022, they numbered only 11. A large enough figure to take note of but not be unduly alarmed by, given that deaths from natural causes are a common fact of life in busy wetland breeding colonies. A week later, however, mortalities had reached 209. By then, tissue samples gathered from the original pelican carcasses had revealed the cause of death as H5N1, or highly pathogenic avian influenza (HPAI). On 9 March, just three weeks after the first deaths had been recorded, the figure had rocketed to 1,003. Witnessing the terrible trajectory of these numbers, it was hard not to draw parallels with the early days of the Covid-19 crisis, when mortality figures rose with staggering exponentiality. And, as with the pandemic, the rising death toll on the Prespa lakes from avian influenza wouldn't stop there.

Through my telescope I scanned the wetland, where movement was largely limited to the more secluded parts of the dispersed colony. Panning from left to right, I eventually landed on an islet entirely wrapped in dead birds. But there was a single living Dalmatian pelican too, starkly alone and standing on the curving white summit of its deceased kin. Up close through the lens, I lingered on its tousled head feathers and the sword-like beak, whose pouch had turned strikingly brick-red for the breeding season; I saw how its eyes were the colour of old ice. Several minutes later, I realised that I was still focused on this one pelican, motionless on its mount. I wasn't sure why it was absorbing so much of my attention except that in standing alone it had become symbolic for me, though I couldn't decide whether it was emblematic of wild resilience or fragility. Or perhaps I was subconsciously projecting onto it the role of witness to the devastation. But then it hit me with sudden force why I was so fixed on that particular bird – it was because in all likelihood it had already been condemned to join those beneath it in a heap. Without a radical change in circumstances, it was extremely unlikely that this bird would survive the coming days, because the scant light of late winter and a period of persistently cold temperatures had conspired to produce the ideal conditions for the transmission of avian influenza. By staying true to a lake that's encoded as home in its tissues and bones, it was almost certainly doomed to die. And it was heartbreaking to be privy to such grim inevitability.

Given the antiquity of the Prespa lakes, it seems only right that they should be home to pelicans, one of the most ancient families

of birds on the planet. They are simply an astonishing and seamless part of being here. In summer, the skies brighten with their
flights, as hundreds of them, their wingspans as great as three and
a half metres when fully extended, catch warm thermals generated
by the earth, tracing rising circles into the endless blue above. Or
they'll shoal together in the shallows to feed, their beaks scatter-
ing spray as they break the still surface, sunlight mirroring off the
water to hold them inside its glow. They have a unique presence
about them – something wondrously familiar yet mysteriously
remote – that's unlike any other Prespa species I know.

Pelicans, however, weren't always considered so convivial and
appealing a neighbour around the lakes. There was a time when
the Greek government offered a bounty on them – 50 drachmas
for a dead bird and 5 for an egg – in the mistaken belief that pelicans competed directly with fishermen for the same quarry. The
fishermen of Prespa, living a long way from the nearest municipal
offices where they could easily transport proof of the killed birds,
often just broke up the nests and smashed the eggs and any young
birds instead. But the fortunes of the Dalmatian and great white
pelicans of these lakes began to change unexpectedly in 1971,
when Greece's right-wing junta regime, which had claimed power
in a coup in 1967, granted the region protected status precisely
because of the significance of these waterbird colonies. The declar-
ation was, in part, an attempt by the military dictatorship to gain
credibility with European governments by casting themselves in a
favourable light at a time when the regime's horrific human rights
abuses justly garnered most of the international attention, but
largely it was a testament to the formidable resolve and persuasive
charm of the Swiss conservationist Luc Hoffmann.

Hoffmann had been drawn to the Prespa lakes when French
biologists in the late 1960s finally identified the basin as the home
of pelican colonies long speculated about but never confirmed by
scientists. Another sign of just how difficult it was to reach Greek

Prespa until relatively recently, not just in a geographical sense but politically too, given the military control of its access point and the restrictions on entry put in place in the post-Civil War period. Hoffmann, a founding member of the World Wildlife Fund and the Ramsar Convention on Wetlands, had already begun making a positive impact on international wetland preservation by then, using his ornithological training and considerable wealth to help protect places of significant biodiversity by encouraging local conservation initiatives through a mixture of scientific study, community involvement and awareness-raising. His persistent lobbying efforts convinced the colonels in charge of Greece at the time to declare Prespa a 'National Forest' in 1974, the only significant protective designation then available and a status that was officially upgraded to National Park in 2009. Hoffmann's critical involvement in Prespa also led to the founding of the SPP in 1991 in order to help preserve the lakes' natural and cultural wealth.

When those visiting French biologists encountered the colonies for the first time, they estimated there to be about a hundred pairs of both Dalmatian and great white pelicans nesting here, restricted to just two isolated corners of Lesser Prespa Lake: an inner lagoon within dense reedbeds in Greece and an area of reeds in the lake's border zone between Greece and Albania. While the great white pelican's presence in Europe is significant, it's a species that's found in such large numbers in Africa and Asia that it's considered to be of 'least concern' in strict conservation terms by the International Union for Conservation of Nature (IUCN). The Dalmatian pelican, however, is far more unusual. While its colonies can be found from southeastern Europe right across central Asia to Mongolia and eastern China, the Dalmatian pelican's need for extensive, undisturbed wetlands means that its occurrence is largely scattered and scarce – especially since the cumulative pressures of habitat loss and persecution in the eighteenth and nineteenth centuries drastically reduced its global numbers – making Prespa's community of birds all the more note-worthy. These ancient Balkan lakes, formed millions of years ago when movements in Earth's crust created a place for water to swell, shelter something of rare and incalculable value.

Olga Alexandrou was bundled up against the cold air in a fleece and a hat when I joined her beside Lesser Prespa Lake as she pre-pared to fly a drone over the colonies. A conservation biologist, Olga has worked closely with the pelicans of Prespa for over a decade now, carrying out research, satellite tracking, monitoring and wetland management with the SPP.

'It's been absolutely shocking,' she said, as light gradually spilled over the mountains to flood the basin in a pale orange wash. 'Overwhelming to see all these colonies full of adults in their impressive breeding plumage, these beautiful, healthy-looking birds that had just arrived to nest, and to suddenly see more and more dead ones. Tens of them. And then hundreds. Many hun-dreds. It's crazy. From our calculations, during the first two weeks of their arrival, we lost 60 per cent of the first one thousand birds that arrived in Prespa.'

Olga – who is a good friend of ours living in the same vil-lage and Julia's running partner three mornings a week – sent the white craft up into the sky, deftly guiding its movements from a control panel in her hands. Within moments I'd lost sight of it, but the screen in front of us relayed the image from above. It was small but stark, a composite of empty nests and dying birds. Of still, white silence.

'Could you have ever imagined this scene in Prespa?' I asked her.

'No way,' she replied straight away. 'I don't think anyone could have imagined this disaster here.' Olga landed the drone

at our feet, the images on its SD card to be reviewed up close
on her computer to assess the spread of the disease. I remembered the excitement that Chris and I used to feel when we
removed the SD card from our camera trap; the mysteries of
what it might hold, such as the mother bear and her cub playing
with the device. This, however, was an entirely different mystery – the number of dead or dying pelicans that would change
from unknown to known because of what Olga decoded from
the images. As we loaded the gear into her truck, I asked how
she kept going. 'It's obviously intense and hard, but you can't be
paralysed by sadness and sentiment, because there are a lot of birds
that need our help. In these really awful circumstances, being
part of their world is so important, knowing what's happening
to them, living with them.'

   With so many birds still at risk, a decision was made on the
advice of avian-influenza experts to remove as many of the dead
pelicans as possible in an attempt to reduce radically the viral load
in the wetland. As the virus is primarily transmitted through bod-
ily secretions, a busy colony of waterbirds who frequently rub and
knock bills together as they engage in courtship rituals and jockey
for position on crowded nesting islands is an absolute boon for the
circulation of the disease. And this ease of transmission makes for
a logistical nightmare given the season, because migratory birds
were constantly arriving to take their place in the shared wetland,
including some 600 pairs of great white pelicans and a significant
number of Dalmatians still to come. As these and countless other
potentially vulnerable waterbirds – squacco herons, little egrets,
night herons, glossy ibises – had already embarked on their journeys, with no knowledge of what awaited them at their end, there
was a grave urgency to the operation.

   Getting the recovery plan in motion not only required a
complex degree of cooperation, something that isn't always easy
to deliver in a nation as bureaucratically inclined as Greece, but

demanded the rapid action and coordinated response of the SPP,
the Prespa National Park Management Body, multiple governmental agencies, the veterinary services, municipal authorities and
the local community. But in a sign of how the perception of pelicans has changed around the lakes in recent decades, from a bird
seen as a nuisance to one that's increasingly upheld as a positive
emblem for the region, no one turned down a request for help.
In fact, offers of assistance were numerous. Prespa's agricultural
cooperative (which is called Pelecanos and uses the pelican as its
symbol) made its commercial weighing station available for determining the precise mass of dead birds. The Greek Army provided
three flat-bottomed boats small enough to navigate the narrow
wetland channels in the reedbeds but sufficiently sturdy to convey
the cumulative weight of gathered pelicans safely to shore. And the
local municipal council let their flatbed truck with accompanying
crane be used to unload from the boats the collection containers
that were to be picked up by a bio-hazard company and trucked
to an incinerator site two hours south of Prespa.

Due to a mix-up about times, I arrived just as the recovery
team was finishing its first shift. 'Don't worry,' said Giorgos
Paraskevopoulos, one of two young, local fishermen tasked with
hauling the carcasses aboard the boats. 'We'll be working for several days yet.'

I watched them go and then climbed the small hill above the
colony again. It was brutally cold, a snapping wind raising white-
caps on the lake. I couldn't imagine what it had been like out on
the water for Giorgos and Manolis, the other young fisherman.
Clouds scudded low over the mountains, unfurling sheets of rain
that obscured whole valleys from view. From the height of the
hill, it was easy to see where the dead birds had been cleared.
In places, living pelicans had even returned to the nesting isles

despite the disturbance. Elsewhere, however, hundreds of lifeless ones remained.

I dropped down the hill and started driving home as rain gusted across the lake. By the shore, in the car park of a long-closed taverna, I could see the orange collection crates stacked ready for the following day's stage of the operation. I pulled in and walked over during a break in the weather, deciding to take a few photographs of the containers while they were still empty. There were two rows of six crates, each stacked double – making twenty-four in total. I was within arm's reach of them when I saw a silvery-white wing hanging over a side. And then the stench knocked me back like a punch. The containers weren't empty but full; between them, they held more than 200 Dalmatian pelicans waiting to be picked up and burned to nothing.

How can such remarkable lives end like this? That's all I could think of as I left, grateful to drive away from the overwhelming smell of death, the image of that silvery wing clinging to me in the sudden, slanting rain.

When I was hospitalised with the back issues that signalled the official end of our farming years, I realised that I'd reached a significant point of change in my life. For a start, it meant a recognition of restrictions when it came to certain physical activities unless I wanted the condition to seriously worsen. But as I was wheeled upstairs after X-ray imaging to the fluorescent room that was to be my home for the following days, I also instinctively understood that there was perhaps something to be learned from what was happening to my body, too. Despite all that I'd gained from working the land, I'd never set out to be a farmer. I had wanted to use our move to Prespa as a catalyst for committing to writing. Until then, I'd been more in love with the *idea* of being a writer than the act of writing itself. And it became clear to me with the doctor's warning that I was being given another chance to follow that path.

That night, just as Julia kissed me goodbye and prepared to drive back home over the mountains, I asked her if she could go downstairs to the small hospital shop and see if they had a pen and pad of paper for sale. Sitting up in bed, beneath the bright light and alongside an elderly patient who snored incessantly throughout much of the night, I used the Bic pen and a children's exercise book that Julia had found for me to sketch out nearly an entire short story called 'Pelicans'. It was the first piece of creative writing I'd attempted in years, and it told the story of a Greek husband and wife out fishing on Great Prespa Lake decades earlier when a sudden and violent summer storm had upended their wooden boat, their lifelines forever tied to the brief, life-saving appearance of pelicans through the drifting mist and beating rain that day. I can no longer remember whether it was the sense of freedom that I associate with Prespa's pelicans that led to the sudden outpouring of words about them, stuck there in a hospital bed having been told there were things that I physically couldn't do any more, or whether it was seeing them as an enduring symbol of resilience after surviving the bounty that had been placed on their heads. All I do know for sure is that it was pelicans, the birds I'll forever regard as a principal essence of this place, that pulled me back into the world of language, creativity and stories.

Like stories, lifelines evolve, change, get remade; they shift course through choice and circumstance. And, sometimes, seemingly small things can alter whole arcs.

Even with the protection of the area in the 1970s, the growth of Prespa's pelican colonies was slow, held back by a combination

of disturbance and a lack of suitable nesting sites. But the presence of biologists and the eventual founding of the SPP at least
enabled the colonies to be wardened, keeping them safe as much
from tourists and photographers trying to get close to the birds
as from any deliberate acts of destruction. In the end, though,
the transformative moment for Prespa's pelicans came from two
entirely unexpected places: fishermen and drought.

So little precipitation fell in the basin between 1988 and 1990
that a drastic drop in the water level of Lesser Prespa Lake left the
pelicans' nesting islands accessible by land. Vulnerable to terrestrial
predators, the birds abandoned their nests. At first, conservationists installed small artificial rafts with moderate success, securing
breeding areas for a few pelicans at least. But in May 1990, just
as the entire nesting season appeared to be lost, the birds, some
of whom had circled the lakes for months in a fruitless search for
suitable sites, began settling on a very different kind of island.

Known as *pelaizia*, these dense floating masses of juniper
branches used to be constructed by fishermen to trap winter fish
in shallow waters. Discovering they could also double as nesting rafts, the stressed pelicans, with no other options available to
them, settled on these artificial islands. Fishermen, understandably,
responded with anger and frustration to the occupation, arguing
that their *pelaizia*, which required considerable labour to cut and
assemble correctly, would be permanently ruined by the nesting
pelicans and the build-up of guano.

It was amid this tense atmosphere, as lake levels continued to
fall and strains were being felt throughout Prespa's human and wild
communities, that the narrative around pelicans began gradually
to shift, as conservationists – including Giorgos Catsadorakis, one
of Europe's foremost pelican experts and the author of the book
that inspired Julia and me to move to this part of the world in
the first place – deepened their dialogue with fishermen about the
significance of these species.

'It's important to remember the evolution of cultural perception here,' said Giorgos when I asked him about that period in the
region's history. His virtual background as we spoke on Zoom was
an image of Prespa, its high mountains and blue water to either side
of him on the screen, a sign of just how much this place means to
him and why he continues working on its behalf even though he
now lives elsewhere in Greece. As I've told him several times over
the years, we owe our own love of Prespa in part to the extraordinary care he brought to the book he so movingly wrote about it.

'When you see pelicans on television and in news reports and
realise that it's a rare bird that people are coming to see here,' he
continued, 'this helps change minds. Some fishermen had already
begun to grasp that Prespa was attractive to tourists because of
pelicans, and that it might mean some additional income in
what was a very poor place, but the cultivation of understanding
through discussion meant that some of the fishermen were gradually becoming more positive about pelicans. They began to accept
them. And bit by bit they also started feeling proud of them,
because this place of theirs, their homeland, hosted wildlife species
that were of immense interest to many people outside of Prespa.'

'Why are pelicans so important to you?' I'd then asked him,
interested in the deeper connection to the species he's devoted so
much of his life in conservation to. 'Pelicans, for me, are the spirit
of the primeval wetland. And Dalmatian pelicans, in particular,
need very specific conditions to nest. So in wetlands with plenty
of fish and clean water, you may have this old spirit of the wetland.
If there are pelicans nesting in a wetland, something is good with
the health of this wetland. And we need to have pelicans here and
there, even if there are only a few, because it means the wetland
is moving in the right direction.'

In that third successive year of drought, an entirely new nesting area emerged for the pelicans of Prespa. It was a place that
had been unavailable to them in the past because of the frequency

with which fishing boats passed through it, but with the eventual agreement of local fishermen to let their *pelaizia* be used that breeding season and, from then on, to concede a part of the lake to the birds, pelicans began colonising natural islands nearby, which finally gave them the necessary nesting space to increase in number when lake levels rose once more. That small, reed-fringed corner of the wetland that I look down on from the hill, out of bounds to the birds until just over three decades ago, is now the very heart of Prespa's pelican colonies.

'If we have pelicans here today,' said Myrsini, the SPP's director, who had once told me that borders can be an opportunity rather than a restriction and who was closely involved in the conversations with the lakes' fishing communities at the time, 'it's because of a few fishermen. Fishermen who are old now but who passed in front of this new pelican colony and turned off their engines and used their oars instead – they didn't even look at the birds, but rowed by slowly, without disturbing them. It was local people that decided they wanted this species for both Prespa and for the world. It's the strongest feeling I've ever had here. And it changed people's feelings about pelicans, even though not that long ago they were paid to kill them.'

Avian influenza is a conveniently deceptive term. While it accurately describes the primary viral host, it also neatly sidesteps the origin of the highly pathogenic variant of the disease by telescoping our attention towards birds. Because the root cause of H5N1, expediently forgotten in many news reports about the waves of infections in recent years, is directly traceable to humans through our food production systems.

While a reservoir of low-pathogenic avian influenza has likely existed in wild bird populations for centuries, rarely manifesting into anything more than minor symptoms in infected individuals, the first confirmation that the low-pathogenic virus had re-sequenced into a more severe strain came when a farmed goose was diagnosed with highly pathogenic avian influenza in 1996 in Guangdong, China. Over the following years, numerous outbreaks would be reported in poultry farms across Asia until the first large-scale emergence within wild birds occurred at Lake Qinghai in China in 2005, when over 6,000 birds died after contracting the virus on a body of water where hundreds of thousands of migratory waterbirds seasonally congregate on their journeys.

'Birds are both victims and vectors,' said Ruth Cromie, lead coordinator of the Scientific Task Force on Avian Influenza and Wild Birds, when we spoke about the wider implications and spread of the disease. 'The genie truly escaped from the bottle with the first big outbreak in wild birds at Lake Qinghai. And following that outbreak, we saw this virus moving with wild birds into various places. Unfortunately, wild birds have been blamed all over the place, even where poultry and people movements are the cause. If you look at the flyway maps of the world, they've been used as "proof" that it was wild birds that have spread the disease, which is a marvellous excuse for having poor bio-security because you can just blame it on them instead.'

It wasn't until low-pathogenic avian influenza was introduced through lax security controls into the cramped conditions of poultry farms or on bodies of water where large flocks of domestic ducks and geese are let loose to mingle with wild species that the virus was able to mutate into a highly pathogenic form which is now decimating both wild and domestic birds alike.

'The way we are managing the planet couldn't be better for creating the settings that generate disease emergence and novel viruses,' said Ruth, 'including the next human pandemic. It used to be that juvenile birds coming off their breeding grounds would be exposed to the low-pathogenic viruses, but now we are seeing these highly pathogenic viruses, with their original source in farmed birds, circulating in the wild. We're watching new, paradigm-shifting relationships forming – and it's massively depressing.'

Avian influenza isn't the only shifting paradigm that the Dalmatian pelican has to contend with. Unlike great white pelicans, which migrate all the way from Prespa to southern Africa at the end of the nesting season and back again in spring, Dalmatian pelicans stay relatively close, moving only as far as lowland coastal waters in Greece or Turkey. As a result of climate change, however, warmer and drier winters around these lowland sites have led to longer periods of favourable weather conditions and more readily available food, which means that Dalmatian pelicans are now reaching their optimal reproductive state far quicker than they once did. While this is positive for the species in the sense that more and more birds are surviving winter when there were once significant losses in the past, the strongest and fittest birds, those with the greatest physical chance of successfully rearing young, are returning to Prespa earlier and earlier each year. In order to secure the best nesting sites, some are even appearing as early as the first half of January. Between 1986 and 2019, the first egg-laying date of Dalmatian pelicans advanced by a remarkable forty days, or 1.25 days on average per year. Given that Lesser Prespa Lake is approximately 850 metres above sea level, that movement from milder lowland waters to this mountain lake is, as Giorgos Catsadorakis describes it, equivalent to travelling 500–600 kilometres due north.

These pelicans arrow straight into the heart of winter, arriving to find falling snow, freezing cold and sometimes even ice on the lake. As it's too frigid for fish to move in the upper layers of

the lakes even when unfrozen, the birds are forced to feed elsewhere, or to endure the low temperatures and extreme weather
conditions of the nesting period without food. This 'temporal
mismatch', as Giorgos calls it, is a reflection of the uneven effects
of climate change, influencing the wintering and nesting sites of
these birds differently. Now, the strongest, most capable and
experienced Dalmatian pelicans, the ones that have traditionally
stood a better chance of continuing their lineage, are frequently
forced to abandon their nests or watch them fail because of mis-
timed reproduction and the adverse seasonal conditions. And
being on the Prespa lakes in the depths of winter – urged home
by shifting climate conditions somewhere else – was when the risk
of avian influenza was at its greatest.

Two flat-bottomed green boats pushed off from shore, steered
through a narrowing channel between reedbeds by the young
Prespa fishermen dressed in hazmat suits and masks. Each boat
carried three large, orange, plastic containers, identical to the
ones I saw in the car park waiting to be collected. From the small
hill I watched the boatmen gather the birds, hauling them from
the water with boat hooks, or lifting them from the islands
where they should have been nesting. Each time a bird was
drawn upwards, its wings fell open, looking from a distance like
an angel rising from the lake. But that's where the comparison
ended, because each of the pelicans was then dumped into a
large industrial crate.

'It was weird when I was putting them in the box,' said Giorgos
Paraskevopoulos, the fisherman I'd spoken to when I'd arrived late
to the first retrieval session. That cold, late-winter day, Giorgos's
face was ringed with red lines when he removed the safety suit
and mask he'd been wearing all morning, his brown hair swept

back with sweat. This time he was relaxed, wearing jeans and a T-shirt as we sat in warm sunshine outside Prespa's library, where he'd just dropped off his son for a music lesson.

'It was as though I was putting a person in their coffin,' he continued. 'I went home and my wife said, *You've changed*. And how could I not? When you see dead bodies, they might not be people, but they're still life. They're still living creatures.'

Each of the boat's containers held ten to fourteen Dalmatian pelicans. When the boatmen turned for shore, they ferried dozens of dead birds between them. With each hour of work, the wetland became increasingly clearer, but so much smaller in meaning than before.

'I think it's good for the birds that remained that we were cleaning up the dead ones,' said Giorgos, who grew up beside the colony on the island of Agios Achilleios with its thousand-year-old basilica and learned to fish on the lake with his grandfather when he was eight. 'I don't know about the psychology of birds, how all of this seems to them, but when they're in an environment where they only see carcasses, I believe it affects them. They might not have the understanding that people have, but I believe all living creatures have feelings. If you're in a pair and you lose your mate – maybe it doesn't have tears to shed or the words to say it, but that creature feels something.'

'Every year when I'm teaching and showing slides of avian flu outbreak data, it's the most recent outbreak that is the worst,' said Ursula Höfle, a veterinary scientist and wild-bird disease specialist at the University of Castilla–La Mancha in Spain who acted as an advisor to Prespa's conservationists during the avian flu episode on the lakes. 'It just gets worse and worse every year. Not every year exactly, but every cycle, because it's quite a cyclical disease.

That cycle used to be every five to ten years, but it's getting far less than that now.'

This most recent cycle would include the deaths of 8,000 common cranes and numerous other wild birds in December 2021 around a lake in the Hula valley in northern Israel, a vital wintering site and stopover point for migratory species. It would also include the deaths of approximately 4,000 barnacle geese wintering in the Solway Firth in Scotland that same month, accounting for 10 per cent of the goose's Svalbard breeding population. And it would include, in the late winter and spring of 2022, the eventual deaths of 2,286 Dalmatian pelicans across thirteen wetlands in Greece – 1,734 of them in the Prespa colony alone – along with several hundred others elsewhere in southeastern Europe, from the coastal lagoons of Albania to the Danube delta in Romania.

Worryingly, as spring became summer in the northern hemisphere that year, new outbreaks were being recorded on an almost daily basis. Until now, warming temperatures and abundant light have typically lessened the virulence of HPAI to such a degree that it would disappear in sync with the seasons. 'We used to only see avian influenza outbreaks in winter,' said Ursula, 'but last year there were cases in May. Unfortunately, we're probably going to see cases throughout the year.'

In June 2022, just as Ursula had predicted, outbreaks of avian influenza began increasing dramatically. The National Trust for Scotland announced the deaths of 120 great skuas at the UNESCO World Heritage site of St Kilda, a remote outcrop of small islands that are home to nearly a million seabirds, including Atlantic puffins, storm petrels, shearwaters and gannets. Gannets had already been turning up dead in the thousands elsewhere – from Shetland right over to the shores of Nova Scotia and New Brunswick in Canada – including two ringed individuals from Bass Rock off the east coast of Scotland, home to 150,000 northern gannets during the nesting season and their largest colony in the world. A few days after the deaths of the ringed gannets, avian influenza was confirmed on Bass Rock; contrasting images of the seabird colony from 2021 and 2022 revealed a staggering decline in the number of nesting individuals. By July, avian influenza was being declared responsible for bird deaths around the much warmer southern coasts of England. And in August, 700 black vultures died at a single roosting site in Georgia in the United States, which means that summer can no longer be considered a period of suspension for viral transmission, at least at certain latitudes. We're now confronting the possibility that HPAI is becoming better adapted to a greater range of climatic conditions as well as to wild birds in general, making its spread all the more unpredictable, and, in all likelihood, utterly devastating.

In the years that we monitored birds, our work took us to long, whale-backed ridges and that vast karstic plateau. It led us upwards into a world of light and sun and sky, where the summering months could crush you with their heat or sway you at the sight of alpine choughs corkscrewing beautifully through the blue. It brought us to remote hills in seasons of wildfire, rain and snow; to landscapes shaped by the roaming herds of the flute-playing shepherd and villagers no longer there because the Civil War had emptied life from their homes. It opened us to the multiple layers of meaning held by these places.

I'll remember those days for the sudden scatter of woodlarks from the mountain grasses, for the way blue rock thrushes stamped pieces of the sea onto stones. I'll remember them for the low, slow glide of a golden eagle across our sunset path between crags, for that brown bear stepping out of the shadows to face me in a meadow. But from the rich register of experiences, when the contours of those places were deepened by repeated visits, to the point where our bodies seemed to fit more closely with the uplands than anywhere else in the basin, it will be pelicans that I remember most.

If asked to name the one thing that best captures the essence of pelicans, what it is they're made for, I would once have said *water* – that it's to lakes, coasts and estuaries that they cleave; that it's to wetlands they express their fidelity. But the living world, as I learned in the mountains above the lakes, is never so simply demarcated or defined, nor reducible to any single, categorisable thing. Neither species of pelican feeds exclusively on the Prespa lakes, even when breeding. They regularly travel to other bodies of water for sustenance; some of which, such as Lake Kerkini to the north of Thessaloniki, are as much as 200 kilometres away. While one of the paired pelicans remains on the nest, its partner goes in search of food, returning a day or two later with its crop full of fish to take its turn in the colony. To reach those distant wetlands – to reach the water I thought of them as being so intensely attached to – the birds must first cross the high mountains encircling the basin.

Up there, standing as much as 2,000 metres above sea level, I'd watch how those journeying pelicans, in assemblies of as many as a hundred birds at a time, would be released by thermals as easily as a balloon let stray from a child's hand, conveyed ever upwards on a ladder of warm air. And the higher they ascended the more unbelievable they seemed to me, until all that could be seen of them were small white gleams as they banked into the sun, like flickers of lightning in daylight. Much that I felt I knew about pelicans shifted during those alpine days; I saw how their lives were hitched to the world in ways far more varied than I'd been able to imagine from the limited vantage point of the lakes. And it was then, when I needed binoculars or a telescope to be certain they were still up there at all, that they seemed to me to be made for mountains and sky just as much as they were wedded to water.

Many of us are prone to thinking of the world as divisible. As capable of being broken down into elements in the same way that I regarded the pelicans' experience when I looked at them solely through the lens of wetlands, neglecting their wider presence and the threats they face when in the air: from collisions with power lines and poorly sited wind turbines in the mountains to the increasingly violent storms they encounter on their migratory journeys. This perspective arises, in part, from a cultural failure to recognise the shared nature of the world. An inability to see in the fruition of others a flourishing of our own, or to admit that our lifelines are entwined. Because what affects the wild will always, unequivocally, affect us too; there is simply no way of separating ourselves from the changes we've made to the world.

As well as infecting both wild and domestic birds, avian influenza has now crossed into numerous other species in the past few years, including dolphins, bears, foxes, tigers, otters, sea lions and cows. And while the passage of this particular strain into humans remains rare, at least seventy-six people, most of them in the United States, contracted avian influenza in 2024, while earlier mutations in Asia were responsible for a number of deaths. Given the multitude of possibilities for recombination that the virus is being granted as it races through colonies of wild birds and packed industrial units where it can rapidly circulate among confined poultry bred to grow unnaturally fast and be sold unfeasibly cheap, there's every chance that a mutation could emerge that triggers our next catastrophic pandemic.

But focusing on the impact of avian influenza on humans to the exclusion of other lives is endgame thinking; when all you have left to play are just the last few pieces on the board. Given that everything on this planet is interwoven, and each interaction between ourselves, livestock, wildlife and the wider environment affects others further down the line, the only way to care for human health credibly is to consider all the pieces from the very beginning. 'We share a lot of pathogens, pollutants and toxins, and these affect us all,' said Ruth from the Task Force on Avian Influenza, highlighting the fact that of the dozens of infectious diseases discovered in humans in the past three decades, more than three-quarters of them originated in animals. But in acknowledging the shared world and responding to its indivisibility by ensuring, first and foremost, the protection of intact ecosystems and the planet's biodiversity as the fundamental building blocks of thriving societies, both human and wild, we begin to shift notions of well-being, both at the ethical and the practical level, towards the health of the whole.

It was midsummer. I was standing on the hill above the colonies again, where heat haze glazed the lakes to a bright shimmer. By then, the skies of Prespa should have been turning with the lengthening coils of pelicans, as adults and juveniles converged and rose as one through the air. The wetland was strangely quiet, and so unusually empty. In contrast to the 1,450 pairs of Dalmatian pelicans that nested in 2021 – when this was the largest colony of these birds in the world, accounting for as much as 20 per cent of their global breeding population – only ninety pairs nested in Prespa in 2022. But the difficult clearing of dead birds and the subsequent drawdown of the wetland's viral load gave this many, at least, a chance to breed successfully. In the end, it was the only species of bird affected on the lake.

Seeing so few pelicans, it was easy to think that we'd been here before; that we'd returned to a time before Luc Hoffmann first became involved in safeguarding these birds and the SPP began working towards their conservation. And that, of course, is entirely possible, because in an age of extinction, when pressures on wildlife exist on multiple fronts and are increasing in severity, there's no certainty that any particular species will survive. Ancient wetland spirits such as the Dalmatian pelican could easily become another kind of spirit: one of loss, a ghost haunting the waters where it once lived. But while the situation on the Prespa lakes and throughout the bird's southeastern European range is unquestionably critical in light of the unprecedented number of deaths in 2022, things are vastly different today too, because the carefully tended groundwork for protection endures.

'It's not the number of birds that's so important,' said Myrsini of the SPP with reference to Prespa's pre-crisis population, 'but the system we have established. It's the system of long-term cooperation of which I'm proud.'

This system has rearranged relationships. When we moved here in the summer of 2000, Dalmatian pelicans nested in only two of Greece's wetlands: on the lake beneath the village where Vassilis found us a house to rent and in the Amvrakikos Gulf on the west coast. But as a result of decades of concerted conservation efforts in Prespa and the rising population numbers that followed, Dalmatian pelicans now breed in six of the country's wetlands, naturally spreading from these high-altitude lakes and making other places their home. And when pelicans began dying of avian influenza on Lake Cheimaditida, a lake two hours southeast of Prespa first colonised as a nesting site only seven years earlier, it was fishermen who went out onto the water of their own volition to collect the carcasses. Without a local conservation body working around the lake, they contacted biologists in Prespa to ask what else they could do to help the species – acts that would have been unthinkable just two generations earlier, when the Greek government's reasoning for placing a bounty on a dead bird or an egg was explicitly clear: 'Pelicans are to be considered vermin. They feed on fish and constitute a threat to the productivity of the fishing industry. They are the enemies of fishermen.'

'I think people have realised that, generally, birds and nature aren't our enemy,' said Giorgos Paraskevopoulos of the contemporary relationship between fishermen and wildlife in Prespa. 'In the past, the pelican was seen as a competitor. But I don't see people thinking like that any more. Okay, they eat some fish, so what? It won't kill us — and we wouldn't have got rich on what little they're eating anyways.'

Above the water, a dozen Dalmatian pelicans glided smoothly in a line through the heating air. I followed their course until they began turning into the light, shining in sequence with the sun in their feathers, lifting above the water with barely a tremble of wings. Watching these survivors, the ones who'll return again next year to this place they call home, I remembered something that Giorgos had said back in the darkest days of the crisis, when he spent countless cold hours gathering the bodies of dead birds from the lake.

'You see a pelican now and you watch it, thinking, *I only hope it will live*. When they're common around you, you don't imagine that you could lose them. The moment when you understand that the population is being increasingly lost, then you see a pelican and you're thrilled, so you value what you have even more. I hope many people will now appreciate them that much more.'

In an age of thinning forms, when the sum of wild lives on the planet grows smaller by the hour, this rising spiral of Dalmatian pelicans parting the summer air above the lakes is also a reminder that we carry within us an extraordinary capacity for change. That our cultures and traditions aren't closed books but just pages to be turned — lifelines still to be written in relationship to a shifting world. And that the old spirits — wild, resilient and still with us — are vital to our shared story.

11

Homecoming

On the small hill beside the lake, the March sun was warm on my skin. It was the vernal equinox once more and three years on from the closure of the country at the start of the pandemic. I'd climbed through lengthening grasses to reach the top of the rise. Underfoot, the small white blades of star of Bethlehem split the damp earth. In our mountain valley, spring can be a stuttering thing, getting going as reluctantly as an old car in the cold, lurching back and forth between the seasons until the engine is warmed through, but down here, by the brilliant blue lake, it felt as though everything had been moving forward for some time. Green reeds lanced upwards from the edge of the marsh and a black redstart shivered its tail, as though dusting the stone it stood on. All around me I could smell blossom and sap and soil. As the land unlocked, it felt like a sense of promise was spreading, as if we were all being given another shot at renewal. Somewhere to the south, a hoopoe called its name. And from the top of the hill, I could see an archipelago of white islands beside the tawny sweep of reeds. It was the first day of spring. Not an end, but another beginning.

A year earlier, the lake had been scattered with dead Dalmatian pelicans. From a distance, it could have been an ice floe. So many of us had feared the worst after the disaster, expecting the spring to come – the spring unfolding around me on the hill at that moment – to be unbearably quiet for the species. But instead, the blue sky was spun with white threads, Dalmatian pelicans circling and turning above me, while others lowered over mountains still capped in snow. I sat in the grasses and watched the birds rise from their islands, heaving free of land, momentarily lumbering and clumsy until they caught a column of warm air and spiralled high as the most graceful shape in the sky. There was nowhere near the same density or profusion of life around the colony as in previous years, but it was a homecoming far greater than anyone had imagined possible.

I turned to follow a group of them gliding over the hills of juniper where trees had once been cut to make *pelaizia*. Although this winter fishing-trap tradition has since died out in Prespa, the lifeline it provided for the nesting pelicans in the desperate years of drought is still vividly remembered. As I sat there, I found myself thinking about the ancient junipers up on that ridge above the lakes. Because they're survivors, too. Some of them twisted into extraordinary and surprising shapes, the flow of expanding energies transformed after whatever pressures and challenges they faced long ago, whether from lightning strikes and buckling winds or storms that heaved them halfway out of the earth. The resilience they must have needed to remake their arrangement with the world, counterbalancing a radically altered centre of gravity, or reshooting from a fire-scorched or shattered crown. In their heartwood, as in the spiralling flights of Dalmatian pelicans returning to these ancient lakes, are held stories of endurance. Stories of persistence and fortitude scored deep into their lifelines.

I packed up my telescope and dropped down the hill as a pair of pelicans lowered towards the colonies, their beaks like tongues of fire in the breeding season. 'We used to shoot them, you know,' said Nikos as I loaded my gear into the car. A farmer from a nearby village, Nikos and his wife, Eudoxia, run a stand selling their agricultural produce at the foot of the hill. So friendly and generous are they that I'm rarely able to walk away without a bag of beans or chickpeas to take home with me. 'We didn't know any better,' continued Nikos, tilting his head as a lone pelican flew over us, the sound of its wings like gusts of wind. 'But you know what, these big birds, I now think of them as people.'

Migration is one of the incontestable wonders of the world. Whether scores of salmon finning upriver after years in the ocean to lay eggs on the same gravel bed where they were spawned themselves or caribou *becoming* a river as they pound in their thousands across the Canadian tundra each spring and autumn, these seasonal cycles of movement are emblematic of the living world's transformative force. And the movements of people can be no less dynamic and compelling. When we were still farming, an elderly woman dressed entirely in black would ride side-saddle on a mule down the mountain track each summer evening. Strapped to each side of the animal were metal jugs filled with milk that she would occasionally tap at with a wooden cane. No matter what work we were doing in the fields, we always stopped to watch her descend from the high slopes. It seemed like such an ancient pastoral image to us – and the woman herself must have been in her eighties by then – that each time it felt as if it might be the last time we saw that older world in motion.

The woman we watched in the thick glow of evening light with her mule and her milk was Sarakatsani – a transhumant people that traditionally moved with their animals on foot from their winter grounds in lowland and coastal Greece to summer pastures in the high mountains, chasing spring as it sped northwards across the country. Only once did I have the chance to spend time with the Sarakatsani community in Prespa before the traditions of movement and seasonal settlements in the uplands largely faded from the basin. That morning, beneath a brilliant summer sky, I was walking in the mountains with my friend Sid, the same friend who'd been considered a potential Bolshevik for wearing a floppy-eared hat in the snowy cemetery. No sooner had we rounded a curve in the granite folds than we were waved over to a set of beehive-shaped dwellings constructed from reeds cut from the edge of the lakes. Giorgos and Antonia, a middle-aged Sarakatsani couple who'd been journeying to this same spot for as long as they could remember, insisted we sit down with them for breakfast. Within moments a table was brought out from their makeshift yard and laid with cucumbers and tomatoes from their small garden and tangy cheese made from their animals' milk. Giorgos then poured each of us a large glass of *tsipouro* and removed from the pocket of his shirt an unopened packet of cigarettes. He stripped away its cellophane and crumpled off the foil, teasing out a single cigarette so that it stood proud of the others as he laid the packet before us on the table.

Until then, I'd thought of transhumant movement – and perhaps all movement if I'm honest – as essentially rootless, but that morning, under an alpine sky in the company of the Sarakatsani couple, I began to understand that the whole mountain was in fact their hearth. They'd welcomed us with the same gracious and generous hospitality common to so many Greek and Balkan houses. And as they began to describe their lives to us – the joys, the difficulties, the fears and hopes – I suddenly realised that each direction in their seasonal movements took Giorgos and Antonia closer to home. Journeying north to the mountains with their animals in spring signalled a homecoming for them; as did travelling south in the autumn after leaving the highlands behind. Home was both the beginning and end of their journeys.

Journeys take many forms.

There are few people I know whose lifeline reflects the shape and shared nature of the Prespa lakes as much as Haris Nikolaou's, the friend who tried helping me with our pipes when they froze on a winter's afternoon. Haris is Vlach, another of the wider region's transhumant peoples. Although Haris's family came from Albania, their pastoralist routes with their animals meant they ended up crossing the highlands and living for a period in what is now North Macedonia but was then Yugoslavia, where Haris was born. And from there the Nikolaou family traversed the mountains into Greek Prespa, where they've been settled ever since. Haris is a soft-spoken and gentle soul whose ancestral connection to movement feels as though it has left a genetic imprint on him even when sedentary. 'I can't sit still, even to read a book,' he once told me while we were walking through deep snow beside a river during a storm. 'I always prefer to be outside, or with my bees.'

Haris, who's married to Myrsini of the SPP, keeps bees on a plot of land at the foot of the mountains close to our old fields and stores his spare hives in the outbuildings at the back of our house. But he's also spent a large part of his life working as a conservationist with Prespa's pelicans, charged with a range of field duties including monitoring the colonies from the moment the birds first arrive in the basin at the beginning of the year.

'I don't think I expected more than a couple of hundred pairs of Dalmatian pelicans to return after the avian flu crisis, to be honest,' he said to me while dropping off beehives one afternoon. 'It was amazing to see so many coming back.'

This homecoming, in which just over 600 pairs of Dalmatian pelicans eventually nested in Prespa in the year after the H5N1 outbreak (having developed, it's believed, at least some degree of immunity to the virus), was possible only because of the decades of work put in by conservationists including Haris to protect the integrity of the wetland and build resilience within the population. As those efforts ultimately helped enable the establishment of colonies elsewhere in Greece, so too did the increase in population size mask a significant number of non-breeding birds that were suddenly able to take advantage of the additional space at the nesting sites to mate.

'I was so relieved when I saw them nesting and having nothing go wrong,' said Olga, the friend and pelican conservationist I'd accompanied when she was monitoring by drone. 'Looking at the footage on the tablet, I would smile and talk to them whenever I saw a few new nests being built here, a new breeding group in an inlet there, watching the young ones grow. *Wow, fantastic,* I thought, I was so happy.' And it wasn't just in Prespa that the homecoming unfolded but also on nearby Lake Cheimaditida, where the colony that had been founded only seven years earlier had been entirely wiped out. But in 2023 fifty-one pairs of Dalmatian pelicans raised a total of fifty-eight young on the lake.

Watching these magnificent birds gather again at a time when considerable uncertainty surrounded their future made clear to me just how similar their lifeways are to those of the Sarakatsani and other pastoralist peoples. The winter grounds of migratory species are just as critical to their well-being as their summer sites, because in either direction these birds are travelling home. And what makes those journeys home possible, just as it would have made the Sarakatsani's journeys possible when crossing mountains and plains with their herds of animals, is everything in between. Which further highlights the need to see the places and species of the world, including ourselves, not in isolation from one another but as inherently linked.

Wetlands are a good example of this, as they can be sites of incredible connectivity or devastating severance. Not only do they act as home for migratory and resident species, but they are essential stopping-off points for journeying creatures. And their benefits radiate outwards through human communities too, being essential for pollution filtration, flood protection, recreation, tourism, fishing, agricultural irrigation, carbon sequestration and food. Yet despite their significance, wetlands are being erased from the world. According to the UN's biodiversity platform, IPBES, more than 85 per cent of the wetlands in existence in the year 1700 had been destroyed by 2000, a rate of disappearance three times greater in percentage terms than global forest loss. In Europe, roughly two-thirds of the continent's wetlands have been destroyed in the past century alone. Which is why it's essential to understand wetlands – and to intensify work towards their protection when in good condition and restoration where degraded – within the context of an interconnected *network* of waters. Remove even a part of it and you rupture a vital lifeline for both people and wild species. There was only a homecoming for Prespa's Dalmatian pelicans in 2023 because of the presence of healthy wetlands at both ends of their journeys as well as along the way; finding any of them destroyed would be just as ruinous as had the Sarakatsani arrived in the mountains or the lowlands only to discover their home was no longer there.

'One of the most important aspects of conservation is water and that's utterly indivisible by the lines on a map,' said Julia as she waded through a pool in rubber boots. 'It knows no borders. And much of the biodiversity doesn't either.'

We'd been walking upriver and talking about the impetus behind PrespaNet and other approaches to transboundary environmental issues. It had been her idea to drop down the steep sides of one of the river channels in our valley to alter our perspective on that intimate world. We'd discovered water falling into bowls of stone and willow stumps bearded in moss like old river gods. Being within the river instead of above it shifted our focus just enough for it to feel as if we were exploring both the same and yet an entirely different place, which is effectively what so much cross-border work is ultimately about. It reminded me of once being in a café on the Albanian side of the lakes and seeing a wall covered with black-and-white photos of French troops in Prespa during the First World War moving in long lines through deep snow with their horses beside the water. 'It's the same place,' said a young man when he brought my coffee to the table and saw me looking at the photos, 'but it feels so different seeing it like that.'

'One of the key things we discovered when we did the bear study,' said Julia as she clambered over a boulder in the river, 'was that the bears are moving around. Which we know, of course, but to see it so clearly takes it to another level in terms of how you feel about it and approach it. So there are animals moving around all over the place; there are birds moving around all over the place. And with the fall of the water, the habitats particularly on the North Macedonian side of the lakes are becoming more and more attractive to birds. For feeding herons, for example. At some point we think that heron colonies might set up there as things shift in the basin. The birds don't think, *Well, we like our Greek colonies*, or *We like our colonies here or there*; they'll go wherever it's best for them to find food and refuge and a space to breed in. If that happens to be the other side of the lake, then it makes no difference to them, because for them it's not the *other* side. And, of course, our challenges are equally non-border-related. Climate change doesn't stop at the border; climate change affects all of us. If you are even remotely going to stand a chance of tackling or mitigating climate change, then you have to work together. Because it's one watershed, it's one ecological unit or space.'

Because it's one watershed, the socio-economic issues faced in each of the three countries sharing the basin, together with the emerging challenges of climate change, are surprisingly similar given the radically different modern histories and phases of economic development they've experienced. The reality of depopulation and the departure of young people in particular for urban centres and other countries – a movement away from agriculture and fishing that's common to many rural communities throughout southern Europe – is making itself increasingly felt in Prespa. While there are incomers like ourselves, along with others bringing their own energies and ideas drawn here by work in the environmental and tourism fields or who decided to stay on after falling in love with Prespa after visiting or volunteering here, there are significant departures, too.

'You were hungry, but everyone was hungry, so it was simple,' said Kosta Trajce when I asked him what it was like in Albanian Prespa under the rule of Enver Hoxha. We were drinking pale green *raki* flavoured with nettles in his house in the village of Tuminec on Great Prespa Lake. A fisherman for the past forty-five years and president of the Fishery Management Organisation, Kosta is responsible for monitoring lake practices on the Albanian side of the water. 'But after 1990,' he continued, 'when the country opened up after Communism, people left and saw other things. And now they don't want to come back. Or they come back, but they don't want to raise children here.' According to Kosta, there were 1,250 people living in Tuminec in 2011. Now there are fewer than 500.

The situation in North Macedonia is no different. At a café-bar in Resen, a town of around 9,000 inhabitants and the only urban centre in the Prespa watershed, Nikola, the server, told me that very few of his friends from school were still living there. 'Where have they gone?' I asked him. 'Different places. Germany, Italy. About a dozen people I know were working in Israel but came back when the war started.' Nikola himself was soon to leave for Alaska, where he'd started spending a few months every year after seeing an ad for jobs in a fish-canning factory on the coast. 'I've heard every song on my playlist about a thousand times,' he laughed. 'I just go there, put my headphones on, put my head

down and work. Then I have some money to come back home
to Prespa with.'

Despite the ongoing issue of depopulation, there are numerous
positive developments throughout the basin. According to Kosta,
fish harvests in Albania have steadily increased since greater efforts
were made to regulate and control the closed season for spawning. In North Macedonia, several excellent eco-tourism initiatives
have started up, focusing on the region's culinary wealth and its
stunning mountain landscapes as a place for walking holidays at
a time when receding water levels make reliance on lake-based
tourism activities increasingly precarious. In Greek Prespa, a
long-touted drip irrigation system that will increase agricultural
efficiency while reducing water take from the lakes will soon
be operational. And during recent local elections, the political
grouping that was to end up winning the mayor's office mounted
a distinctive campaign based around young people bringing new
ideas and fresh perspectives to the region's issues, several of whom
were ultimately elected as councillors, heralding a potentially new
era on our side of the waters.

Prespa has always been an essential blend of the human and
more-than-human worlds for me. You can't separate out the different forms of life and the varied challenges they face and still
have the same place. Nor can you ignore the entanglement of the
borders if you aspire to elevating living conditions in the region.
Despite a history of frequently acrimonious relations between the
three nations, traced back to land disputes, demographic suspicions, ideological models and the movements of people, some of
the hard work needed to overcome these schisms is already under
way. It's a place where bridges can – and are – being slowly built,
seen in the joint monitoring of wintering waterbirds by environmental NGOs, the sensitive, trilateral management of water
resources that emerged out of the grassroots protection of pelicans on the lakes, workshops on joint fire-protection strategies,

educational, scientific and artistic exchanges, the collaboration of cross-border municipalities on mutually beneficial projects and the ongoing conservation efforts of PrespaNet. With the reopening of the border crossing within the basin between Greece and North Macedonia, expected by the end of 2027, another opportunity for strengthening relationships will begin. It took nearly two decades for the Transboundary Prespa Park to officially become a political and institutional reality, a sign of the difficulties in healing national differences and divisions, but also a reminder, especially at the local level, which is where nearly all of the above initiatives originated rather than at state level, of what is always possible through connective cooperation. Through inclusion, solidarity and exchange. A shared endeavour forged at a crossroads, whose catchphrase sums up its vision – *Prespa: Three Countries, Two Lakes, One Future.*

Journeys take many forms.

It wasn't until I shared breakfast with Giorgos and Antonia in the mountains of Prespa that I finally understood how home can be both a place and a way of getting there. And that sometimes you have to trust the path that's being shown you to find your way back. At the end of our travels through southern India, where our relationship properly began, Julia returned to London and I travelled north into the Himalayas. My destination was Dharamshala, a town spread over the forested foothills of the imposing, snow-covered Dhauladhar range that has been home to the Dalai Lama and the Tibetan government in exile since 1960. Once there, I found a basic room in a guest house in a nearby valley and walked into town through a wood each morning to attend the Dalai Lama's yearly teachings on Buddhism. Dozens of other travellers from around the world had gathered there for the same reason, sitting in the spacious courtyard of his residence while monks in maroon robes poured yak butter tea into the cups we were each asked to bring. And then the Dalai Lama – gentle, funny, thoughtful and engaging – began his public teachings while sitting cross-legged in front of us.

One of the first things he had said while talking about meditation and its relationship to the openness and posture of the body was to sleep on our left-hand sides so that our hearts were closer to the earth. As an extremely light sleeper, I struggled immensely with this practice, rolling over umpteen times a night when woken by owls or dogs or the wind through the pines in that valley outside of town. But I stuck at it, consciously trying to make myself aware of my sleeping patterns and to stay true to that side as much as I could. In the meantime, I attended the teachings each day, listening attentively to the Dalai Lama's words on emptiness, non-attachment, suffering, awareness and compassion within the Buddhist tradition. In the afternoons, when the teachings were over for the day, I would sit at a table outside my guest house and try to work on a novel that I was writing at the time, but mostly I just observed the movements of wild creatures in the valley with increasing wonder and fascination. I'd hauled north with me on a series of trains and buses some of the classic field guides to Indian birds written by the ornithologist Salim Ali that Julia and I had found in a bookshop while in the south, and whenever I saw a species for the first time – red-headed tit, verditer flycatcher, Himalayan whistling thrush – I would write up a brief description of the bird and its behaviour so that my workbook for the novel increasingly resembled a natural history guide to the small valley. That was the shape of my days; and come morning, I would set off again into town for the teachings.

After a week of sticking with this routine, I woke at dawn and knew that something had changed. My desire to attend the teachings had shifted to an intense need to walk higher into the mountains. All these years later, I can see how that path in my

lifeline had already been signposted for me should I wish to follow it. There were those vibrant green clearings in the London
landscape that became so incredibly vital to me. There was Sid
suggesting that I bring binoculars to India and the sarus cranes and
extraordinary days of discovery that followed in Keoladeo National
Park. There was that emergent and shared love of birds as Julia and
I fell in love with each other on our journey. And there were the
wild creatures of the valley that so entranced me. But that morning,
when faced with a physical choice of paths, either left into town
to the teachings or right into the mountains for whatever came
next on the journey ahead, all I knew with any certainty was that
even if I wasn't able to sleep on one side I could try *living* with my
heart closer to the earth instead. And so I followed a winding track
towards the snowfields and encountered griffon vultures and mon-
gooses and wild rhododendron forests. I met red-vented bulbuls,
Himalayan tree creepers and a great barbet calling from the dark
green tip of a pine. I felt an immense world opening up to me with
each step. When I now look back at the twenty-seven-year-old that
never returned to the teachings but just kept walking in the hills,
there's a part of me that thinks, *What were you doing, man, giving up
a week in the company of the Dalai Lama like that?* But the other part,
the far greater part, understands that the teachings had done exactly
what they were meant to do for me, in that they provided answers
to a set of questions I didn't even know I had. They showed me
that the living world was my place of homecoming.

I'm sometimes asked if I have a favourite place in Prespa. Given
the many options, my answer tends to vary according to the season and the mood I'm in at the time. There's that porous spine
of limestone above the lakes with its sacred grove of junipers and
the playful bear cub and its mother. Or the point at the top of

the Galičica mountains in North Macedonia where I proposed to Julia on an autumn afternoon, the stunning blue panorama of Lake Ohrid and both of the Prespa lakes visible at the same time with a single turn of the head. Or there's the glorious, heart-singing karst country, which is still intact and with us at the time of writing. Although a government permit was granted in early 2024 for the construction of wind turbines along the highest ridge in what is meant to be an EU-protected Natura 2000 area (a different proposal to the one we had carried out ornithological surveys for over a decade earlier), Prespa's municipal council voted unanimously against it after canvassing opinion from local residents, issuing what it called a Commitment to the Future, which stated that 'Prespa is and will remain "something wild for tomorrow". This means we are committed to preserving the natural beauty and ecological value of our area, protecting it from actions that could alter its character.'

But if I had to choose just one from the numerous places that have come to mean so much to me, I would pick a place that is completely new rather than enduringly old like these others. So new, in fact, that it doesn't even show up in any of the photos in Giorgos Catsadorakis's book that held us spellbound while reading it over wine in our London flat the day it arrived. And it's a place that might just tell us something important about how to move into the future in an uncertain and shifting world.

We know that Great Prespa Lake, in particular, is receding. The drop in its water levels and surface area is unmistakable. Made clear by the satellite photos and the old, sloping shorelines. We know, too, of the considerable worries shared by nearly everyone in the basin: the serious concerns about how this decline will affect fisheries, agriculture, water supplies, tourism and wildlife. But the loss of water isn't the only story about the shrinking lake that needs telling, because the other story of the shrinking lake is the story of a forest.

Years ago, on another of Sid's several visits to Prespa, the two of us went walking along the shore one afternoon. Neither of us can now recall the conversation we were having or who stopped first to emphasise the point they wanted to make, but we suddenly came to a halt on the sandy track. Which is when we heard the great *whoosh* of wings and looked up to see an enormous eagle owl tumbling from the top of the tree we were standing beside, its piercing, flame-coloured eyes growing larger and larger as it fell towards us before the bird gained enough lift to clear our heads and fly away. Sid and I dropped to the ground, joyfully laughing at the shock and beauty of having serendipitously stopped beside precisely the same tree chosen by the owl to roost in that day. A tree that wasn't in any of the photographs in the book that first brought us here because the forest didn't yet exist.

I pulled Giorgos's book from the shelf while writing this closing chapter, flipping through its beautiful and evocative pages in search of a specific image nearly a quarter of a century after first seeing it. And there it was, the photograph that had felt so magnetic to us, so spectacularly unlike anything either of us had seen in a landscape in Europe until then that it convinced us that this was the place to make a leap of faith for. It had been taken in winter from the mountains behind our house and contains within its frame the compressed topographical layers of the basin, so that it flows from the red-tiled roofs of the stone village we now live in down to the flat tawny plain and steely blue waters of Great Prespa Lake right across to the snow-streaked mountains of Albania rising high in the distance. It's an epic image that stunned us when we first saw it, but what strikes me about it today is the significance of the southern shore being entirely devoid of trees. No matter how close I look, there's nothing there to interrupt the meeting of land and lake.

At the beginning of this other story – at the beginning of the forest – are reeds. Reeds that anchored themselves in the shallow water when lowering lake levels made conditions ideal

for colonisation. Over time, as the reeds gained a greater foot-
hold, they expanded their extent, chasing after the receding water.
Those reeds stranded higher up the shore, however, began breaking down into what is known as reed litter, the perfect base for
bramble scrub and moisture-loving trees such as alder, willow,
poplar and silver birch. In the decades that the lake has been leaving, this cycle of reeds and scrub and trees has kept repeating until
a unique forest surfaced where once there was water.

This forest – little more than three decades old now – is the
only one of its kind in all of Greece. Nowhere else can its specific composition of tree species be found living alongside one
another. After Chris and I ran a camera trap in it for a few weeks,
we quickly came to see that it acted as a vital ecological corridor
between the granite and limestone halves of the basin, enabling
the movement of large numbers of animals without the attendant
risk of having to cross farmers' fields or the open terrain and road
along the isthmus. Seen from above, it follows the curves of the
shore precisely: receding lake lines becoming another lifeline.

Inside the forest, it's the sheer generative entanglement and
agency of the living world that astonishes me each time I'm there.
The way it has filled a space as water fell away. Its profusion of life
– the thick spread of silver birch and poplar, the songs of night-
ingales and warblers, the paths of wolf and wild boar, the mother
bear shepherding her three cubs across the track when I'd turned
back for my hat – is the result of resilient adaptability. And as I witnessed when the avian influenza crisis unfolded on Lesser Prespa
Lake, which demanded an urgent and unprecedented response,
adaptability is key to weathering our current and future ages. And
not just the adaptability of individuals, communities, organisations
and governments to fit as best they can to the altered reality of the
physical world, but an adaptability of ideas and perspectives. An
adaptability, ultimately, of stories – so that a flexibility of thinking enables practices, approaches, associations and coalitions to

be embraced that might once have been considered unfeasible or even unheard of. To think outside the box that is no longer a box because we've made everything a radically different shape. To become a forest when a lake is leaving.

Journeys take many forms.

The blue pick-up truck that Vassilis helped us buy in our second season of farming had been built in 1980. You wouldn't have guessed it from how it looked, though, as it had largely spent the twenty-one years of its life from the production line until we bought it in 2001 resting under a canvas cover in a car port in our village, needed only for occasional local forays when its elderly owner fancied a coffee in one of Prespa's cafés. Like all Greek vehicles considered commercial, our pick-up truck had its agricultural purpose and the place where it was registered for use stencilled in white paint on the side panelling. That August, as our crops were flourishing but the restaurant we primarily supplied in Thessaloniki had taken its summer break, we loaded up the truck and took a much-needed weekend off from work ourselves to spend some time by the sea.

We drove out of the basin that day and crossed the mountains to Florina, continuing onwards through wine country around Amyntaio and the fruit orchards near Lake Vegoritida. We passed the waterfalls of Edessa and dropped down off a plateau to cross the expansive lowland plain planted with rice and cotton and industry towards Thessaloniki. We skirted that vibrant city at the head of the Thermaic Gulf, the lone mass of Mount Olympus rising in the distance across the water, and turned south towards Halkidiki and the first of its three large peninsulas. As we neared the coast, windblown and dripping with sweat from driving 330 kilometres in the summer heat with the windows down because there was no air-conditioning in the old truck, we followed a winding road from the clifftop village of Afytos and came to a stop beside a beach as traffic stalled ahead of us. As we sat there, a woman in a green bathing suit, the sea burning blue behind her, began crossing the road from the beach. She had a towel over her shoulder and a book in one hand. Glancing over at us, her eyes dropped to the name of our village printed in small white letters on the side of the pick-up. As soon as she saw it, she made her way towards us.

'Hello,' she said, smiling as she lowered her face to our open window in a queue of idling vehicles. 'You must be the English couple from Prespa. I'm so happy to meet you,' she continued, 'and I hope you enjoy living in Greece. Bye bye.'

The woman finished crossing the road just as the traffic edged forward and we never saw her again. We had no idea who she was, or how she knew about us, only that in the extraordinary moment of serendipity by the sea she had kindled a connection hundreds of kilometres from the place in which we were still trying to put down roots. It was as though home, just as it was for the Sarakatsani on their migrations and the countless pelicans we've watched cross the mountains over the years, was both the beginning and end of our journey that day. And her intimate gesture of welcome reminded us that the physical journey we'd embarked on to Prespa after reading a book was only the very beginning of that journey. Because the real journey – the far greater, more difficult and ultimately rewarding one – was the journey *into* a place. A journey that was never ours alone because it involved so many people and wild species for it to be made meaningful. I don't think we'd ever imagined in our wildest dreams what this journey – this homecoming of ours – might grow into over time. Yet from its earliest days, it was shown to us that home is a relationship above all else. A way of living connectively. And it's a relationship built on kinship, reciprocity and solidarity – a relationship sometimes given heart by complete strangers.

It was late on a December afternoon when I stopped in the village of Glloboçeni on the Albanian side of Great Prespa Lake. The sun was tilting away and I could see from a distance that the headland I wanted to walk was already deep in shadow. An elderly woman in a floral headscarf and apron was wheelbarrowing firewood up the lane. She stopped and then smiled, greeting me in Macedonian and Albanian. When I'd exhausted the few words I knew in each language, I continued in Greek. Together we raised our arms and laughed loudly, as if to say that at least we'd tried. A pair of bee-keepers in white suits smoked their hives and a donkey broke away from its clan to nudge at my elbow, smelling the apples I had in my bag. As I followed the curve of the village, I passed traditional haystacks shaped like thimbles at the edge of the sloping shore. My friend Meto Velevski, an ornithologist with MES, once told me about a pair of storks that had nested on top of a haystack like these on the Pelagonian plain in North Macedonia. Each time a villager removed feed for their animals they'd added a long post to the stack, so that by the time it had been emptied of hay the stork's nest was supported solely by a wigwam of wood. Another small story of the kind of care that shifts how we see the world and what's possible within it.

I reached the edge of the village and found a path that felt no different from the paths I'd walked hundreds of times on the Greek side of the basin, where the reddish soil is stony and boul-dered and the dense stands of juniper and box squeeze you into a narrow seam like a lead of open water in sea ice. Wild boars had peeled back the autumn soil in search of roots; wayside stones glowed with emerald mosses. Downslope of me, a sparrowhawk spooked from a stunted oak, shooting off across the water. It passed over a yellow wooden boat and a pair of fishermen haul-ing a net aboard. I tracked it across the bay towards the village of Tuminec, where I'd sat with Kosta and heard his stories of the lakes.

'We need wet snows from the south to raise the level of the water again,' I remembered him saying, a little confused until he explained that warm winds melt a snowfall into the watershed while dry air from the north can result in evaporation, a process I would later learn is called sublimation. 'It's been many years since we had snow like that here,' he'd added.

As the sparrowhawk swept landward, slipping away from me as it grew small in the distance, I saw for the first time what looked like a monastery around the coast that I'd never noticed from the main road before. Even after all this time in the basin, there's no shortage of surprises.

To journey around the lakes is to see home from a different angle, like the day Julia and I had dropped down into the river in our valley, walking through the water with a shifted perspective on its flow. It rearranges views, patterns, shapes and forms, revealing previously unseen connections and commonalities. And it highlights differences, too – because what makes this place unique is that it's a watershed of variations and contrasts brought together and blended into one.

The path grew stonier and more rutted as it descended, the slick mud and ankle-twisting roots keeping my eyes focused on the ground. After ducking beneath a low branch of oak, I suddenly stepped into a bowl of stunning light. The trees had thinned to a grassy clearing where the headland bent south, stilted on white cliffs above the water. The whole of the lake was beautifully blue. Not the same blues that grace these lakes in summer, like the rich magnificence stitched into the feathers of a kingfisher, but a paler and more reflective radiance: the blue of swimming pools and ice and eyes. An egret lifted like a white flag from the shore, the sound of its wings as they worked the air the only thing I could hear in the huge silence of the headland.

I sat on a slab of limestone and looked out over the lake. The island of Golem Grad, that remarkable place of snakes and tortoises that feels like a world within a world, wore a ring of brilliant white stone, its reflection in the water making it seem as though it was floating free of the basin. Beyond it, along the eastern shore in North Macedonia, rose the crinkled ridges of snow-capped mountains clad in forests of leafless beeches, the granite folds so different from this evergreen limestone headland. Nestled within those peaks are a pair of glacial lakes called Pelister's Eyes, the rising route to them a track built by French soldiers during the First World War and still known locally as the French Road. As I swivelled to the right and reached Greece, I pulled my binoculars from my bag, finding at the same time the apples that the donkey must have smelled in the lane. I named the villages out loud as I saw them: Miliona, Laimos and, finally, our own, Agios Germanos. From the perspective of this other shore – a distinction not made by the birds of these lakes – everything seemed so small against the vastness of the basin. But it wasn't, of course, because the stories of this shared place, like the stories of so many places called home around the world, are anything but minor when held close to the heart.

In the sinking light, I could see the alpine slopes that Giorgos and Antonia had journeyed to each spring when they made the mountains their home. I could see the bay of Psaradhes where Germanos and Alexandra remembered high water against the houses and where the restored skeleton of a brown bear stands on a table in the pale windowlight of the old schoolroom. I could see the tip of the Roti peninsula where monks once dwelled and great crested grebes still gather in the winter cold. I could see the isthmus that thousands of years ago split an ancient lake into two and where the falling waters bring bombs to the surface while seeding an astonishing forest. And beyond the isthmus, I could just make out the reeds marking the nesting islands where nearly 400 Dalmatian pelican chicks fledged in 2023, raising hopes that the colony will recover and thrive on these shared waters once more.

I look back now, at what seems like another lifeline ago, to the day we arrived in Prespa on that summer's afternoon with no idea of what lay ahead of us, and I realise that none of the extraordinary thrill at being in this crossroads place has ever left me. Whenever I've been away and crest the pass on my way home to see the lakes shimmering inside a bowl of mountains it still feels like the first time. Only it's a first time deepened by experience, so that the layers of the place lend it an even greater depth and beauty than before. A beauty not without its wounds and scars, as we've seen throughout the course of this book, where the complex and sometimes contested lifelines of people, history, ecosystems and wild species are entwined, but a beauty worth knowing even more because of what this place has lived through and endured. What's helped shape it into the unique and extraordinary shelter that it is today. Not only is it the place that has so fundamentally changed our lives, but it's the place that will go on changing them because there's still so much more of it to grow into as a home. So much of it still to hold, to learn, to love.

I rose and readied to go. What was left of the day was being gathered up at its edges, the winter blue of the lake fading to evening grey as the reflection of the island fell away from the water. I took a last look at our valley on the far side of the lakes, where the snowfields of the mountains caught the sun's dipping glow, blazing like beacons before dark. A lone boat on the water turned for shore and the egret resettled on the rocks. It was time for me to leave. It would soon be wren-light, the hour of wolves and bears in the shared shelter of the basin. I pulled an apple from my pack and found the path heading home.

WRENS IV

I open the door to a cold blue sky and a thin layer of snow that fell two nights ago. A little early, as it's only November, but not unheard of for this time of year in the mountains. I sort through some of the seasoned beech beside the porch that Julia barrowed down from the back garden the week before when we were clearing space for our new stacks of firewood. I gather a few logs in my arms to split into kindling and look up at the nest above the door.

Two years earlier, the wrens had returned for a third and final winter with us. That last season was so mild that the birds didn't even appear until the end of February, when a late cold snap ushered them back into the nest. All week I'd watched them at dusk as they arrived, swelling to a dozen as they took refuge above our door. And in the mornings I counted them back out again, seeing them streak into days of ice and snow. Since then, I've heard the occasional clicking of a single wren as the sky dimmed on the coldest of nights but haven't witnessed any birds settling into the swallow's nest again. Perhaps those wrens with the strongest attachment to that cup of dried mud had died in the intervening time, or they'd found another roosting site that offered even better protection from the elements. Either way, for three whole winters that nest of another's lent them vital shelter.

With an armful of beech, I cross the garden to my splitting stump. I drive the heavy blade of the axe into each piece, shaving off slivers that will catch easily from the coals in the grate. Replacing my axe in the shed, I gather up the pieces of kindling that have fallen to each side of the stump. As I turn around and start walking back to the house something suddenly stands out to me at that different angle. Beside the path in the snow that we've worn smooth since it first fell are the steps of someone else.

The night before, Julia and I had gone outside into a world of white light. It was nearly eleven o'clock and the full Beaver Moon was as bright as we'd ever seen it. It illuminated the meadows and hills around the house so that we could make out each shrub and tree against the stark pallor of snow. Clouds spun past so fast that it seemed as if it was the moon itself that was being propelled across the sky. Jupiter hung shining to the south of us and stars flickered in the fastness.

'If there was a bear about tonight we'd see it easily,' I'd said to Julia, a faint halo ringing the moon as ice particles high in the atmosphere reflected its scattered light.

'Definitely, look at how bright everything is,' she'd replied. We'd stood there in the cold for another minute or two, scanning the moonlit snow for any sign of movement before returning indoors.

I set the kindling on the ground and kneel beside the prints, bewildered by what they're telling me. Looking up, I now see others in front of it, lined up in a row in the direction of the house. I quickly pull my phone from my pocket and snap a photo of my hand beside one of the impressions, messaging it to Julia at work. *OMG! Is that what I think it is?* she immediately replies. *Pretty sure, can't think what else it could be!* I stand up, trying to decide if there could be any other explanation for what I'm seeing. But the more I stare at the prints in the snow the more it becomes startlingly clear. On the night of the full moon, a brown bear visited our garden.

I follow the tracks in reverse to see where the bear entered the yard and find paw prints sliding down a set of wooden posts leaning against the stone wall. From there the bear had rootled through leaves in search of walnuts beneath the tree that I see from my window each day while writing. It then lumbered past the splitting stump and shed, joining the path that we'd flattened through snow, which is why Julia hadn't noticed anything when leaving for work earlier in the morning. But on the steps at the front of our house I find a single paw print with its distinctive pads and claws clear in the snow. It had walked right past our front door while we were sleeping. I follow its prints across the garden to the stone wall beside the stream, where it had turned around and lowered itself down to the water more than two metres below by clinging on with its front paws. In the long raking lines left behind by its claws, the snow told a story of the dangling bear that we wouldn't otherwise have known.

That evening, when Julia gets home from work, we walk the bear's path by torchlight, still buzzing and overwhelmed by what the snow shows in the dark. We take turns placing our hands beside the prints and reckon from the size of them that it's a young bear that still lacks experience or has got confused by the early snowfall while foraging. It's the first time we've been certain of having a bear in the garden – and the experience carries an intense and heightened blend of beauty, astonishment, nervousness and awe.

'I followed the tracks on the other side,' I say as we shine our lights over the claw marks on the stone wall.

'Where did it go?' Julia asks.

'Under the elderberries and then over the stream. It circled around the meadow to that other walnut over there and dug around a bit before heading up to the dirt track towards the mountains.'

We hold hands as we look at the silhouette of the walnut in the meadow, our breaths clouding in the glow of the torches. The stars so bright in the endless mountain sky.

'Did you ever imagine when we were living in London that we'd end up in a place where a bear would walk past our house?' Julia asks.

We both laugh in the dark and follow the steps of the bear back to the old swallow's nest above the door and to the warmth of the fires inside.

Bibliography

Abram, David, *Becoming Animal: An Earthly Cosmology* (New York: Vintage, 2011)
——, 'On Being Human in a More-Than-Human World', *Centre for Humans and Nature*, 22 July 2012
Aguon, Julian, *No Country for Eight-spot Butterflies* (London: Penguin, 2022)
——, 'To Hell with Drowning', *The Atlantic*, 1 November 2021
Alexander, Kurtis, 'Rush to rescue thousands of endangered abalone buried in Big Sur landslides', *San Francisco Chronicle*, 3 April 2021
Ashworth, James, 'Bird flu kills thousands of South American sea lions as outbreak continues', Natural History Museum (UK), 9 March 2023
Bahnson, Fred, and Jeremy Seifert, 'The Church Forests of Ethiopia: A Mystical Geography', *Emergence Magazine*, 11 January 2020
Bangstad, Sindre, and Torbjørn Tumyr Nilsen, 'Thoughts on the Planetary: An Interview with Achille Mbembe', *New Frame* (2019)
Bauhaus Earth, 'Toward re-entanglement: a charter for the city and the earth' (Rome: 8 June 2022)
Bautista, Carlos, et al., 'Large carnivore damage in Europe: analysis of compensation and prevention programs', *Biological Conservation*, vol. 235 (July 2019), pp. 308–16
Bearfoot, Cheyenne, 'Land Back: The Indigenous Fight to Reclaim Stolen Lands', KQED, 21 April 2022
Bersi, Eurydice, 'Too much of a good thing? Wind power and the battle for Greece's wild heart', Reporters United, 7 October 2021
Beyer, Robert M., and Andrea Manica, 'Historical and projected future range sizes of the world's mammals, birds, and amphibians', *Nature Communications*, 11 (2020); doi.org/10.1038/s41467-020-19455-9
'Biodiversity highest on Indigenous-managed lands' (press release), *UBC Research and Innovation*, 31 July 2019
Bounas, Anastasios, 'Large pre-migratory roost of Lesser Kestrels (*Falco naumanni*) in Ioannina city, Greece: Trends, roost characteristics, and implications for conservation', *Journal of Raptor Research*, vol. 50 (2016), no. 4, pp. 416–21

Bourke, India, 'Saving our Wild Isles is David Attenborough's most political show yet', *New Statesman*, 9 April 2023

Bridle, James, *Ways of Being: Animals, Plants, Machines: The Search for a Planetary Intelligence* (London: Allen Lane, 2022)

Burston, Cole, and Leyland Cecco, '"There's nothing left in Lytton": The Canadian village destroyed by wildfire – picture essay', *Guardian*, 25 July 2021

Burton, Nylah, 'Learning a new language can help us escape climate catastrophe', *Vice*, 15 April 2021

Butler, Judith, 'Creating an inhabitable world for humans means dismantling rigid forms of individuality,' *Time*, 21 April 2021

Bytyci, Fatos, and Ognen Teofilovski, 'Locals fear disaster as North Macedonia's Lake Prespa recedes', Reuters, 14 September 2023

'California to truck young salmon to the Pacific because of low river levels', *Los Angeles Times*, 29 April 2021

Cámara-Leret, Rodrigo, and Jordi Bascompte, 'Language extinction triggers the loss of unique medicinal knowledge', *PNAS* (June 2021); doi.org/10.1073/pnas.2103683118

'Canada Lytton: Heatwave record village overwhelmingly burned in wildfire', BBC, 1 July 2021

Canavan, Claudia, 'You use 140 litres of water a day: here are 6 ways to get through less', Huffpost, 23 May 2018

Carrington, Damian, 'Arctic stronghold of world's seeds flooded after permafrost melts', *Guardian*, 19 May 2017

——, 'Climate emissions shrinking the stratosphere, scientists reveal', *Guardian*, 12 May 2021

——, 'Fossil fuels being subsidised at a rate of $13m a minute, says IMF', *Guardian*, 24 August 2023

Cassella, Carly, 'This frozen cave lion is so well preserved you can still see its whiskers', *Science Alert*, 6 January 2023

Catsadorakis, Giorgos, *Prespa: A Story for Man and Nature* (Agios Germanos: The Society for the Protection of Prespa, 1999)

——, *The Book of Pelicans* (Agios Germanos: The Society for the Protection of Prespa, 2002)

Cílek, Václav, *To Breathe With Birds: A Book of Landscapes* (Philadelphia: University of Pennsylvania Press, 2015)

Cocker, Mark, *Birds and People* (London: Jonathan Cape, 2013)

Coles, Terri, 'Indigenous languages are in danger of becoming extinct – here's how you can help save them', Huffpost, 21 June 2018

'Collecting water is often a colossal waste of time for women and girls' (press release), UNICEF, 29 August 2016

Colliopoulou, Hélène, 'Desolation in Greece's Dadia Park after Europe's biggest fire', Phys.org, 3 (November 2023)

Cooney, Chris, 'How songbirds island-hopped their way from Australia to colonise the world', *The Conversation*, 30 August 2016

Crook, Mackenzie, *Detectorists*, season 2, episode 2 (BBC Four, first aired 5 November 2015)

Danforth, Loring M., and Riki Van Boeschoten, *Children of the Greek Civil War: Refugees and the Politics of Memory* (Chicago: University of Chicago Press, 2012)

Davis, Wade, *The Wayfinders: Why Ancient Wisdom Matters in the Modern World* (Toronto: House of Anansi Press, 2009)

Earthquake Hazards Program, 'A glossary' (USGS: Science for a Changing World); https://www.usgs.gov/glossary/earthquake-hazards-program

Evyenidou, Despina, Ioannis Kanonidis and Thanasis Papazotos, *The Monuments of Prespa* (Athens: Archaeological Receipts Fund, 1991)

Fa, Julia E., et al., 'Importance of Indigenous Peoples' lands for the conservation of Intact Forest Landscapes', *Frontiers in Ecology and the Environment* (January 2020); doi.org/10.1002/fee.2148

Farge, Emma, 'Sand crisis looms as world population surges, U.N. warns', Reuters, 27 April 2022

Ghosh, Amitav, *The Nutmeg's Curse: Parables for a Planet in Crisis* (London: John Murray, 2021)

Gill, Victoria, 'Regent honeyeater: Endangered bird has "forgotten its song"', BBC, 17 March 2021

Gonev, Andrej, et al., 'Dietary habits of the brown bear (*Ursus arctos*) in the transboundary Prespa basin', *Macedonian Journal of Ecology and Environment*, vol. 25, issue 2 (2023), pp. 101–12; doi.org/10.59194/MJEE23252101g

Gonzalez, John-Paul, and Gavin Macgregor-Skinner, 'Dangerous viral pathogens of animal origin: risk and biosecurity', *Zoonoses: Infections Affecting Humans and Animals* (2014), pp. 1015–62; https://link.springer.com/referenceworkentry/10.1007/978-3-031-27164-9_41

Goodfellow, Maya, '"We can't pretend the ecological crisis is separate": The economist thinking differently about the climate crisis', *Guardian*, 10 January 2024

Gorenflo, L. J., et al., 'Co-occurrence of linguistic and biological diversity in biodiversity hotspots and high biodiversity wilderness areas', *PNAS* (2012); doi.org/10.1073/pnas.1117511109

'Greece wildfires "worst ecological disaster" in decades, says PM Mitsotakis', Euronews, 12 August 2021

'Greece witnesses hottest winter on record', ekathimerini.com, 3 March 2024

Greenfield, Patrick, 'Farm plan poses "catastrophic" threat to Zambian park vital for fruit bats', *Guardian*, 21 June 2021

——, 'Court halts land clearance on edge of protected park in Zambia', *Guardian*, 7 February 2022

Guasco, Anna, 'Upwelling: Ecological Memory on the Coast', *The Scholar*, 18 May 2021

Guha, Nabarun, 'Gangetic river dolphins in Assam decline in wake of anthropogenic pressures', Mongabay, 24 August 2022

Hanson, Eric, et al. 'The Residential School System', *Indigenous Foundations*, First Nations and Indigenous Studies UBC, 2020

Harvey, Fiona, 'Almost 2,000 children die every day from air pollution, report finds', *Guardian*, 19 June 2024

He, Megan, et al., 'Total organic carbon measurements reveal major gaps in petrochemical emissions reporting', *Science*, vol. 383, no. 6681 (January 2024), pp. 426–32; doi.org/10.1126/science.adj6233

Hochkirch, Alex, et al., 'A multi-taxon analysis of European Red Lists reveals major threats to biodiversity', *PLOS One* (2023); doi.org/10.1371/journal.pone.0293083

Hoffman, Julian, 'Faith in a Forgotten Place', Terrain.org, issue 28, 11 November 2011

Horton, Helena, 'Thames Water pumped at least 72bn litres of sewage into Thames since 2020', *Guardian*, 10 November 2023

Hu, Jane C., 'The record-breaking high temperatures aren't even the worst part of the Pacific Northwest heat wave', *Slate*, 29 June 2021

Hwang, Su, *Bodega* (Minneapolis: Milkweed Editions, 2019)

Ingold, Tim, *The Perception of the Environment: Essays on Livelihood, Dwelling and Skill* (London: Routledge, 2000)

'Intensive search underway for survivors of destructive flooding in Western Europe', CBS News, 17 July 2021

IPBES, 'Global assessment report on biodiversity and ecosystem services of the Intergovernmental Science-Policy Platform on Biodiversity and

Ecosystem Services' (Bonn, Germany: IPBES secretariat, 2019); doi. org/10.5281/zenodo.3831673

Jackson, Tim, 'Care over growth', Project Syndicate, 29 September 2021

Jamail, Dahr, 'Grieving My Way Into Loving the Planet', *Yes!*, 21 May 2021

James, Ian, 'Violence over water is on the rise globally. A record number of conflicts erupted in 2023', *Los Angeles Times*, 22 Aug 2024

Johnson, Jake, '"Code Red for Humanity": IPCC report warns window for climate action is closing fast', *Common Dreams*, 9 August 2021

Jones, Benji, 'Indigenous people are the world's biggest conservationists, but they rarely get credit for it', *Vox*, 11 June 2021

Kassabova, Kapka, *To the Lake: A Balkan Journey of War and Peace* (London: Granta, 2020)

Kati, Vassiliki, et al., 'The biodiversity-wind energy-land use nexus in a global biodiversity hotspot', *Science of the Total Environment*, vol. 768 (2021); doi.org/10.1016/j.scitotenv.2020.144471

——, 'The overlooked threat of land take from wind energy infrastructures: quantification, drivers and policy gaps', *Journal of Environmental Management*, vol. 3248 (2023); doi.org/10.1016/j.jenvman.2023.119340

Kingdom, Sarah, 'Kasanka bat migration: The largest mammal migration on planet Earth', *Africa Geographic Stories*, 24 March 2021

Krishnamurti, Jiddu, *Krishnamurti's Journal* (Chennai: Krishnamurti Foundation India, 2003)

Krznaric, Roman, *The Good Ancestor: How to Think Long Term in a Short-term World* (London: W. H. Allen, 2020)

'La Palma volcano: how honey bees survived the eruption', *BBC*, 7 December 2021

La Tray, Chris, 'I was raised beside "Squaw Peak" – it's time to change America's offensive place names', *Guardian*, 21 December 2021

Lakhani, Nina, '"A continuation of colonialism": indigenous activists say their voices are missing at COP26', *Guardian*, 3 November 2021

——, 'Record number of fossil fuel lobbyists get access to COP28 climate talks', *Guardian*, 5 December 2023

Laville, Sandra, 'Raw sewage discharged into English rivers 375,000 times by water firms', *Guardian*, 31 March 2022

Li, Lingshan, 'Small green spaces can help keep cities cool during heat waves', *The Conversation*, 8 June 2022

Lialios, Giorgos, 'Endangered trout possibly wiped out by flood works', ekathimerini.com, 29 November 2022

Lohan, Tara, 'Biodiversity solutions also fight climate change', *The Revelator*, 13 May 2022

Louchart, A., N. Tourment and J. Carrier, 'The earliest known pelican reveals 30 million years of evolutionary stasis in beak morphology', *Journal of Ornithology*, vol. 152 (2011), pp. 15–20; doi.org/10.1007/s10336-010-0537-5

Lovatt, Steven, *Birdsong in a Time of Silence* (London: Particular Books, 2021)

Lyons, Kate, 'How to move a country: Fiji's radical plan to escape rising sea levels', *Guardian*, 8 November 2022

Magnason, Andri Snaer, *On Time and Water: A History of Our Future* (London: Serpent's Tail, 2021)

Mam, Kalyanee, *Lost World*, Emergence Magazine (online film), 2018

Marques, Nuno, 'Dead Languages and the Man Trying to Revive Them', *Babbel Magazine*, 21 February 2018

Marshall, Tom, 'People and Nature Survey: How has Covid-19 changed the way we engage with nature?' *Natural England*, 18 May 2022

McSweeney, Ella, 'The Barrow begins life with enormous potential but by the time it flows into the sea it is in a bad way', *Irish Times*, 19 August 2023

Mead, Jill, 'Capital Scenes: London's Third Lockdown – in Pictures', *Guardian*, 23 February 2021

'Merkel describes German flood devastation as "terrifying"', *Al Jazeera*, 18 July 2021

Michelin, Ossie, 'A new dawn rises in the Arctic: the Inuit plan to reclaim their sea', *Guardian*, 27 August 2023

Miller, Brittney J., 'Why unprecedented bird flu outbreaks sweeping the world are concerning scientists', *Nature*, 26 May 2022

Miller, Daegan, 'Reading in the Anthropocene', *Guernica*, 16 June 2021

Miller, Sarah, 'The Millions of Tons of Carbon Emissions That Don't Officially Exist', *New Yorker*, 8 December 2021

'Μητσοτάκης: «Η πολύ καλή απόδοση της οικονομίας αντισταθμίζει το κλίμα των φωτιών»', *Η Βραδυνή*, 30 August 2023 ('Mitsotakis: "The very good performance of the economy compensates for the climate of the fires"', *The Evening*, 30 August 2023)

Moss, Stephen, 'Geese, skuas, cranes and even foxes: avian flu takes growing toll on wildlife', *Guardian*, 2 June 2022

Moss, Todd, and Jacob Kincer, 'Bitcoin, gaming and the schism of global energy inequality', *Energy for Growth Hub*, 10 July 2019

——, 'Global energy inequality goes deeper than bitcoin', *Medium*, 10 September 2019

'Vanessa Nakate's Full Keynote Speech at Youth4Climate Pre-COP26', YouTube, uploaded by DohaDebates, 29 September 2021; https://www.youtube.com/watch?v=W71eBGN2iSw

Nardone, Anthony, et al., 'Redlines and greenspace: the relationship between historical redlining and 2010 greenspace across the United States', *Environmental Health Perspectives*, vol. 129, no. 1 (January 2021); doi.org/10.1289/EHP7495

Niranjan, Ajit, 'Toxic air killed more than 500,000 people in Europe in 2021, data shows', *Guardian*, 24 November 2023

Nowak, Katarzyna, et al., 'Poland's border wall will cut Europe's oldest forest in half', *The Conversation*, 15 December 2021

'Online survey shows more than 3 out of 10 women were abused during first lockdown', ekathimerini.com, 26 November 2020

Ortega, Rodrigo Pérez, '"They were destined to drown": How scientists found these seabirds a new island home', *Science*, 29 June 2021

'Our use of sand brings us "up against the wall", says UNEP report' (press release), UN Environment Programme, 26 April 2022

Pablo, Ofelia de, and Javier Zurita, '"I got to know the wolf": how Spain's shepherds are learning to live with their old enemy', *Guardian*, 19 October 2023

Pandian, Anand, 'Look around you. The way we live explains why we are increasingly polarized', *Guardian*, 16 January 2022

Parissis, Nikolas, 'The wind of change: how Greece loses its natural heritage', *Medium*, 26 July 2021

Pettifer, James, and Miranda Vickers, *Lakes and Empires in Macedonian History: Contesting the Waters* (London: Bloomsbury, 2023)

Petridou, Maria, et al., 'Do husbandry practices reduce depredation of free-ranging livestock? A case study with wolves in Greece', *Biological Conservation*, vol. 283 (2023), 110097

Phillips, Sara, 'Green space key to better mental health in cities and towns', *The Canberra Times*, 2 June 2022

Pigott, Anna, 'Butterflies in the Blue Zone? Some thoughts on #COP26 and Anthropocentrism', *Environmental Politics Journal*, 12 November 2021

Pyne, Stephen J., 'Our children will need to find the beauty in our burnt planet', *Psyche*, 2 November 2022

Radford, Tim, 'Shrinking world leaves less room for wild creatures', Climate News Network, 18 November 2020

Ramsar Convention on Wetlands, 'Global Wetland Outlook: State of the World's Wetlands and their Services to People' (Gland, Switzerland: Ramsar Convention Secretariat, 2018)

Rannard, Georgina, '"Chemical cocktail" polluting English rivers – MPs warn', BBC, 13 January 2022

Rawlings, Alex, 'The man bringing dead languages back to life', BBC, 22 March 2019

Readfearn, Graham, 'How an endangered Australian songbird is forgetting its love songs', *Guardian*, 17 March 2021

Rees, Martin, 'Astronomer Royal on science, environment and the future', *The Conversation*, 12 September 2013

Reid, John, 'Whether humans can survive climate change is the wrong question', *Mongabay*, 17 November 2022

Ritchie, Hannah, 'Who has contributed most to global CO_2 emissions?', *Our World in Data*, 1 October 2019

Robbins, Jim, 'How Returning Lands to Native Tribes is Helping Protect Nature', *Yale Environment 360*, 3 June 2021

Rufo, Yasmin, 'Thames Water: 72 billion litres of sewage pumped into river in two years', BBC, 10 November 2023

Saikia, Jaideep, 'The Chinese threat to Lower Brahmaputra riparians India and Bangladesh', *The Diplomat*, 19 February 2022

Salam, Elum, and Aliya Uteuova, 'How America's treeless streets are fuelling inequality', *Guardian*, 28 June 2021

Saulitis, Eva, *Into Great Silence: A Memoir of Discovery and Loss among Vanishing Orcas* (Boston: Beacon Press, 2013)

Saville, Samantha M., 'Towards humble geographies', *Area*, vol. 53, issue 1 (2021) pp. 97–105; doi.org/10.1111/area.12664

Schriek, Tim van der, and Christos Giannakopoulos, 'Determining the causes for the dramatic recent fall of Lake Prespa (southwest Balkans)', *Hydrological Sciences Journal*, vol. 62 (2017), no. 7, pp. 1131–48; doi.org/10.1080/02626667.2017.1309042

——, 'Establishing the influence of climate, water extraction and tectonics on the water level of the Prespa Lakes (N Greece)', National Observatory of Athens – proceedings paper; http://uest.ntua.gr/adapt-toclimate/proceedings/full_paper/PresATC_TvdS_vs2.pdf (2012)

Schuster, Richard, et al., 'Vertebrate biodiversity on indigenous-managed lands in Australian, Brazil, and Canada equals that in protected areas', *Environmental Science & Policy* (2019); doi.org/10.1016/j.envsci.2019.07.002

Shin, Yunne-Jai, et al., 'Actions to halt biodiversity loss generally benefit the climate', *Global Change Biology* (January 2022); doi.org/10.1111/gcb.16109

Simard, Susanne, *Finding the Mother Tree: Discovering the Wisdom of the Forest* (Toronto: Allen Lane, 2021)

Singh, Ananya, 'How unequal access to green space impacts health', *The Swaddle*, 19 October 2022

Skinner, Anna, 'Bird flu outbreak kills hundreds of vultures at animal sanctuary', *Newsweek*, 22 August 2022

Skrbinšek, Tomaž, et al., 'Analysis of non-invasive genetic samples from brown bears (*Ursus arctos*) from the transboundary Prespa basin', University of Ljubljana, 2021; doi.org/10.13140/RG.2.2.18738.27848

Smith, Georgina, 'Why the world's biggest mammal migration is crucial for Africa', *Guardian*, 5 January 2021

Smith, Helena, 'Rescue efforts stepped up after deadly floods in central Greece', *Guardian*, 9 September 2023

Soanes, Kylie, and Pia E. Lentini, 'When cities are the last chance for saving species', *Frontiers in Ecology and the Environment* (April 2019); doi.org/10.1002/fee.2032

Solnit, Rebecca, '"If you win the popular imagination, you change the game": Why we need new stories on climate', *Guardian*, 12 January 2023

Soria, Juan, and Nadezda Apostolova, 'Decrease in the water level of Lake Prespa (North Macedonia) studied by remote sensing methodology: relation with hydrology and agriculture', *Hydrology* (2022); doi.org/10.3390/hydrology9060099

Stancil, Kenny, 'Canadian official says Trans Mountain pipeline revenue needed to fight climate crisis', *Common Dreams*, 10 August 2021

Standring, Kevin, et al., *Prespa Walking Guide* (Agios Germanos: The Society for the Protection of Prespa, 2009)

Staufenberg, Jess, 'Cows officially the most deadly large animals in Britain', *Independent*, 9 November 2015

Strid, A., E. Bergmeier and G. Fotiadis, *Flora and Vegetation of the Prespa National Park, Greece* (Athens: The Society for the Protection of Prespa, 2020)

Taylor, Matthew, 'Canadian tar sands pollution is up to 6,300% higher than reported, study finds', *Guardian*, 25 January 2024

Temelkuran, Ece, *Together: A Manifesto Against the Heartless World* (London: Fourth Estate, 2021)

Thiery, Wim, et al., 'Intergenerational inequalities in exposure to climate extremes', *Science*, vol. 374, issue 6564 (September 2021), pp. 158-60; doi.org/10.1126/science.abi7339

Thomson, Jess, 'A million migrating birds expecting Kansas wetlands will find dust', *Newsweek*, 21 November 2022

Union of Ontario Indians, *An Overview of the Indian Residential School System* (Nipissing First Nation, 2013)

Vidal, John, 'As forests are cleared and species vanish, there's one other loss: a world of languages', *Guardian*, 8 June 2014

Vougiouklakis, Theodore, 'Fatal brown bear (*Ursus arctos*) attack: Case report and literature review', *The American Journal of Forensic Medicine and Pathology*, vol. 27 (2006), pp. 266–7

Wallace, Alfred Russel, *The Malay Archipelago* (London: Penguin, 2014 [1890])

Watts, Jonathan, 'Pandemic made 2020 "the year of the quiet ocean"', say scientists', *Guardian*, 17 April 2020

Weston, Phoebe, 'Knowledge of medicinal plants at risk as languages die out', *Guardian*, 8 June 2021

——, 'Number of species at risk of extinction doubles to two million, says study', *Guardian*, 8 November 2023

Whiting, Kate, and Madeleine North, 'Sand mining is close to being an environmental crisis. Here's why – and what can be done about it', World Economic Forum, 21 September 2023

Woods, Hiatt, 'How billionaires got $637 billion richer during the Covid-19 pandemic', *Business Insider*, 3 August 2020

'World's wetlands disappearing three times faster than forests', WWF, 27 September 2018

Wuthnow, Joel, Satu Limaye and Nilanthi Samaranayake, 'Brahmaputra: a conflict-prone river takes a step backwards', *War on the Rocks*, 23 December 2020

Yong, Ed, 'The Story of Songbirds is a Story of Sugar', *The Atlantic*, 8 July 2021

Yonovski, Cyril Y., *Prespa* (Skopje: General Impex, 2000)

Yurk, Valerie, 'Pacific Northwest heat wave killed more than one billion sea creatures', *Scientific American*, 15 July 2021

Zahed, Shakeri, 'Sacred groves as a safe shelter for biodiversity and culture in Kurdistan', *People, Nature, Landscapes*, 5 April 2021

Acknowledgements

It's hard to sum up all the gratitude I owe for a book that has been nearly a quarter of a century in the making, but special thanks must go first to those who appeared in these pages: Alejandro Onrubia, Nikos Delkos, Chris 'Ray' Mounsey (with extra thanks for the supply of fresh water that winter!), Germanos and Theodora, Sid 'Chris' Dance, Jimmy, Myrsini Malakou and Haris Nikolaou, Ross Crates, Jaydev Mandal, Anthi Oikonomou, Karak, Germanos and Alexandra, Stavros and Eleni, Sinéad Corcoran and Angelos Nikolaou, Yannis Ziogas, Bledi Hoxha, Maria Petridou, Vassiliki Kati, Milica Ivovic, Dimitris Vavylis, Ritsos, Tasos Bounas and Ellie, Olga Alexandrou, Ruth Cromie, Ursula Höfle, Giorgos Paraskevopoulos, Nikos and Eudoxia, Meto Velevski, Giorgos and Antonia, Nikola, Kosta Trajce, and the woman by the summer sea.

My heartfelt appreciation also to those whose names I never knew because of the briefness of our encounters but who nonetheless enriched my understanding of this shared place: to the passing shepherds, berry-pickers, mountain-tea gatherers, field-workers, arriving immigrants and returning emigrants that we've crossed paths with in the landscape, I'd like to say thank you.

A special note of thanks to Vassilis and his mother Chrysoula – for generously offering us shelter and being our first friends here all those years ago. We'll be forever grateful for it.

My gratitude to Luc Hoffmann for his tireless work on behalf of Prespa and other wetlands around the world throughout his long and inspiring life. It was a true honour to have known him and he is greatly missed by so many. Special thanks to friends and colleagues at the SPP, PPNEA and MES, from whom I've learned so much about the ecological integrity of the lakes' basin through their joint work with PrespaNet and the rich possibilities for cooperating across borders with the aim of protecting the cultural and natural values of our shared world.

It's hard to express just how much Giorgos Catsadorakis's book about Prespa changed our lives. Without it, Julia and I would be somewhere entirely different right now and this book wouldn't exist. We'll always be immensely thankful for being shown a place just at the moment when the need to turn towards home was at its greatest. Ευχαριστούμε πολύ, Γιώργο.

There are many friends who have been fundamental to our experience here and who've helped shape our understanding of Prespa and the wider issues introduced in this book over the years. Thank you to Miki Ambrózy, Artemis Anastasiadou, Zenia Anastasiadou and Kiriakos Poukamisas, Nikos Arambatzis and Eleni Tamba, Marie Archer, Dragan Arsovski, Josh Barley, Tina Bernot, Pippa, Hannah-Louise and the much missed Robin Blackall, Andrea Bonetti, James Bridle and Navine Dossos, Robert Caskie, Mathilde Chanvin, Mark Cocker and Mary Muir, Apostolis Christakis, Loring Danforth, Tasos Dimalexis, François Doleson, Claudio Donadel, Vera Eftimova and family, Ida Eliaou, Nicole Fowler, the Gemenetzidou family, Nikos Giannakis and Angela Georganta, Giorgos Giannatos, Judy Greenwell and Bruce Thorndike, Jimmy Ioannidis and family, Jan Jordan, Apostolis Kallioras, Thanos Kastritis, Ross Kaufmann, Yiannis Kazoglou, Vera Kolatskou, the Konstantinou family, the dearly missed Maria Kouli, Irene Koutseri, Sam Lee, Stefanos Levidis and Sofia Georgovassili, Vladimir Levidis, Annita Logotheti, Sevi Louiza and Yiannis Theodoropoulos, Lisa MacDonald and family, Glenn Manarin, Don Matthews, Lydia Matthews, the greatly missed Ljupčo Melovski, Paul Miller and Begoña Samaniego, Marcia Nickerson, the Nikolaou family, Dimitris Nikolaou and Fani Christaki, Elli Nikolaou, Dimitris Noulis, Nikos Papadopoulos, Thymios Papayiannis and Ivy Nanapoulou, James Pettifer, Romina Queralt, Vivi Roumeliotou and family, Matthew Ryan, Fanikos Sakellarakis, Victoria Saravia, Despina and Fanis Shaho and family, Spase Shumka, Caroline Simmonds, Ruth and Kevin Standring, Martin Stewart, Jørgen and Kirsten Stubgaard, Máté Tálas, Toula Tamba and family, Caterina Tiveron, Spyros Toutountzis and family, Dimitris and Zoe Tsikos, Yvonne Tsorogouni and family, Nash Tysmans, Margarita Tzali, Panos Valatidis, Helen Vatsikopoulos and Mark Corcoran, Marianna Veneti and Stelios Christakis, Miranda Vickers, Kostas Hantzaras and Petroula Boitsi, Daniela Zaec, Sofia Zouzeli and family, our wonderful neighbours in the house by the square, Antigone, Giorgos and Ioanna, the postmen Vassilis and Yiannis, who worked below an eave of swallow nests across from that house, and Filbert and Pushkin, our beloved cats that were born in the barn beside the distillery where Germanos kept his barrels of wine.

A special note of gratitude to Sandor Veldman and Camilla Huss, Trudi Clamp and Pete Bell, and Hilary Koll and Steve Mills for helping in the fields and stacking tonnes of firewood on their visits to keep us warm through winter!

Deep thanks to Kathleen Jamie for a few encouraging words one evening in Prespa that encouraged me to tell this story.

With immense love to the family of Nina Mesner – Marjan, Peter, Alina, Urban and her parents, Bogo and Ida – a dear friend that we lost far too young. Nina adored Prespa. She would often visit us from her native Slovenia and sit on the shore of Great Prespa Lake looking out at the villages of North Macedonia and say, 'That used to be my country.' A reminder that it was all still Yugoslavia only a decade before we moved here and that borders and belonging don't necessarily equate to the same thing.

To Robert Hogg – a brilliant poet, organic farmer and professor of literature who fundamentally shaped me as a writer while at university. Twenty-nine years after we'd last seen one another we met over coffee and a pile of books and it felt like barely a day had passed. Sadly, we never had another chance, but I'll always be grateful for everything you taught me. *Light and love forever far.*

To the kindness of Annabelle, Philip and Alexander Louvros and Alex Preston for inviting me to talk about Prespa at the wonderful Corfu Literary Festival for several years now. Thanks as well to Jaime Turner, John Kittmer and Sudha Nair Illiades for opportunities to publicly expand on this shared place in ways that fundamentally helped formulate my thinking in this book.

I'd like to express my deepest thanks to Su Hwang for granting me permission to quote from her remarkable poem 'Witness Marks' that's found in her collection *Bodega*. And to *Emergence Magazine* for permission to quote from Kalyanee Mam's moving and powerful documentary *Lost World*. I highly recommend seeking out both of these important works.

Thanks as well to *Elsewhere Journal*, *The Clearing* and *Zoomorphic*, where short sections of this book first appeared. And to *Emergence Magazine* for publishing an earlier version of the chapter 'Of Water, Mountains, Sky' as 'The Spirit of the Wetlands'.

Deep gratitude to my fantastic agent, James Macdonald Lockhart, for his kindness, generosity and sensitivity. He saw something in *Lifelines* at a time when I wasn't sure about its ultimate direction, suggesting a path forward before we were even formally working together. I owe the final shape of this book to his astute recommendations.

Immense appreciation to the extraordinary and lovely team at Elliott & Thompson. From the moment they expressed interest in the book it has felt like I was coming home. I'm deeply grateful to my brilliant editor, Sarah Rigby, for not only championing this book right from the very beginning but for her deft and thoughtful suggestions that infinitely improved the manuscript. Huge thanks as well to Katie Bond,

Amy Greaves, Pippa Crane, Meg Humphries and Jill Burrows for all their incredible and essential work behind the scenes that have made this book what it is.

It can be an anxious moment when a writer sees an email with the words 'proposed cover' in the subject line, but as I gradually scrolled down the image of Ola Galewicz's beautiful artwork I knew in an instant that it was perfect for the book. Immense thanks to her for capturing so richly this place of mountains and lakes. And my deepest gratitude to my dear friend, Matina Galati, for her gorgeous and engaging illustrations and for crafting such a wonderfully playful map to help guide readers around the shared basin. It's an honour to have such incredible work gracing the book.

With enormous love to my parents – Pam and Ken – for believing in this journey right from the very beginning. So much so that they'd booked flights to come and see us in Prespa before we'd even found a house to live in. And to Julia's dearly missed and much-loved Mum, Pat Harker, who supported this journey of ours wholeheartedly. Finally, to my very talented brother, Justin Hoffman, for the author photograph for the book.

To our beloved Mitzi, who was born on our sofa when a friend asked us to look after his pregnant cat while he went to France on holiday. 'Don't worry,' he'd said, 'I'll be back home in plenty of time before she gives birth.' A day or two later we had five mewling newborns on our hands, one of whom ended up staying with us. For fifteen years Mitzi filled our hearts and home – both in the house by the square and then in the one of the wrens. The sadness of her loss last year is eased by the memory of so much love.

Prespa wouldn't be Prespa without its extraordinary communities of wild species, nor would our experience here be anything like as rich as it's been without them. My profound thanks to our wild neighbours for all the years of beauty, wonder, mystery and fascination you've given us.

I can't even begin to truly express my gratefulness to the people of Prespa and especially the village of Agios Germanos, along with friends in nearby Florina and Kastoria who've helped and encouraged us count-less times over the years. You not only welcomed us when we arrived with no idea of who we were but you gave us a chance to make this place a home. Thank you for everything – your friendships mean the world to us.

Finally, my deepest love and gratitude to Julia. Not only for all that we've shared over the years but for making this leap of faith together. I could never have made this journey on my own, nor would I have wanted to. It's being in Prespa alongside you that has made it so reward-ing. Onwards, my love, to the days and journeys ahead.